THE WORLD'S
MOST DIFFICULT QUIZ

THE WORLD'S MOST DIFFICULT QUIZ

King William's College
General Knowledge Papers
from 1981 to 2010

Edited by Pat Cullen

LIVERPOOL UNIVERSITY PRESS

First published 2011 by
Liverpool University Press
4 Cambridge Street
Liverpool
L69 7ZU

British Library Cataloguing-in-Publication data
A British Library CIP record is available

ISBN 978-1-84631-695-1 limp

Typeset by Carnegie Book Production, Lancaster
Printed in the UK by Bell and Bain Ltd, Glasgow

Contents

Acknowledgement

I am particularly grateful to Tony Glover, who was responsible for all the papers up to 1996–97, and who, rightly or wrongly, felt that I was the right person to try to maintain the high standards which he had set.

Introduction

December 2004 saw the unleashing of the one hundredth King William's College General Knowledge Paper and for the fifty-fourth time it was published in the *Guardian*. That newspaper heralded the latest paper with the headline 'A century of bewilderment', and it has previously used such adjectives as 'fiendish', 'legendary' and 'impossibly difficult'. Almost all the questions and answers which follow have previously appeared in the *Guardian*, which continues to publish the Paper annually, during the week before Christmas. I have however prepared a bespoke set of questions for this book.

The story of Bishop Barrow's Charity, dating from 1668, the establishment of King William's College at Castletown on the Isle of Man in 1833 and the development of a highly successful co-educational day and boarding school has been vividly described by Michael Hoy in *A Blessing to this Island* (London: James and James, 2006). Further details regarding King William's can be found on the school's website: www.kwc.im.

The GKP began life in 1905 much as any other school quiz, with masters contributing questions of very variable difficulty and subtlety, so that 'Who wrote *Pickwick*?' was considered a bright and suitable type of question. It was not until 1917 that W. G. Wilson became sole editor and established the rigid format of 18 sets of ten questions. W. G. had been a master at King William's since 1898, became Vice-Principal in 1926 and died in harness in 1930. Not only was he the architect of this world-famous quiz, but he was also hugely popular amongst the boys – 'a scholar, a true gentleman and a sportsman in every sense of the word'.

His successor was Denis Thompson, another Oxonian, who was a master from 1919 to 1949 and was to continue as quizmaster until 1958. Known to all as Denis, or sometimes D. T., his whimsical mannerisms were used to cloak his serious outlook on life and customs. The four most serious interests in his life at King William's, namely School House, music (he was a great organist), English literature and history, and the General Knowledge Paper, were all coloured by a delightful conservatism. His great favourites, which emerged repeatedly in the GKP, were Queen Elizabeth I, Charles

Dickens, Jane Austen, Edward German, Bruges and Delft (the name which he gave to his retirement house in Castletown). But the extent of his reading and knowledge was phenomenal and certainly unequalled by any of his successors. Denis's voice is easily recalled to this day – an audible in-drawing of breath and 'My dear boy...' coming from somewhere seemingly well beyond the larynx! And who could forget that figure, astride a bicycle, riding up the Hundred some windy day and holding his trilby on with the handle of his walking stick?

There followed an interregnum during which the paper was prepared by Basil Hartley, the formidable housemaster of Junior House, who had come to College in 1939 and who served as Vice-Principal from 1960 until his retirement in 1965.

Most people would agree that after D. T., the high standards which he had set for the GKP dwindled somewhat, but they were to be restored by Dick Boyns, who produced excellent papers, with questions also contributed by other enthusiasts, in particular Ean Wood, one of his pupils in School House. The son of a Methodist minister, Dick went to Kingswood and then St John's College, Cambridge, where he won blues for cross-country and athletics. A master at KWC from 1948 to 1982 and editor of the GKP from 1965 to 1981, he was Head of History for 33 years (nobody will have forgotten his heroine, Lady Margaret Beaufort, or, for that matter, his feigned distaste for boys from Peel), housemaster of School House for 31 years, master in charge of the library for 17 years, and in charge of both the GCE exams and rugby for 13 years. He had a unique capacity for getting the best out of his charges, whether academically or on the sports field. The sheer quantity of work which he got through was staggering and whatever the weather, however tired he may have been, he never failed to turn up for early morning dip (6.55 am for School House) or for chapel services every morning. The ideals of toughness, tempered by good manners; of hard work, undeterred by apathy; of service without a thought of self-interest; of a lively rapier-like wit were unfashionable virtues. Times changed but not Dick. A staunch upholder of traditional standards and discipline, he stood four-square against the forces of permissiveness and laissez-faire, which seemed at times to threaten all walks of life. Tough, but always a gentleman, Dick is remembered with affection and respect by many generations of boys and his name will not be forgotten. He died at the age of 63, just four years after his retirement.

Art master at King William's from 1952 to 1984, Tony Glover succeeded Dick as quizmaster and continued, after his own retirement, for a further thirteen years. He was the popular and kindly housemaster of Junior Day Boys House and an outstandingly talented craftsman. Very much an archivist, a repository of facts and knowledge, Tony had a penchant for crosswords, and the clues certainly became more cryptic during his stewardship. He is a loyal member of Yorkshire County Cricket Club and it was fitting that one set of questions in his final paper was devoted to his home town, Wakefield. During much of Tony's period of editorship, I had sent him questions, thirteen of which appeared in his final GKP for 1996–97. Little did I realise that having made my own bed, I would now be asked to lie in it!

In fact, far from being a chore, I have found preparing the GKP a very enjoyable change from other activities. Denis Thompson reckoned to sit down with a blank sheet of paper in September and have the questions ready for the printers by early November. For me it is a year-long activity, so that even in January I will have several sets awaiting the finishing touches. Research into one subject (jazz comes to mind) will spawn one or two further sets for different treatment in future years. I would get occasional sets of questions from old boys, notably Ken Wilson, Geoffrey Kinley, Brian Crookall, Brian Trustrum, David Jones, Gordon Stuart and my brother Tim; in fact I feel the need for fresh ideas, as my own particular interests are, I suspect, dominating my efforts.

Traditionally, on the final day of the autumn term we would sit the GKP, unseen, under strict exam conditions. Over Christmas, the more enthusiastic would spend long periods in public libraries, while ambitious parents would distribute copies to friends and relatives. The answers would start to come in early in the New Year and there followed a hectic period of checking and learning. One would return to school with perhaps 120 answers, some sections complete, while in others the theme might not have been cracked. That first evening back at school was devoted to swapping answers, often in whispers, as there were always eavesdroppers, and sometimes giving away some of the easier ones to the less academically inclined. The following morning we re-sat the paper under the same conditions and without notes. Marks were eagerly awaited, the more successful earning a free half, while those in the bottom fraction would have a session in detention. This system continued until the late nineties, when it was decided that, with the current programme of national exams, it was inappropriate that pupils should be deflected from more meaningful revision during the Christmas break. Participation is now voluntary, but competition no less intense.

Prizes were awarded, the Mitchell for the unseen winner and the Edgar Healds for Senior and Junior first, second and third – based on aggregate scores for both unseen and prepared. Mrs Vowles (née Mitchell) had presented £20 in 1929 in memory of her three brothers, who had all gone to King William's in 1882, while in 1946 Edgar Heald, father of a further three boys, gave £175.

Two books have been published. In 1954 the Cresset Press produced *General Knowledge Papers. 1905–1953. Prepared for King William's College, Isle of Man.* Denis Thompson inscribed one copy *"'General Knowledge?' said Sir Oliver Lodge – 'I call it General Nonsense.' I hope you don't. DT"*. The preface alludes to an occasion when one daily newspaper begged that the GKP might not be issued until after Parliament had risen for Christmas, as the two could not be dealt with at once, and to the Paper's being broadcast from Chicago and of a rumour of its being handed round during a session of the United Nations. There is also a reference to 'a sheaf of letters, some abusive and some appreciative' – this still happens! In 1982 came *The King William's College Tests*, published by Hutchinson and the *Guardian*, and carrying the slogan '30 of the most confoundingly difficult tests ever set'. In editing the present book, I have inevitably detected occasional errors, which I have corrected, but I have little doubt that there must be others undetected, at least by me.

To the long-established format of eighteen sets of ten questions must be added the tradition of the first set relating to 100 years before and the last to the current year. In 1923 section 17 related to the current year, as it did in both 1930 and 1931, but the topic occupied the section 18 slot the following year and has remained there ever since. After a set in 1951, section 1 has been devoted to one hundred years ago every year since 1965. Other recurring themes have been colours and given names, with which I still persist, while more recently I have done European countries (now just about exhausted!), works of individual authors and food/drink.

The impact of the internet, and more particularly the search engine Google, has had a significant impact on quizmasters and has influenced the way in which questions are presented. Most proper names should really be excluded – easier said than done – and it is inevitable that questions are therefore more convoluted and, dare one say, irritating. I was recently very disappointed when I tried a number of what I thought were quite tricky questions by offering them to Google. Even the mistresses of supposedly obscure Danish kings were revealed. Realistically the GKP cannot be made entirely Googleproof and I see no reason why the pupils of KWC should not use every device at their disposal. However, *Guardian* readers settling down for their annual masochistic Boxing Day entertainment, and readers of this book, will probably regard referral to Google as unsporting and, if so, I am content!

Pat Cullen
Cronkbourne
Isle of Man
2011

Questions

'Scire ubi aliquid invenire possis ea demum
maxima pars eruditionis est'

1981–1982

• 1 • *In 1881:*

  1   who was first entertained at the Rectory Field on 14th February?

  2   whom did Piet Joubert defeat on 27th February?

  3   what had Georgium Sidus become at its centenary on 13th March?

  4   who was the victim of Charles J Guiteau on 19th September?

  5   whose birth at Salonica heralded a new look for women?

  6   where were widows and spinsters enfranchised?

  7   what Goldfish was spawned and named Samuel?

  8   where did free primary education start?

  9   what nation was born?

10   what nation acquired both shares of the straits?

• 2 • *What lovers:*

  1   corresponded as Florizel and Perdita?

  2   met making *To Have and Have Not*?

  3   begot Caesarion?

  4   were shot down in a Ford V-8 Sedan?

  5   received the press from their honeymoon bed?

  6   were sundered by Canon Fulbert?

  7   begot Frankenstein?

  8   discovered element number 88?

  9   were recognised by Captain Kendall?

10   caused the death of Uriah?

• 3 • *What divination is by:*

1   fire?

2   dreams?

3   communication with the dead?

4   a wand?

5   ashes?

6   water?

7   melted wax in water?

8   arrows?

9   the hand?

10   turning a sieve?

• 4 • *Who failed to finish writing:*

1   *Weir of Hermiston?*

2   *The Mystery of Edwin Drood?*

3   *The Watsons?*

4   *The Ivory Tower?*

5   *Wives and Daughters?*

6   *Denis Duval?*

7   *The Poodle Springs (Story)?*

8   *Emma?*

9   *Slattery's Sago Saga?*

10   *The History of England from the Accession of James II?*

• 5 • *Who was:*

1   circumscribed at Alexandria?

2   invented by Steinbeck?

3   given Baghdad on Christmas Day 1638?

4   the only English one?

5   content to amass his capital?

6   insomniac from his headgear?

7   Paphlagonian?

8   compelled to abdicate for the second time at Bayonne?

9   principal Disk-worshiper at Amarna?

10   alleged to be the father of the false Dimitri?

• 6 • *Who or What or Where:*

1   sang runaway?
2   is woody in Cheshire?
3   is literally a land of fire?
4   is a Greek triangle?
5   was the Academy of Chaff?
6   is a security printer?
7   is the Diamond State?
8   was the seat of an Oracle?
9   was beautiful but treacherous?
10 could view the Celestial City?

• 7 • *Who or What:*

1   had the Manor of Mells for his plum?
2   is an ignis fatuus?
3   appeared to guide steamships off New Zealand?
4   is epithetically auric and ursine?
5   sailed with guzzling Jimmy?
6   could consume only muscular tissue?
7   is proverbial for brevity in utterance?
8   was claimed to insist on 'reg'lar rotation'?
9   was known as Amend-All?
10 wrote from hell to Mr Lusk?

• 8 • *Identify:*

1   the Bald
2   the Bold
3   the Fat
4   the Long
5   the Well-Beloved
6   the Well-Served
7   the Posthumous
8   the Short
9   the Simple
10 the Stammerer

• 9 • *What song contains:*

1 mulligan stew?
2 a little bacon and a little beans?
3 schnitzel with noodles?
4 yesterday's mashed potato?
5 a wienie bake, steak, and a layer of cake?
6 a figgy pudding?
7 burning toast and prunes?
8 penny ice and cold meat?
9 a sugar cake?
10 Napoleon brandy?

• 10 • *What assassin chose:*

1 The Ambassador Hotel?
2 A bath tub?
3 The bridge over the Mijacka?
4 The Pan-American Exposition?
5 The Prinsenhof?
6 A masked ball?
7 The Dakota?
8 The Lorraine Motel?
9 Avenida Viena in Coyoacán?
10 Birla House

• 11 • *For what:*

1 the Lugano?
2 the Thomas?
3 the Bermuda?
4 the Courbillon?
5 the Arthur Dunn?
6 the Silver Dagger?
7 the Maskeleyne?
8 the Stanley?
9 the Huxley?
10 the Schneider?

• 12 • *Where:*

1 an aristocratic bibliophile philosophises in Snowdonia?
2 a Liverpudlian foundling pursues a vendetta in Yorkshire?
3 a Glaswegian provision merchant adventures in Galloway?
4 a reverend Albino plays false in Cornwall?
5 a military widower excites suspicion in Cornwall?
6 a rowing daguerreotypist reminisces in New England?
7 a mononymic crossing sweeper initiates a quest in London?
8 a gigantic spectre disintegrates an edifice in Italy?
9 a juvenile clown gains enfranchisement in Virginia?
10 a suburban clerk solicits charity in Hertfordshire?

• 13 • *What misnomer is commonly given to:*

1 a bird brought from Mexico via Spain?
2 an obelisk lost at sea but subsequently recovered?
3 a stiffener for stays?
4 the sliced pith of a Formosan tree?
5 a peninsula south of Weymouth?
6 iron dipped in molten zinc?
7 the root of a species of sunflower?
8 an alloy of copper, zinc and nickel?
9 a hydrous silicate of magnesium?
10 a double-reeded tenor woodwind?

• 14 • *Locate:*

1 Druk-yul
2 Shqiperia
3 Bharat
4 Chung-Hua Min-Kuo
5 El-Djemhouria el-Djazairia
6 Tuvalu
7 Sakartvelos Sabchota Sotsialisturi Respublica
8 Kibris Cumhuriyeti
9 Daehen Minkuk
10 Ittihad al-Imarat al-Arabiya

• 15 • *What or who did the following become:*

1 Fort Duquesne?
2 Norma Jean Mortenson?
3 NKVD?
4 The France?
5 O'Neill's Mourning?
6 Idlewild?
7 Sackville Street?
8 Mary Magdalene von Losch?
9 Christiania?
10 Leopoldville?

• 16 • *What engineer:*

1 turned Turbinia loose among the Spithead Review?
2 had most of his masterpieces re-erected on Plymouth Hoe?
3 invented a parallel motion?
4 named his micrometer 'The Lord Chancellor'?
5 turned himself into a timber top hat?
6 had even his coffin made of iron?
7 ran 'Catch-me-who-can' at Euston?
8 compared refreshment-room coffee to bad roasted corn?
9 had his great disaster commemorated by McGonagall?
10 admitted that a collision with a cow would be 'very awkward – for the cow'?

• 17 • *Who exclaimed:*

1   My God, Mr Chairman! At this moment I stand astonished at my own moderation!

2   Oh? He is mad is he? Then I wish he would bite some other of my generals!

3   Another damned thick square book! Always scribble, scribble, scribble? Eh! Mr Gibbon?

4   Published and be damned!

5   O Diamond! Diamond: thou little knowest the mischief done!

6   What, is it you, you dogs? I'll have a frisk with you!

7   What a parcel of fools and dastards have I nourished in my house, that not one of them will avenge me of this one upstart clerk!

8   Was there ever such stuff as the great part of Shakespeare? Only one must not say so!

9   I know not what course others may take; but as for me, give me liberty, or give me death!

10   Die, my dear doctor, that's the last thing I shall do!

• 18 • *In 1981:*

1   when was theirs the 444th and he became the 40th?

2   from what did Stephanitur acquire 431?

3   whose 63rd was revived on 11th November?

4   whose centennial cake was consumed at Keighley Station?

5   who involuntarily vacationed in Barbados?

6   why hail Columbia?

7   who arrived to become 'bright as the dawn'?

8   what recalled Jacques Pelletier?

9   who completed a trans-oceanic double?

10   who had 'merci' bestowed upon him after 39 years?

1982–1983

• 1 • *In 1882:*

1   what Swan alighted in Coxon's of Newcastle?

2   what made its first sheepish appearance?

3   how did half a zebra disappear?

4   who arrived to become 32 in 33?

5   what destination found ag in search of au?

6   what came for a long stay, bailfully?

7   what came from Kano with Dan, Dan, etc.?

8   whose first was St Thomas's undoing at Lambeth Palace?

9   who decreased with electrical assistance?

10 who lighted where, following Winstanley and Smeaton?

• 2 • *What is or was:*

1   consulted before the Battle of Gilboa?

2   Sir Walter Scott

3   Matthew Hopkins

4   Hamamelis virginiana?

5   a successful raid by those magnificent men?

6   Thomas Alva Edison?

7   discovered by Reginald Scott in 1584?

8   'Bysshed' in 1820?

9   Frank Morgan?

10 periodically discriminating?

• 3 • *Locate bibliographically:*

1 Matthew Dodd

2 Josiah Peabody

3 Charles Allnutt

4 George Krause

5 Hugh and Carlos O'Neill

6 Colonel Jean-Baptiste Caillard

7 Captain Miles Troughton-Harrington-Yorke

8 Colonel Lord Wychwood

9 The Prince of Seitz-Bunau

10 Don Julian Maria de Jesus de Alvarado y Moctezuma

• 4 • *Where would you ride in a:*

1 Shikara?

2 Dolmus?

3 Sheroot?

4 Dandy?

5 Norimon?

6 Celesa?

7 Conestoga wagon?

8 Karrozzin?

9 Carozzo?

10 Pulka?

• 5 • *What twins:*

1 circulate for Mars?

2 followed St Elmo's fire?

3 failed to match their hundred children?

4 included a great labourer?

5 counted vultures?

6 included a hairy one?

7 produced a Rock King?

8 left before Khomeini?

9 were really Shakespearean?

10 were record recorders for porter?

• 6 • *Who or what:*

1 was the chronicler of the five towns?

2 station was 5XX?

3 dissolved the Council of Five Hundred?

4 failed to arrest five MPs?

5 was told 'Full fathom five thy father lies, of his bones are coral made'?

6 were controlled by the Five Mile Act?

7 imposed the Five Articles of Perth?

8 five made the Danelaw?

9 five for silver are followed by six for gold, seven for a secret?

10 solved the Five Orange Pips?

• 7 • *Amend:*

1 Bugges

2 Murderers

3 Printers

4 Sin on

5 Forgotten

6 Sting

7 Vinegar

8 Wife

9 Cease

10 Camels

• 8 • *Who or what:*

1 wrote the *Red House Mystery*?

2 was the Red Baron?

3 painted a large red interior?

4 wrote the *Red Shoes*?

5 wrote *Red Rover*?

6 led the Red Shirts?

7 was the Red Dean?

8 featured a singing red shadow?

9 Red early went to Greenland?

10 was capital of Red River Settlement?

• 9 • *Who is or was:*

1   George IV?
2   Tank?
3   Harry Lime?
4   Death?
5   Monmouth?
6   James I?
7   Enoch?
8   Van Buren?
9   Lindley?
10   Sappho?

• 10 • *Who or what:*

1   were the Castles with matching steps?
2   Scottish international visited Castle Gay?
3   castle was haunted by Murgatroyds?
4   castle is The Corbie's Nest?
5   castle was the last to surrender to Cromwell?
6   castle was Oflag IV C?
7   castle produced a Constable compliment on landscape?
8   described what castle as 'the most romantique that is in the world'?
9   deserted what castle in *Love and Friendship*?
10   Castle stood in Blackburn?

• 11 • *What line follows:*

1   Two Sticks and Apple?
2   Sep. No. Iun Ap. dato trigenta: religuus magis vno?
3   Cackle, cackle, Mother Goose?
4   Hana, mana, mona, mike?
5   Who kill'd John Keats?
6   The king sent his lady on the first Yule day?
7   Hushie ba, burdie beeton?
8   A Soldier and a Sailor, a Tinker and a Tailor?
9   ich wollte gern über die Magdeburger Brück?
10   I, William, of the Wastle?

• 12 • *Who or what:*

1 were defeated at Vinegar Hill?
2 led the way into Coppenburg Hill?
3 surrendered on Carberry Hill?
4 battle was truly fought at Breed's Hill?
5 were crowned on Tara Hill?
6 came off best on America's Fisher's Hill?
7 is nationally situated at Bickenhill?
8 Hill is an adhesion of pasta?
9 Hill hears in summertime the bells sound round both the shires?
10 Village has heather on the hill even in the mist of May?

• 13 • *What:*

1 role was played by Marshal Royal for the Count?
2 King (1897, 1903, 1908) swerved over the Lord's sword?
3 Duke was named as a President's brother – and how?
4 Duke made the Conqueror, reel and reel again?
5 Lord from Lord St. made quite a pile?
6 King bore the Government's warning?
7 Peer was driven from the Kings' Hall?
8 Count follows a dispute involving Dukes?
9 Pope might take a beating from a Priest?
10 King was proclaimed by Senator Hammond?

• 14 • *Identify the measure:*

1 in which my sister Kate excelled.
2 for Latin sons and daughters near the Adriatic.
3 when the foot goes out and is then brought back.
4 in which the whiting needs to increase the pace.
5 when the upstairs' maid was joined by other staff.
6 indicated by Jealousy.
7 of the Maidens of Cadiz.
8 when I like coffee, I like tea.
9 arising when you meet me in St Louis.
10 of up on your heels, down on your toes.

• 15 • *Who or what:*

1 was an aide to Poirot?

2 is when two's company…?

3 … and the third is a crowd?

4 is 13′ 1″ x 5′ 3⅘″ and 4′ 5½″ high?

5 may be summoned to the library with lead piping?

6 was cast as Thisbe's father?

7 is found on both fiddle and bow?

8 together with Buckhorn ended by assisting Groundsel on the Belt?

9 is eponymously Dickensian?

10 expresses audible disfavour?

• 16 • *Who wrote:*

1 and said 'I propose to give a ball at Christmas … it will cost a thousand pounds'?

2 and who said 'One Christmas … years gone … I went the round with Dilbeach choir'?

3 'I dined, today being Christmas Day … with poor old people … (and) Joseph Smith, my clerk'?

4 'The Christmas tree was a sprig of pine … (with) lights on milky white plastic-covered wire … connected to a battery'?

5 the ballad of 'It was Christmas Day in the workhouse'?

6 in what work 'At Christmas I no more desire a rose Than wish a snow in May's new fangled mirth'?

7 in what work 'I am a poor man, but I would gladly give ten shillings to find out who sent me the insulting Christmas card received this morning'?

8 and who said 'I have often thought … it happens very well that Christmas should fall out in the Middle of Winter'?

9 in what work 'I have two children of my own … (who) are full of wonder at the German Christmas Tree and its candles'?

10 describing what Christmas as 'its success is prodigious. By every post all manner of strangers write about their hearths and homes'?

• 17 • *What was:*

1   the fare on the Runcorn Ferry?
2   the price of yer maple?
3   killed by a cork near Crewe?
4   the diet of beefeaters on night duty?
5   the West Wigan Whippet's opposition?
6   Nelson's gift to J Moggeridge?
7   Little Aggie – and her position?
8   William's answer to rude words in Saxon?
9   the price of gas?
10   the lion's name?

• 18 • *In 1982:*

1   what extravagant gull scarcely got off the ground?
2   who were inseparable down under?
3   who is now walking a greased tightrope with a prison yard beneath?
4   what did Shao-Shao have to show?
5   who ended a masterly performance by stepping from one green to another?
6   who zoomed to success with an Oscar?
7   what band-waggoner said 'goodbye' to his play-mates?
8   whose strong arm raised, as directed by Rule?
9   who returned to the Thames after 315 years – this time by invitation?
10   what dear departed said 'Hello Dolly'?

1983–1984

• 1 • *What, in 1883:*

   1   was undertaken by Auguste Bartholdi?

   2   was the contribution made by the Prefect of the Paris Police towards cleaning up the streets?

   3   achievement was notched up by Heckmondwicke?

   4   was led by Littlechild?

   5   brought Shakespeare to Shakespeare Street?

   6   went bang just once in a blue moon?

   7   averaged just 15 degrees a time?

   8   resulted when Mr Haig, the butcher, ordered chops, eight at a time?

   9   was seen at Fort Wayne by the first light of night?

  10   had its business all wrapped up?

• 2 • *Define:*

   1   St Giles's carpet.

   2   St Stephen's loaves.

   3   St Nicholas's clerks.

   4   St Hugh's bones.

   5   St Patrick's purgatory.

   6   St Johnstone's tippet.

   7   St Francis's distemper.

   8   St Luke's bird.

   9   St Lubbock's day.

  10   St Geoffrey's day.

• 3 • *What:*

1   spied for Odin?
2   appears to be trying to walk on water?
3   is the axe of Ishtar?
4   inhabits caves and lives in caverns?
5   gave birth to the Shang Dynasty?
6   removed a bone from the throat of a wolf?
7   gave a lift to Sinbad?
8   did Lear consider Regan and Goneril?
9   takes its parent's remains to Heliopolis?
10 was white until it failed Apollo?

• 4 • *Patefiat venditor:*

1   'Good morning! Have you used – – ?'
2   'That schoolgirl complexion.'
3   'Which twin has the – ?'
4   'worth a guinea a box.'
5   'Every picture tells a story.'
6   '– – pink pills for pale people.'
7   'You should see me on Sunday.'
8   'Friday night is – Night.'
9   'Even your best friends won't know you.'
10 'Body Odour.'

• 5 • *Who was:*

1   The Citizen of the World?
2   The Rev. Dr. Dryasdust?
3   Mr John Jorrocks?
4   Diedrich Knickerbocker?
5   Richard Prentis?
6   Walter Ramel?
7   H. Scriblerus Secundus?
8   John Sinjohn?
9   Samuel Titmarsh?
10 Yorick?

• 6 • *Who is:*

1 Colin Tampon?

2 Robert Macaire?

3 Jean Baptiste?

4 Brother Jonathan?

5 Mynheer Closh?

6 Cousin Michael?

7 Johnny Warder?

8 Scowegian?

9 Johnny Bono?

10 Sinister Bosey?

• 7 • *Who:*

1 represented Lady and Rachel Verinder?

2 defended Charles Darnay?

3 acted for Cecily Cardew?

4 was solicitor to Ko-Ko?

5 acted for the Fentiman brothers?

6 took the case of the missing postal order?

7 advised Robert Carne?

8 spoke up for Mrs Bardell?

9 was adviser to Mrs Lomax and met Miss Heron?

10 prosecuted the Utopian?

• 8 • *What first happened:*

1 in late 1835, featuring Mr Wilson and his eagle?

2 on 6th January 1938, in an adapted horse box?

3 in 1842, on the journey from Slough to Paddington?

4 in 1848, involving an antelope from Boston?

5 in July 1864, on the 21.50 from Broad Street to Poplar?

6 on 26th September 1877, when 'Lochee' left Wormit for Magdalen Green?

7 in 1880, which was cooked up and commemorated in song?

8 on 5th June 1883, departing from Paris?

9 in November, in dining car No. 2419?

10 in May 1969, at Harwich after a journey of 7,600 miles?

• 9 • *Locate:*

1 d e g b.
2 e g c c b g c a a a g e.
3 a a e e e b c b a.
4 g g g c c c a f c.
5 a g f a g f f a f.
6 a a a b b b.
7 b b b b c d e d.
8 a g f c c d c a b g.
9 c b a g f g a c b a g f e.
10 g d e d c b a g.

• 10 • *Which Monarch:*

1 still has his queen packed eightfold?
2 was on his own, I, II, III and IV
3 owned Minoru?
4 was married to a May bride who on becoming queen naturally acquired an 'R'?
5 was the first Guelph?
6 married a Schleswig-Holstein-Sonderburg-Glücksburg?
7 was four short of Francis Joseph, who was four short of Louis XIV?
8 is reputed to have said that he would have sold London itself if a buyer rich enough could be found?
9 had ridden six winners in three years?
10 lost 67-68?

• 11 • *Anglicise:*

1 Young Scarface.
2 Tight Little Island.
3 The Randolph family.
4 The Outsider.
5 Mister V.
6 The Invaders.
7 High and Dry.
8 Break to Freedom.
9 Suicide Squadron.
10 The Creeping Unknown.

• 12 • *Who or what:*

1 lies mainly in SC but partly in NX?

2 should answer question 18/11?

3 houses a Scottish minister?

4 being almost 8½ miles around scored six to Ickx?

5 are one of one to ten plus eleven?

6 is a way, by the addition of ore, to boost a claim for sale – perhaps in Siberia?

7 are well-jammed sandwiches?

8 is an attack, not for 'our lax and divided powers' – according to Jefferson?

9 followed Lanfranc from Bec?

10 were Iosif and Gregorievich and Dzhugashvili?

• 13 • *What:*

1 is BART?

2 arrived in 1860?

3 is the significance of 415?

4 was Andrew Hallidie's contribution?

5 is the crookedest street in the world?

6 is the occupation of the Giants of Candlestick Park?

7 closed for business on 21st March 1963?

8 lies at the other end of Interstate Highway 80?

9 was left by Tony Bennett?

10 was Yerba Buena?

• 14 • *What or who:*

1 danced with Frank, Vic and Jaroslav?

2 springs from Monte Viso?

3 is a form of oriental theatre?

4 was tormented by Hera's gadfly?

5 is an oriental investigator?

6 married Dr Bhaer?

7 is played on stoney ground?

8 is a yak cross?

9 confirmed Mr Lillywick in his opinion of the French language?

10 featured with Moore herein?

• 15 • *What comes midway between:*

1   a light breeze and a hurricane?
2   afternoon and last dog?
3   a loom with a grip and a blade with a copper band?
4   'My vessel is stopped and making no way through the water' and 'My vessel is healthy and I request free practique'?
5   Rear Admiral of the Blue and Admiral of the Red?
6   Juliett and November?
7   51°S and 4°N?
8   a square of leather with a hole in it and a piece of cord with two knots in it?
9   worming and serving?
10   . - - - - and - - - - . ?

• 16 • *Identify:*

1   Darsie Latimer.
2   Sir Willoughby Patterne.
3   Helen Graham.
4   Cedric Errol.
5   Edward (later, VI) and Tom Canty.
6   Michael Henchard.
7   Mulvaney, Ortheris and Learoyd.
8   Anne Catherick.
9   Dr Charles Primrose.
10   Harvey Birch.

• 17 • *Define:*

1   'That period of time in which our affairs prosper, our friends are true and our happiness is assured.'

2   'A person who talks when you want him to listen.'

3   'One who in a perilous emergency thinks with his feet.'

4   'A minor form of despair, disguised as a virtue.'

5   'An instrument employed in the rectification of national boundaries.'

6   'Refusing to pay your tailor's bill because he addressed you as "Mr." instead of "Esq."'

7   'In international affairs, a period of cheating between two periods of fighting.'

8   'A person of low taste, more interested in himself than in me.'

9   'A popular entertainment given to the military by innocent bystanders.'

10   'The part of eternity with some small fraction of which we have a slight and regrettable acquaintance.'

• 18 • *In 1983:*

1   what ornament and safeguard appeared, to join its Manx precursor?

2   who was the first to become 656th?

3   who ran two hundred metres faster on 3rd July?

4   with whom will there be no more 'Champers at Twickers'?

5   what appeared in company with an eagle and a long spanner?

6   whither did Sally Ride ride?

7   why did the pip leap?

8   which paintings were for a time thought to be not so hot?

9   who was dragged in an orderly way?

10   what was overtaken by John Bertrand?

1984–1985

• 1 • *In 1884:*

   1   what went from A to Anat?

   2   for what 'Silence Cabinets' was authority given?

   3   who made a first oval contribution to tsardom?

   4   whose holey aspirations began to take shape?

   5   who embarked on a life involving the Walkers on Water?

   6   what was taken by Germany and shared by Britain?

   7   who was given 'out' but is still '120 not out'?

   8   who was ginned?

   9   who, with mugwump assistance, beat St John into fourth place?

  10   what won 'Picture-Frame' Jennings his Gold Medal?

• 2 • *Delineate:*

   1   a beer glass

   2   a nap raiser

   3   a light heavy

   4   a kitchen (within)

   5   a golf-blouse

   6   a salt meat

   7   soiled

   8   twenty-one

   9   a party-starter

  10   a Pools return

• 3 • *What was represented as:*

1 Viola?

2 Béatrice et Bénédict?

3 Chimes at Midnight?

4 West Side Story?

5 A Place Called Rome?

6 Sir John in Love?

7 Kumonosu-Djo?

8 The Boys from Syracuse?

9 I Capoletti ed i Montecchi?

10 Kiss Me Kate?

• 4 • *What:*

1 necessitates the handling of Ailsa Craig?

2 sees gentles scattered?

3 scores with a chase made in a grille?

4 involves pearling and tubing?

5 has the counters finishing in beds?

6 is pétanque?

7 was Baggataway?

8 could see one score a behind?

9 must have a cradle and probably a corkscrew?

10 requires the propulsion of a dishcloth?

• 5 • *Who created:*

1 *Trouble in Tahiti?*

2 *The Force of Destiny?*

3 *The Siege of Corinth?*

4 *The Battle of the Huns?*

5 *A Survivor from Warsaw?*

6 *The Attack on the Mill?*

7 *The Rise and Fall of the City of Mahagonny?*

8 *The Mines of Sulphur?*

9 *Death in Venice?*

10 *The Triumph of Time and Truth?*

• 6 • *Who or what:*

1   flower is the 'String of Pearls'?

2   was worn when 'I met a pearl of a native girl'?

3   sings 'take back your mink, take back your pearls'?

4   is the Pearl of French West Africa?

5   melodrama was originally 'The String of Pearls'?

6   Pearl penned *The Good Earth*?

7   said 'Her bed is India; there she lies, a pearl'?

8   Pearl advocated the rhythmic beating out of Bizet on a drum?

9   was the Pearl of York?

10   composed the 'String of Pearls'?

• 7 • *What:*

1   struck at 2.15 on 7th May 1915?

2   was the last Delage?

3   sought Saharan skies in '65?

4   failed to reach its Indian destination in 1930?

5   was the only midget to return from Kaa Fjord?

6   silver class had the blue bird of York as its flyer?

7   was topped by Desio?

8   caused the cancellation of a summit?

9   slices through spaghetti?

10   was Who's?

• 8 • *What covering is or was:*

1   felt and mesmerised?

2   fixed at the front?

3   originally red but could be a currant biscuit?

4   headed N.E.?

5   a reminder of that daring young man on the flying trapeze?

6   Genoese and usually tight?

7   almost caught by Cutty Sark when very tight?

8   scanty, just a section of chain in two sections?

9   plaited in Ecuador, much further south?

10   in charge in charge?

• 9 • *Whose death was depicted by:*

1 Copley?
2 West?
3 Munkacsy?
4 Maclise?
5 Delacroix?
6 Piero di Cosimo?
7 Delaroche?
8 Shahn?
9 Bree?
10 David?

• 10 • *Terminate:*

1 Shinkansen
2 Étendard
3 Hiawatha
4 Flèche d'Or
5 Indian Pacific
6 Rheinpfeil
7 Daylight
8 Settebello
9 Ghan
10 Southern Belle

• 11 • *Who:*

1 rolled ball-bearings and worried about strawberries?
2 mastered a craft found by Dei Gratia?
3 lost the old Bethia to a Christian?
4 was ignored by his tenants?
5 endeavoured in the Earl of Pembroke?
6 flew from Batavia?
7 took Anna to the Far East?
8 may have trained his band but not his horse?
9 was 'proficient' in Slwuggagond?
10 had a treasure revealed by the Gold Bug?

• 12 • *What:*

1 lady pin'd in thought with a green and yellow melancholy?
2 June operation had a gold centre?
3 when red is gules and black is sable, is purple?
4 is a cuttlefish?
5 was once Arausio?
6 links blue and yellow with green and red?
7 emberiza makes its stately home betwixt the magnolia and the peach?
8 hue is 125 years old?
9 comes from Cambodia?
10 when red became brown, and black became blue, happened to green?

• 13 • *In what work appears:*

1 Bly?
2 Manderley?
3 Tara?
4 Brandon Abbas?
5 Dorincourt?
6 Pemberley?
7 Robin Hill?
8 Nampara?
9 Ellangowan?
10 Woodstock?

• 14 • *Top and tail:*

1 John Moreton Drax Plunkett.
2 Augustine Aloysius.
3 Loomis.
4 Arthur St. John.
5 Henry Hall.
6 Chawner.
7 Hilaire Pierre.
8 Ronald Reuel.
9 Marlais.
10 Fingal O'Flaherty Wills.

- 15 - *What was lit up:*

    1   when Mrs O'Leary's cow kicked the lantern?

    2   it would seem, by van der Lubbe, after all?

    3   when Callinicos mixed in his mortar?

    4   in Cumberland county, blazoning the bicentenary of Master Farryner's handiwork?

    5   heralding reprieve from a dark and stormy night, if the twins are to be believed?

    6   after excessive horseplay?

    7   by Friml?

    8   and named after the Christian who rebuilt it?

    9   and, being admired from afar, was accompanied by the reciting of verses concerning the city of Paris?

    10 and spread from Pudding to Pie?

- 16 - *Puzzle:*

    1   The polished mosaic floor

    2   of the stage had beneath it a room

    3   in which a Neapolitan beggar

    4   on his grey

    5   did fraudulently appropriate

    6   soft Italian cheese

    7   from a Muslim official caller

    8   who used a method of copperplate engraving

    9   for colouring (to give an impression of life)

    10 cheese and tomato pie

• 17 • *Who married:*

1   his namesake?

2   Geneva?

3   in London?

4   in the Blue Room?

5   the same woman twice?

6   'The Inquiring Camera Girl'?

7   'Pat – who also ran'?

8   a planter of Japanese cherry trees?

9   Lemonade Lucy?

10   not at all?

• 18 • *In 1984:*

1   what shell cocked its snook at lighter opposition?

2   to whom did the Archers give a bow?

3   who (middle name, Fauntleroy – and for whom Clarence Nash always spoke out well) celebrated his 50th birthday?

4   why, at last, may Flash flush with pleasure?

5   what duo recalled the double double double of D G A Lowe?

6   who took Stockton on his ninetieth birthday?

7   how many stood beneath a crooked spire to make a record?

8   ironically, on what day was the Torch of Freedom put out?

9   who took his name from his very long time resting place?

10   who was 6079?

1985–1986

• 1 • *In 1885:*

1 who took over as caretaker?

2 what was fought for a fortnight?

3 what Wanderer travelled 1,300 miles without leaving the Stables?

4 what grew from a smallish plot on Sulphur Mountain?

5 what, with an extra dozen, reached 670 (only 37 short of its record)?

6 what address, later illuminated, bore witness to the appearance of Michael Holroyd Smith's conduit system?

7 who launched a Viking ship on two wheels?

8 where did Home Insurance rise steeply for William Jenney?

9 who turned out crackers in Dublin?

10 what (B C for this last stage) had reached across a continent?

• 2 • *What is or was:*

1 a skipper's daughter?

2 sucking the monkey?

3 a Spithead nightingale?

4 an anti-guggler?

5 blowing the grampus?

6 jibbering the kibber?

7 a donkey's breakfast?

8 a pusser's medal?

9 taking a caulk?

10 a Scarborough warning?

• 3 • *Locate:*

1 *aptrik*

2 *slowit*

3 *foi*

4 *ensö*

5 *web'li*

6 *hoik*

7 *mouz'l*

8 *lärn*

9 *stērz*

10 *bōnes*

• 4 • *Whence came:*

1 Olive Blossoms?

2 Epaulettes?

3 Bombas?

4 Black Swans?

5 Chain-breakers?

6 Farley's Follies?

7 Bantams?

8 Bluenoses?

9 Tyrian Plums?

10 Small Falls?

• 5 • *Who or what:*

1 five overlook Duich and Shiel?

2 launched a Five-Year Plan – 1928 to 1932?

3 was a five pot-piece?

4 was the 'Five-and-Ten'?

5 whizzed them over the net, full of the strength of five?

6 suggested Tattycoram take five-and-twenty?

7 five 'birds are flown'?

8 were extirpated by five-and-thirty pipers?

9 if the Nations were Five, were the Soldiers and the Seas?

10 was 'Mr Five Percent'?

• 6 • *Produce:*

1 mentha x piperita
2 cowslip x primrose
3 stallion x she-ass
4 grapefruit x tangerine
5 lion x tigress
6 mandarin x seville
7 greyhound x spaniel
8 white rose x red rose
9 bison x domestic cow
10 blackcurrant x gooseberry

• 7 • *Detect:*

1 Antony Hamilton and Jennifer O'Neill
2 James Warwick and Francesca Annis
3 Lewis Collins and Martin Shaw
4 Don Johnson and Philip Michael Thomas
5 Sharon Gless and Tyne Daly
6 Fred Dryer and Stepfanie Kramer
7 Michael Brandon and Glynis Barber
8 Brian Keith and Daniel Hugh-Kelly
9 Don Henderson and Siobhan Redmond
10 Clayton Moore and Jay Silverheels

• 8 • *Who or what:*

1 gave a second-hand ring to Mordecai?
2 ring is a young golden-eagle?
3 wears the Fisherman's Ring?
4 ring is at Zetweg?
5 sold a ring for one shilling?
6 ring involves Mime and ends in a wash-out?
7 married the sea annually, with a ring?
8 ring preceded a couple of sneezes?
9 nightly … look you sing, Like to the Garter's compass in a ring?
10 ring is not a 'a place' within the meaning of the Act of 1853?

• 9 • *Who is or was:*

1 recently overworked by a bear, having rejected a rose?
2 Arthur Lucan?
3 Sinbad's burden?
4 produced for Elizabeth, Christmas 1598?
5 the not-so-neat admiral, despite his silken coat?
6 a Royal Irish Fusilier of the 87th Foot?
7 the seventh President?
8 Isocrates?
9 featured in the *Comic Adventures of Sarah Catherine Martin?*
10 the holder of the 51st card?

• 10 • *Realise:*

1 Dumble
2 Chatteris
3 Mudfrog
4 Bevishampton
5 Stoniton
6 Steepway
7 Weatherbury
8 Priorsford
9 Oldcastle
10 Doomington

• 11 • *From what and from where:*

1 Batzi?
2 Pulque?
3 Pinga?
4 Zibib?
5 Kislav?
6 Bagaceira?
7 Enzian?
8 Akvaviittee?
9 Skhou?
10 Rakia?

• 12 • *Who or what:*

1   is the Lychnis chalcedonica?

2   is topped apparently by the Boston Stump?

3   steps lead to the Chapel of the Three Kings of Cologne?

4   left in the 'Matthew'?

5   European first was opened in 1792 at 37 Queen Square?

6   World first is the New Room off Horsefair?

7   promising and delightful business was started by a doctor, a potter and a typefounder?

8   is understood locally to be the Spy Glass of a sterling character?

9   were counter dealings in Corn Street?

10   was Bricgstoc?

• 13 • *Isolate:*

1   Solid brawn, sane and great scout altogether.

2   Let me shop for five old batteries.

3   Newly in salad, straight off barrow.

4   Escort red-skins, yielding ground to Kiwis.

5   Flame is on highest at 621.

6   Final diners find tables at the Plough Inn, Beal.

7   'All's fine' sounds the nearby roach.

8   Uncle, babe and Betty Burke left here.

9   Mun (Scottish male) holds pitfall for Jack's giant.

10   A land – one nine thirty two saw the completion of its fortress.

• 14 • *What school:*

1   came from Brazil in 1914?

2   would sound mammalian?

3   is No. 55 in E flat?

4   was the Buchanan view of Rossetti poems?

5   was Southern 927?

6   features the screen scenes?

7   discovered the Mississippi sources?

8   is Dent's version of *I quattro rusteghi*?

9   features in the Stanza della Segnatura?

10   was attended by N Molesworth, England, Europe, the World, the Universe, Space?

• 15 • *What force:*

1 is an act of God?

2 figured in the Clapham sect and would not tolerate a triangle?

3 is of necessity?

4 featured de Carlo, Lancaster and Bickford?

5 is operational under unified command?

6 plays light airs?

7 claims 'offence defence'?

8 'should be *well* flavoured … and firm enough to be fried without breaking'?

9 is to abscond with the punters' stakes?

10 is visited by the Green Dragon?

• 16 • *Who or what:*

1 is the first arrival at the Woolpack?

2 is M'bwa m'kubwa M'bwa mamwitu?

3 said nothing until the 1960s but may eat eggs without restriction?

4 was not said by Charles Boyer?

5 was not said by James Cagney?

6 was not said by Humphrey Bogart?

7 was not said by Sherlock Holmes?

8 is run in plimsoles and without spoken orders (almost)?

9 said of his extra father, 'My God, there he is on the dock, waving goodbye, and there he is on the ship waving goodbye to himself on the dock'?

10 ended with 'The rest is silence'?

• 17 • *What (or who):*

1   could be dug-out?

2   is, literally?

3   was claimed by Michael Flanders?

4   comes from barren-ground or woodland and offers no help to its cousins at Christmas?

5   is a Bentley Quattro?

6   is a cavity in snow over a seal's breathing hole?

7   is a pigtail?

8   caused general distress at Greasy Grass River?

9   before STD could cause Trans-Atlantic confusion?

10   lived at Gill's Lap, Hartfield?

• 18 • *In 1985:*

1   what had had its final shove?

2   who, finding himself in a corner, finally blacked out the world?

3   who left Clacton for a whale of a time at Windsor?

4   what biennial bloomed belatedly before coming to a strange brown end?

5   who took command of the Fleet when the Crusader sank to a mighty punch?

6   what visitor's course had been plotted by the captain of HMS *Paramore*?

7   who was taken off course by a wind from the west?

8   what notable all-rounder signed off?

9   where was Adam Hughes' picnic pitched?

10   who became a cygnet?

1986–1987

• 1 • *What, in 1886:*

1 first flowed as Dr Pemberton's 'Esteemed Brain Tonic and Intellectual Beverage'?

2 visitor to Turkey returned and wrote *Biritch*?

3 iconoclast was sworn in?

4 bascule construction began its eight-year span?

5 was established ahead of St Anne and St Hilda?

6 New York Country Club welcomed Grisworld – the man in black?

7 Bill ensured Uncle Bob's speedy return?

8 was first savoured in Californian guise as Shakespeare hawker McConnell's giveaway gimmick?

9 king had his birthday?

10 explosions were created by a WWII admiral for his grandfather?

• 2 • *Where lie:*

1 Aurora?

2 Mark Twain?

3 Santa Maria?

4 Rose?

5 Lady Hopetown?

6 Nancy?

7 Burza?

8 W P Snyder?

9 Gjøa?

10 Belfast?

• 3 • *Name the three:*

1 'A's

2 Andrews Sisters

3 'F's

4 Emperors

5 'L's

6 Festival Choirs

7 'P's

8 Smart Girls (three years on)

9 'R's

10 In Happidrome

• 4 • *Wot:*

1 Some criminals have underestimated Royal Canadian Mounted Police.

2 Is perpetual zeal the means?

3 Camels often sit down carefully. Perhaps their joints creak.

4 At the Canine Club never give viscous vegetables to Dalmatians.

5 Lazy French tarts sit naked in anticipation.

6 No plan like yours to study history wisely.

7 How I want a drink, alcoholic of course, after the heavy chapters involving quantum mechanics.

8 Sergeant Major hates eating onions.

9 Roll out your Guinness, boys, in vats.

10 Men very easily make jugs serve useful nocturnal purposes.

• 5 • *Localise:*

1 Arkell's Ark.

2 Smith's Magnet.

3 Flower's Bard.

4 Young's Victory.

5 Hammond Hub.

6 Hyde's Anvil.

7 Wadsworth's North Gate.

8 Hartley's Crown.

9 Tamplin's Phoenix.

10 Holt's Lighthouse.

• 6 • *In sport:*

1 what is played by Manchester Football Club?

2 where is the New Zealand Golf Club?

3 what is the LCF of walking – and around the snooker table?

4 who are the reigning Olympic Rugby Champions?

5 how many Olympic silver medals have been won for cricket?

6 … who lost that match?

7 … and who was the flop of the 1968 Olympics?

8 what may be squopped with a squidger?

9 where does a pepper-box on a step cause problems?

10 what can never be said to be over when delivery is without the pig's ear?

• 7 • *Account for:*

1 Tincture of aloes and myrrh.

2 Normal horse serum.

3 Elixir of vitriol.

4 Pig, salol.

5 Imperial drink.

6 Dessicated stomach.

7 Compound syrup of creosote.

8 Sumatra dragon's blood.

9 Yohimbae cortex.

10 Wormseed.

• 8 • *Who said:*

1   'Science is the first sin, seed of all sin – thou shalt not know'?

2   'Science is the greatest antidote of … superstition'?

3   'Science advances with gigantic strides; but are we aught enriched in love and meekness'?

4   'Science is the religion of the suburbs'?

5   'Religions die when they are proved to be untrue. Science is the record of dead religions'?

6   'I … fear that Science will be used to promote the power of dominant groups rather than to make men happy'?

7   'Remember that Science demands from a man all his life'?

8   'Science grows and beauty dwindles'?

9   'His proud Science never taught to stray'?

10 'Science … hast thou not dragged Diana from her car'?

• 9 • *Entitle afresh:*

1   Tomorrow is Another Day.

2   The Chronic Argonauts.

3   Mag's Diversions.

4   The Various Arms.

5   The Tree and the Blossom.

6   Before this Anger.

7   The Summer of the Shark.

8   Something that Happened.

9   The Incident at West Egg.

10 The Sea Cook.

• 10 • *Who or what:*

1 is a wild carrot?

2 became of Abraham Lauritz Jonsson?

3 carries on affairs on the left bank?

4 took on St Ives at 31 to end it all?

5 dummy was quite capable of striking back?

6 merchant carried concealed weapons?

7 according to Greek legend was forbidden in Eden?

8 depression was left behind as Monty prospered?

9 were Dannay and Lee?

10 borders on Nassau to the east and Jamaica to the south?

• 11 • *Who:*

1 produced a running commentary – stop or go?

2 did, in fun, meet me inside, all buttoned up?

3 portrayed the maestro, and studied birds, bees and storks?

4 presented nothing but Max and offered Max presents?

5 drew round the bend, going on up the straight (and over the line)?

6 came up with inventions and some frightful war pictures?

7 described a top dog and added a leg at each corner?

8 fashioned the female approach and drew back to the slaughterhouse?

9 made progress at Pelvis Bay, sailing to Byzantium?

10 caught the early morning milk train and remembered the forgotten tramcar?

• 12 • *Who:*

1 eloped following canine hilarity?

2 received acetic acid treatment for capital repairs?

3 took flight after sinister dealings?

4 had a row, appropriately?

5 practised porcine pilferage?

6 was a snappy sconce skipper?

7 was failed by the cavalry?

8 was an arachnophobe?

9 tried tripe, beer, wine and fruit as petfood?

10 succumbed after an eventful sennight?

• 13 • *Identify the card dealers to:*

1   J Baker.

2   Mr Donald Bass.

3   J Marshall.

4   Mrs A M Healy.

5   J N Travers.

6   M Stephens.

7   Susan James.

8   Mr Leslie Porter.

9   Mr X K Davis.

10   Jacques LeGrand.

• 14 • *Who might be:*

1   set to take over after a take-off?

2   safe?

3   quail in Virginia?

4   made accountable?

5   linked across a manly front?

6   a sheep of one colour and another?

7   understood when out?

8   a lot of interest?

9   a weight-lifter?

10   recognised by the initials WC?

• 15 • *An 'L' test:*

1   to what did Polk agree despite his campaign slogan?

2   what comes in order between DFM and IOM?

3   who, when elevated, was impressed by an advertisement for '21 Styles of Shoes'?

4   what are disposed according to Hoyle?

5   who lost at Vesontium?

6   whose Scotch was first appreciated in Leipzig after taking twelve years to mature?

7   what extends capitally from Dover to Honolulu?

8   who was praised to his face with courtly foreign grace?

9   what green twin weighs in at just over 140?

10   where did Heston, Niven and Gardner spend almost eight weeks?

• 16 • *Gild:*

1   what was done in WWII by an idling GI.
2   Andalusia.
3   oil.
4   the setting for a little chap's enjoyment of a well-cooked sole.
5   the one unbearably disruptive of food and furniture.
6   the winner of $100 from the Dollar.
7   the smallest bird of Europe.
8   iron pyrites.
9   the hypothesis that every even number greater than two is the sum of two prime numbers.
10 a colonel of the Life Guards.

• 17 • *State which is or was:*

1   Hitler's 'provocation' in 1939.
2   strictly 'Men Only'.
3   the smallest and policed by foreigners.
4   a Herculean pillar.
5   to despatch Mickey, Minnie, Donald and Goofy to all parts in 1970.
6   Letzeburgesch spoken.
7   cleaned out six times in three days of 1891 by the Martingale system.
8   the home of the Viguier Francais and the Viguier Episcopal.
9   noted for the quality of its beguiling grins and sausage skins.
10 to lose its 'Freedom' in 1954.

• 18 • *In 1986:*

1   what was sold up in the 'Greatest Sale on Earth'?
2   what watchdog took a consuming interest in its patrol beat?
3   where was Peter O'Sullevan received in comfort (and with a cup of tea)?
4   for whom did six years become six hours (because of a widow's might)?
5   for whom was Gulfland lucky 13?
6   what egg-eating emigrants left their home to walled-out seaweed-scoffing sheep?
7   who faced a spear (not an arrow) at Hastings?
8   what was kept by a Bill, two Bobs and a Bruce?
9   with whom did the Dutch sign a peace treaty after 335 years of war?
10 for what did the rampant lion of Hawick pay £2,587 a letter?

1987–1988

• 1 • *In 1887:*

1 what cut was first cut?

2 what patent was to treble the Mint's copper coin output ten years on?

3 what was lost by George Thomas Morton?

4 what brigade recorded its first turnout?

5 in what first did George Benton 'walk over'?

6 who was Thorkell Mylrea of Slieu Dhoo?

7 whose appearance was to bring an avalanche of centenary congratulations upon the head of Sue Brown of the Abbey National?

8 who was 'the man who …' man who first drew breath?

9 what stretched onto British shores for a suspenseful if scanty stay?

10 kio estas tio?

• 2 • *Study:*

1 beer mats

2 folklore

3 tree-ring dating

4 birds' nests

5 life on other planets

6 astronomy

7 money boxes

8 political economy

9 the art of lying

10 Methodist circuit plans

• 3 • *Who embodied:*

1 Melina Havelock?

2 Honeychile Ryder?

3 Tiffany Case?

4 Holly Goodhead?

5 Tatiana Romanova?

6 Anya Amasova?

7 Kissy Suzuki?

8 Fatima Blush?

9 Stacey Sutton?

10 Tracy Bond?

• 4 • *Where is there:*

1 a 6½ pound batman?

2 a fuss about a foot?

3 a gun weighing 1⅓ pounds?

4 18,000 pounds of candy?

5 a kettle holding over 17½ pints?

6 a pond over a pound?

7 a one yard war?

8 a mile, 4½ times that length?

9 mud covering almost 2½ acres?

10 a chum over ten times the fun in Hong Kong?

• 5 • *Track down:*

1 U.B.A.

2 V.R.

3 P.C.A.L.

4 C.F.L.

5 T.C.D.D.

6 P.K.B.

7 R.F.F.S.A.

8 M.A.V.

9 K.C.R.

10 S.Z.D.

• 6 • *What:*

1   came with Tangier as Catherine of Braganza's dowry?

2   are the bunders?

3   are sports shorts in Strine?

4   transferred from Surat in 1687?

5   is the harpadon nehereus?

6   number are the 'Towers of Silence'?

7   is a glass of milk with a double dose of castor oil?

8   bade imperial welcome monumentally?

9   became of Alexandra Dock in 1972?

10   is Ptolemy's Heptanesia, supposedly?

• 7 • *Where the … are:*

1   Bray?

2   Wickham?

3   Bolton?

4   Markham?

5   Blackpool?

6   Chester?

7   Peel?

8   Barley?

9   Trent?

10   Fleetwood?

• 8 • *What is or was:*

1   empty for years after aspiring to 33 in '66?

2   kept in the first four hours?

3   the final setting of Church Road?

4   bridged by three ossicles?

5   Meriden?

6   the Africa – West Indies/US stage?

7   an aid to stability that started with junk?

8   Royal China

9   the Association's number 9?

10   Ynis Badrig, where St Patrick foundered?

• 9 • *Name the chief castle captive at:*

1 Ashby-de-la-Zouche.

2 Gloucester.

3 Pevensey.

4 Middleham.

5 Knaresborough.

6 Berkhamsted.

7 Carisbrooke.

8 Odiham.

9 Kenilworth.

10 Bamburgh.

• 10 • *Who aired in what:*

1 L'amour est un oiseau rebelle?

2 Où va la jeune Hindoue?

3 Casta Diva?

4 Ora e per sempre addio?

5 Connais-tu le pays?

6 Vissi d'arte?

7 Nothung! Nothung!?

8 Un bel di vedremo?

9 Di tanti palpiti?

10 Ombra mai fù?

• 11 • *What has come from:*

1 an antipodean greeting?

2 Adolf Dassler?

3 good play by the Danes?

4 a Nicholas Product?

5 the Provincial Incandescent Fitting Company?

6 a French cooking pot?

7 the Via Gellia?

8 Standard Oil?

9 making savings by going Dutch – and being spruce, too?

10 a ball-bearing proclaiming its ability to roll?

• 12 • *Who made his name by:*

1   decorating in plaster?

2   making bits and (suchlike) pieces?

3   feathering tails – but there was also a point to his work?

4   hooping and staving?

5   turning – or was he merely clumsy?

6   using a cleaner earth or cloth?

7   making hay?

8   hunting hares – by rushes?

9   making a pilgrimage with frond in hand?

10   leading the pipes?

• 13 • *What:*

1   by Jeremiah was called Heliopolis?

2   would have received a visit from Buddy but for his aversion to Al?

3   is joined by Tom on the way north?

4   is the art of Riley and Vasarély?

5   field is where the northern lion, Gules, stands rampant?

6   would we be in Scotland?

7   bird is the dunlin?

8   man of substance was said to have survived on the roof of the Ark?

9   force from female finger-tips burns blue?

10   is the US memorial site to the men of Tuscania and Otranto?

• 14 • *Who or what:*

1   charioteer scorched over the deserts of Africa?

2   would be about two-a-penny today, if about (or two-a-penny) today?

3   anchorite founded a monastery at Breuil?

4   provided for a 'beautiful woman' to be as 'a jewel in a velvet-lined casket' and designed Birmingham Town Hall?

5   is for general purposes?

6   is a supporter of Krishna – 'Lord of the World'?

7   had a noted fringe success in 46 or sooner?

8   is divided – by a glass partition?

9   is for a man who wants to be alone – with his horse?

10   was Maria Lee of Philadelphia?

• 15 • *Who:*

1 sees Crystal Falls in the county seat?
2 was better developed in La Tène than in Halstatt?
3 in 1907 was the published forecast from London?
4 arrowy shower hurtles in the darken'd air?
5 Longobardic headgear is cross-nailed?
6 is gorged most deeply by Rouman and Serb?
7 was cover for M. de Marchiel?
8 sort of breather came from a Drinker?
9 was the 'Tin Duck'?
10 a soft set that was!

• 16 • *What:*

1 is the Original Buff?
2 clock was put back one hour 37½ minutes?
3 goes forward with Britain?
4 was shackled for 13 years?
5 appropriately first sported a monocular sun?
6 became the two dailies that disappeared in 1930?
7 resident is to be found in Gloucester?
8 left the city in 1959?
9 came first daily in England?
10 covers 'twixt Trent and Tweed'?

• 17 • *A plump little Christmas robin to dissect:*

1 Falls disregarded by M. Gravelet.
2 Pannier.
3 Peg with a swell job for board on board.
4 Anaglypta.
5 Trainer of trainers.
6 Ledger when lying.
7 Penguin.
8 Norman, work axed and succeeded by dog-tooth.
9 Sumpter.
10 Rider ahead of the rebel tread.

• 18 • *In 1987:*

1   who by coming first came forth to the fourth?

2   where was Viscount Grant supreme?

3   who lies doggo – a stranger unspied?

4   what service, which drove a tennis ball into a klaxon, celebrated its Golden Anniversary … ?

5   … and what Anniversary was doubly Golden with a quarter of a million held up at a hold up?

6   what flower, closely related to a Daisy, flourished on the Green, shading out both Wood and Dell … ?

7   … how many went to Yasuda Insurance Co. at £1¾M. a time … ?

8   … and whose tiger, tiger burnt even brighter?

9   for whom did lightning strike for a second time in the shape of another Hogan?

10   what was occupied by Mrs Angela Bailey putting on a further 15 revs?

1988–1989

• 1 •   *In 1888:*

   1   who came first to see as what where?

   2   what issued forth and now provides 11M subscribers with travelogues gilt girt?

   3   what letter so intrigued George Eastman?

   4   whose was the traverse of Kalaallit Nunaat?

   5   what was declared free and open in Constantinople?

   6   who showed no sign of triskaidekaphobia with tales of an Irishman, a Cockney and a Tyke?

   7   what was won by Bertha Soucaret?

   8   who won despite a smaller final score against Cleveland?

   9   through whose sharp practice did Mary Nicholls become first lady?

  10   what line started doing things by halves and later solved a piano-balancing problem – 'neatly'?

• 2 •   *Identify:*

   1   Neville St Clair.

   2   Godfrey Emsworth.

   3   Violet Smith.

   4   Josiah Amberley.

   5   Robert St Simon.

   6   Eugenia Ronder.

   7   Jonas Oldacre.

   8   Godfrey Staunton.

   9   Henry Wood.

  10   Hall Pycroft.

• 3 • *Who designed:*

1   the President's Palace, Brasilia?

2   the Marshall Field Warehouse, Chicago?

3   the Monastery of La Tourette, Eveux?

4   Grundtvig's Church, Copenhagen?

5   the Opera House, Sydney?

6   the Main Railway Station, Helsinki?

7   Boots' Factory, Beeston?

8   Falling Water, Bear Run?

9   Truyère Bridge, Garabit?

10   the Bauhaus, Dessau?

• 4 • *Who gave an ism for:*

1   a philosophy of positivist system?

2   sanguine autosuggestion?

3   excessively realistic treatment of the grosser side of human nature?

4   the writing of light, witty, painless literary and even legal compositions?

5   profit sharing according to the value of work?

6   an old, old chestnut?

7   edifying Shakespeare?

8   misapplication of a long word?

9   hypnotic fascination?

10   conventional prudery?

• 5 • *Who or what:*

1   leans from a window in Great Marlborough Street?

2   appears in Victoria Tower Gardens – with her daughter (who, of course, came later)?

3   'Roman Senator' with the Magna Carta stands in Bloomsbury Square?

4   bestrides a mount with flying tail in Cockspur Street?

5   is talking to the Brontës in Cornhill?

6   appears outside Guy's Hospital – the only one in the city with the brass to be outside?

7   stands by his chair in Parliament Square just as he does in Chicago?

8   sits cross-legged in Tavistock Square?

9   kitted for flight stand between Terminals 2 and 3?

10   recumbent nude is to be found in Red Lion Square?

• 6 • *Who or what:*

1 lies opposite the Temple in King's Reach?

2 was produced by Sergeant Cuff (with no budding on)?

3 flourished most famously for Joseph William Mayerl?

4 was Nobody junior?

5 received Harry Dacre's proposal?

6 caused his unrequited lover to pine away to just a voice?

7 Mr Porter, is the way to the everlasting bonfire?

8 by elusion foiled Louisette?

9 was Margaret Kelly?

10 outsmarted in bed, wept diurnally?

• 7 • *Identify:*

1 Pongo.

2 Annie Laurie.

3 Andrew Millar.

4 Mutt and Jeff.

5 Johnny Armstrong.

6 Aunt Mary Ann.

7 Clara and Mona.

8 Snowflake.

9 Queen Mary.

10 Archie.

• 8 • *What:*

1 writing desk was ordered from Gillow's by Captain … ?

2 stool is drum-shaped?

3 drawer sets usually came in a double-decker?

4 according to Sheraton was a supper-tray or music-stand made to a bishop's order?

5 set of shelves was named as nothing in particular?

6 has drawers for odds, ends and raggy bits?

7 kept the bottles cool and moved on castors?

8 container was named after its three feet (though sometimes there were four)?

9 moves the meal up and down or round and round?

10 chair is designed for the chamber?

• 9 • *Who or what:*

1   surveyed in Tom Thumb?

2   was the great voyage of the Indian canoe, Tilikum?

3   frozen fish surfaced on 17.iii. 1959?

4   record fell to Orient Trader in 1966?

5   did Rattler prove to Alecto?

6   ships fought the first 'iron-clad' battle?

7   WWII US shipping was originally designed by the Sunderland Co. of Newcastle-upon-Tyne in 1879?

8   completes the 'six': Chesapeake, Congress, Constellation, Constitution, United States?

9   visited Britain in Bonhomme Richard?

10   left Bellerophon for Northumberland?

• 10 • *Who or what:*

1   when 'you were fast asleep at Crewe … was walking up and down the station'?

2   loco became the Titfield Thunderbolt?

3   was murdered in *Beware of Trains*?

4   was hurrayed 'for the life that is in him, and his breath so thick and black'?

5   is the destination when you take the 'A' train?

6   noted Pacific 231?

7   eloping head clerk was killed by a French train?

8   is 'a man who shaves and takes a train and then rides back to shave again'?

9   leaves from track 29?

10   was Stoneface's Western and Atlantic love?

• 11 • *Landscape:*

1   Roseberry Topping.

2   Wills Neck.

3   Midsummer.

4   Sharpenhoe Clappers.

5   Tap o'Noth.

6   Hay Bluff.

7   High Willhays.

8   Burrington Ham.

9   Little Hangman.

10   Brown Willy.

• 12 • *Hatch, match or dispatch*:

1 On 7ᵗʰ April at Cockermouth, to Anne (née Cookson) and John ... a son ... brother for Richard.

2 On 2ⁿᵈ January at Kuruman, Dr ... son of Mr & Mrs Neil ... to Mary, daughter of Mr & Mrs Robert Moffat.

3 On 4ᵗʰ August, peacefully in his 71st year, at Rolighed, near Copenhagen, home of Mr & Mrs Moritz Melchior ...

4 On 18ᵗʰ February, suddenly, overcome in the Tower of London, George ... youngest son of Richard and Cicely of York.

5 On 11ᵗʰ June at East Bergholt, to Anne (née Watts) and Golding ... a son ...

6 On 4ᵗʰ August, in St Stephen's Cathedral, Vienna ... son of Mr & Mrs Leopold ... to Constanze, daughter of the late Mr Fridolin and Mrs Cäcilie Weber.

7 On 25ᵗʰ April, in High Street, Huntingdon to Elizabeth (née Steward) and Robert ... a son ...

8 On 29ᵗʰ July, in a state of mental turmoil following a bullet wound at Auvers ... dear brother of Theo.

9 On 2ⁿᵈ January at Seaham, George Gordon, son of Captain and Mrs John ... to Annabella, daughter of Sir Ralph and Lady Milbanke.

10 On 2ⁿᵈ November, in the sanctuary of Westminster Abbey, to Elizabeth (née Woodville) and Edward a son ...

• 13 • *What mark*:

1 sees q on o?

2 paces no place?

3 died in prison c.68?

4 featured five lions on a cross – for York?

5 left with the words 'Now my spirit is going: I can no more'?

6 came from fluvial sounds?

7 was William Hale White?

8 is just west of Mark?

9 was used invariably by the Hanseatic League?

10 somersaults joyously?

• 14 • *What:*

1 Victorian diva trilled raspberry sauce?

2 French politician had filled a ring with fruit, nuts (and rum)?

3 Patron saint was a case of choux and shortcrust filled with vanilla cream?

4 Italian composer took tournedos and garnished them with truffles?

5 French general sautéed vegetables saucily?

6 Russian ballerina whirled a meringue with cream and fruit?

7 Somerset doctor really took the biscuit?

8 French marshal had crushed nuts – sugar-coated?

9 Westphalian goblin is called 'brown George'?

10 Bath lady cleaned up with a sweet tea cake?

• 15 • *What:*

1 5/3 in gold disappeared in 1762?

2 were tin from 1685–95?

3 reign saw the first minted appearance of Britannia?

4 land saw doubles, doubled, doubled and doubled again?

5 change of arms was made in 1797?

6 date saw the appearance of the Northumberland?

7 was the composition of the dodecagon?

8 was the smallest Jersey coin?

9 value had marigold three hundred years ago?

10 silver oddity was patterned in 1812?

• 16 • *Who or what:*

1 is born every minute?

2 could scream and scream until she was sick?

3 kept on walking?

4 blew, blew, blew, blew, blew?

5 just grow'd?

6 was born in 1820 still going strong?

7 stood on the burning deck?

8 laughed and laughed?

9 couldn't get the wood, you know?

10 had 'em?

• 17 • *What (literally):*

1   land was Biafra?

2   democrat, whose middle name was Goodenham, was secretary to one whose middle name was S?

3   is harrier, shark, bailiff, spy?

4   son of Jehoshaphat was killed by Hazael?

5   was amiss with Olivia's brine?

6   cascades for half a mile in Wensleydale?

7   city saw silversmith rioting against tentmaker?

8   early aviator crossed the sea later named after his son?

9   according to 'Musso' when the suffragettes were triumphant, was Woman's place?

10   was Sykes' missing 'Plank'?

• 18 • *In 1988:*

1   what well-aired and fenestrated place of learning closed down?

2   what old pal and beauty bowed out?

3   what Bluey came uniquely on the double off Arnie's edge?

4   what sailer did TRH present down under?

5   who, with a Spring headache, got gold all stitched up?

6   what doctor departed as three prancing children appeared?

7   who achieved a century and did always remember Marie, all alone with so very many more?

8   what first did Mr Barbara Harris achieve as a result of Mass. Appeal?

9   how were all the eights celebrated by a BEM?

10   whose Diamond Jubilee in Guiseley took place with more salting and battering?

1989–1990

• 1 • *In 1889:*

1 what herald brought news to London in February?

2 who patented his card and is still remembered by IBM?

3 what VET was demanded on four-wheelers?

4 what Liberty Bell came up with horseshoes and, more oddly, bells?

5 what started its course and was soon to influence 40% of the world's population?

6 who became the first arvicoline grandee?

7 where did Raymond give a new meaning to the expression 'show a leg'?

8 what tester featured in an outing on the river?

9 what prize awaited the winner of Harrison's Hoss Race?

10 for what did the Savoy charge 12/- a night?

• 2 • *Identify:*

1 the black hellebore.

2 a squirrel's brush.

3 Gulley Jimson's story.

4 walrus ivory.

5 sandstone veined with chalk.

6 the hazel catkin.

7 the height of Okie's Zea mays.

8 a pattern of broken checks.

9 Canary red in varnish.

10 an absolute honey.

• 3 • *What:*

1 man created King-Post?
2 is Eupagurus Bernhardus?
3 is airtight?
4 are Biblical interpretations?
5 is the situation of the Castle and Harbour of Derain?
6 is Manly red?
7 is lit by Muckle Flugga?
8 boy was Maia's?
9 is Jabal ash-Shaykh?
10 sees Fisherman and Mermaid overlooking the Bear?

• 4 • *Where:*

1 did a bedstead light on Buttermilk Hill?
2 was HMS *Sanderling*?
3 might one expect a greeting from hares?
4 was the Bollin re-bedded?
5 were Allied Airways based?
6 did newspapers arrive on the right day in April 1937 but cease three years later?
7 was there a move from Longman to Dalcross?
8 was land bought by Richard Fairey in 1929?
9 was towered over by the Orangefied Hotel?
10 between '44 and '46 was HMS *Urley*?

• 5 • *What game:*

1 was Hen Pearce?
2 was Caxton's version of Virgnay's 'Liber de ludo scacchorum'?
3 asks for it – and probably gets it?
4 was played by the Gentlemen of the Green Baize Road?
5 was played by Quintus Fabius Maximus?
6 saw Julius Caesar as a top notcher?
7 had Kimball O'Hara as a trainee?
8 was played by Charles I on a long West End green?
9 was Charles Darrow's tour of many cities?
10 was played by James Gibb with champagne corks and cigar boxes?

• 6 •   *What is 1% of:*

1   a kyat?

2   a pa'anga?

3   a leu?

4   a baht?

5   a tughrik?

6   a kwacha?

7   a cordoba?

8   a pataca?

9   a won?

10   a naira?

• 7 •   *Cast:*

1   Chill Wills and Donald O'Connor.

2   William Boyd and Andy Clyde.

3   Chester Morris and George E Stone.

4   Warner Oland and Keye Luke.

5   Arthur Lake and Penny Singleton.

6   Lewis Stone and Fay Holden.

7   Lionel Barrymore and Lew Ayres.

8   Marjorie Main and Percy Kilbride.

9   Gordon Harker and Alastair Sim.

10   Lupe Vélez and Leon Errol.

• 8 •   *Locate:*

1   the bear.

2   grocer's harbour.

3   the white fortress.

4   good hope.

5   the little town.

6   wisdom.

7   the little island of the log.

8   smoky bay.

9   the building in the marsh.

10   'Blackpool'.

· 9 · *What:*

1 voided lozenges?

2 fur is black with white tails?

3 rank would be indicated by a helmet, steel and closed?

4 are multiplied piles?

5 sort of coats make puns?

6 is a pairle that is couped?

7 term denotes natural colours?

8 becomes of a lion guardant?

9 mark on a coat-of-arms is of the eldest son?

10 … and what do younger sons do?

· 10 · *What:*

1 came of Kingsley Amis?

2 was written by Thomas Hardy?

3 was the work of Gertrude Stein?

4 was committed to paper by Compton Mackenzie?

5 came from the pen of Peter Shaffer?

6 was set down by Luigi Pirandello?

7 was put in writing by Max Beerbohm?

8 had as author, Enid Blyton?

9 was penned by Mary Stewart?

10 came from John Reed?

· 11 · *Who was:*

1 Howling Mad?

2 Vinegar Joe?

3 Uncle Bill?

4 Bull?

5 Iron Pants?

6 ABC?

7 Blood and Guts?

8 Tooey?

9 Jumbo?

10 Beetle?

• 12 • *Who:*

1   in 1753 published the first anatomy of the eye?

2   was French Royal Commissioner in Santo Domingo in C 17?

3   wrote *Atlantica* in Swedish?

4   was Court Librarian to Louis XIV?

5   acquired Singapore for the East India Company?

6   from 1535 was Professor of Medicine in the University of Tübingen?

7   is thought to have discovered the conger eel?

8   was Physician to James I?

9   was Van Buren's Secretary of War?

10   was Charles I's gardener?

• 13 • *Locate:*

1   Okuwahaken.

2   Dilston.

3   Ninai.

4   Sutherland.

5   Falefa.

6   Llandovery.

7   Tequendama.

8   Topsail.

9   Tamarind.

10   Ripon.

• 14 • *Which Cunarder:*

1   was the first?

2   was sister of *Franconia, Samaria, Scythia* and *Servia?*

3   sank the cruiser *Curaçao?*

4   was the company's first twin-screw steamship?

5   was the Green Goddess?

6   kept her White Star funnel after 1934?

7   was the first to have a permanent swimming pool?

8   ended her life as a seaplane carrier?

9   was once *Saxonia?*

10   should have been *Queen Victoria?*

• 15 • *Who:*

1   came of droll parentage to show touches of velvet and diablerie?
2   related Hellenistically, and nearly Stranded, 'disappeared' in 1936?
3   came out with 'Oh, Kay!'?
4   wrote of Early Years and Gilbert Penfold?
5   lost many battles by fire at the Doge's Palace in 1577?
6   started a line in stringing that extended melodiously for 100 years – to Geronimo?
7   painted for Queen Christina of Sweden and miniaturised Milton and Cromwell?
8   received fabulous translation by Edgar Taylor and illustration by GC?
9   were Pryde and Nicholson of the flamboyant signature?
10 found his mark at Ford's and became America's first great Shakespearean tragic actor?

• 16 • *Who led:*

1   the Savoy Orpheans?
2   the Band that plays the Blues?
3   the Bobcats?
4   the American Band of the AEF?
5   the Skyrockets?
6   the Telefunken Swing-Orchester?
7   the Georgians?
8   the Creole Jazz Band?
9   the Bluerockets?
10 the Quintette du Hot Club de France?

• 17 • *Try, try, try and try again (in the 20th Century, of course!)*

1   Skin and lay low a hill – deadly!

2   A kettle-handle to ladle a barrier in a stable typewriter bar.

3   Bunker gin to bedeck a light carriage.

4   A meander and fog at sea worry a ridge for strings.

5   Smack a nail and harness fare.

6   A flock of swans lame an object of pursuit – plucky!

7   Yearn for a summer holiday or three 'perfect' breves extended.

8   Hide a military coat and strike bare skin.

9   To turn to leeward believe in dam fashion.

10   Final cargo to continue the foot model.

• 18 • *In 1989:*

1   what became of the baby hedgehog?

2   who took Anti-matter to 150 and went on to 221?

3   how was the Dorsetshire coup-de-grace remembered?

4   what assemblage – the third since 1844 – was completed with eleven ancient chips to spare?

5   who became No. 10 in the Hall of Fame with a medal from Lord Derby … ?

6   … and who remembered an earlier lord with the first Grand Slam?

7   to what was Sydney able to give detailed assistance?

8   what was the significance of shelling at the corner of Anchor Terrace and Park Street?

9   what saint was flat out as a result of an outbreak of contractions and depressions?

10   who said 'th-th-th-that's all, f-f-f-folks'?

1990–1991

• 1 • *In 1890:*

1 who struck to achieve a twelve-hour day?

2 whose work was completed by Glazunov and Rimsky Korsakov?

3 what stellar treatment featured the wedding of Professor Stuart MP?

4 what was the hot-seat of William Kemmler?

5 what Channel crossing was achieved from St Margaret's Bay to Sangatte?

6 what padded-cell seat cost 2d?

7 what appeared jam-packed with jokelets and jestnuts?

8 what gem entered with equality?

9 what sprang forth to become the grand old lady, famed for her cosmesis?

10 who succeeded with help from her mother, Emma?

• 2 • *Who or what:*

1 place could fathom-line never touch?

2 involves the hypothecation of a vessel?

3 suffered temporary bereavement after aural provocation on the Fylde coast?

4 Athenian wove as in a dream?

5 came first in the History of John Bull?

6 cheers suggest inversion?

7 two leagues (poetically speaking) are found in East Anglia?

8 is at the junction of Eye and 23rd?

9 made the woman fundamentally sensible?

10 are bags of tar?

• 3 • *Where:*

1   is Calamity Corner?

2   did Walter Danecki work his two-ton bluff?

3   is Cotton's?

4   did Isao Aoki win a £40,000 house with one shot?

5   are OL and LO?

6   did Wg Cdr Laddie Lucas crash-land on his birthplace?

7   is Sahara?

8   has a Witch's pool engulfed a German fieldgun?

9   is South America?

10   did Bing Crosby sing 'White Christmas' sitting on the steps?

• 4 • *Who or what:*

1   wore no other uniform than a blue dress coat, brass buttons ... and a bright red cloth waistcoat?

2   is the lousewort?

3   are Gen. Sherman, Gen. Grant and the Sentinel?

4   was the state of Marian's nose when roasted crabs did hiss?

5   are the four branches of Mabinogi?

6   was Herries of Birrenswork?

7   was the Haunted Man?

8   came of Ilford, Wanstead and Woodford in 1965?

9   proclaims 'inter arma caritas'?

10   on an errand of mercy fared better in German hands than in French?

• 5 • *What:*

1   pair met at the pole?

2   Turtle attacked an Eagle?

3   was the purpose of UA Deutschland?

4   need had E22 for two further propellers?

5   number of sea-going Type VII U-Boats was built?

6   nationality were the victors aboard *Queen Elizabeth* and the *Valiant*?

7   VC destroyed 101 ships in 96 days?

8   three were 'Fisher's Toys'?

9   country produced a variety of Whiskies?

10   was 'The Trade'?

- 6 • *Number in elementary fashion:*
  1 the sons of earth.
  2 a rose.
  3 Copenhagen.
  4 a fire-stealer.
  5 a budding twig.
  6 Stockholm.
  7 a violet.
  8 a goblin.
  9 devil's copper.
  10 an Argyllshire village.

- 7 • *Who was:*
  1 the Landlord of New York?
  2 the First Grenadier of France?
  3 the Hermit of Walden?
  4 the King of Iceland?
  5 the Lawgiver of Parnassus?
  6 the Master of Flémalle?
  7 the Prisoner of Chillon?
  8 the Sage of Chelsea?
  9 the Oracle of Nuneaton?
  10 the Bastard of Orleans?

- 8 • *Identify:*
  1 Al Norris.
  2 Ruth Jones.
  3 Sophia Abuza.
  4 Norma Dolores Egstrom.
  5 Richard Penniman.
  6 Harold Jenkins.
  7 Benjamin Franklin Peay.
  8 Robert Walden Cassatto.
  9 Eunice Waymon.
  10 Ernest Evans.

• 9 • *Which best friend was named after:*

1   an abbey in the Ardennes?

2   the island of Iviza?

3   a Liddesdale farmer?

4   a butterfly (with a squirrel's tail)?

5   the 'sporting parson' of Swymbridge near Barnstaple?

6   the estate of Capt. John Tucker-Edwardes of Haverfordwest?

7   a Portuguese cartridge?

8   a heap of stones?

9   a little skipper?

10   a mining town in Northumberland?

• 10 • *Who or what:*

1   when they sell good beer in Haslemere, is where a beggar may drink his fill?

2   was Cedric Errol?

3   was the Swift view of Protestants?

4   is Tchaikovsky's Symphony No. 2 in C minor, Op. 17?

5   school was attended by Eisenhower's federal troops?

6   fought the President, by accident, a year too early?

7   was nominated after Praise-God Barebone?

8   was the crusty steward of the Abbot of Glastonbury?

9   was Amorica?

10   brought down the horse, Sorrel (cf. William Hill)?

• 11 • *Which of 3,890,000 broad acres emblazon:*

1   three arches?

2   three harts' heads?

3   three eels?

4   three sheaves?

5   three crowns?

6   three horns?

7   three white swans?

8   three 'B's?

9   three sailing ships?

10   three lilies?

• 12 • *Who painted:*

1   *McSorley's Bar?*
2   *The Copley Family?*
3   *Breezing Up?*
4   *American Gothic?*
5   *Mc Donnell Farm?*
6   *Stag at Sharkey's?*
7   *Colonel Guy Johnson?*
8   *The Passion of Sacco and Vanzetti?*
9   *Flax Scutching Bee?*
10 *The Biglen Brothers Racing?*

• 13 • *When:*

1   was VAT introduced?
2   did Henry Royce run out his first 10 hp car?
3   was Scaffhausen bombed by the USAF?
4   was Lufthansa revived?
5   did the RFC and RNAS disappear?
6   was Hitler jailed?
7   did the TA come into being?
8   did Winston Churchill receive his wings?
9   was Electricity nationalised?
10 did Montgomery become Powys?

• 14 • *On which station stand:*

1   Ralph and Joy Swann?
2   George and Oliver Turner?
3   Joy and John Wade?
4   Walter and Margaret Couper?
5   Roy and Barbara Harding?
6   Peggy and Alex Caird?
7   Joseph Rothwell Sykes and Hilda M?
8   Robert and Dorothy Hardcastle?
9   Babs and Agnes Robertson?
10 Robert and Violet?

• 15 • *Who:*

1 came first with Alice?
2 followed Alice but went to Lantz?
3 started life as Dippy Dawg?
4 are Pippo, Langben and Silja?
5 are Fiddler, Fifer and Practical?
6 is 'America's most original contribution to culture' (Sergei Eisenstein)?
7 is the Swedish Kalle Anka?
8 are Fat, Dandy (Jim), Glasses, Preacher and Straw Hat?
9 served longest with pedal variations?
10 is Yen Sid?

• 16 • *What residence:*

1 was endowed by Henry VII for 100 paupers?
2 was presented to the future Edward II by Bishop Beck?
3 once Bella Court, became Placentia?
4 'the very pearl of the realm' had its site excavated in 1959?
5 was where the Earl of Morton 'discovered' the Casket Letters?
6 caused Sidney Smith to suggest 'that the dome of St Paul's must have come … and pupped'?
7 was Queen Victoria's 'dear little Home'?
8 knew the royal couple at times as 'Lord and Lady Churchill'?
9 had all the clocks running half an hour fast?
10 was conceived by Princess Marie Louise?

• 17 • *Reveal:*

1 54, jokingly.
2 76, euphoniously.
3 650, sedentarily.
4 673, blunderingly.
5 969, genetically.
6 1400, strangely.
7 4077, carefully.
8 4468, pacifically.
9 4472, tenderly.
10 65000, engagingly.

QUESTIONS

• 18 • *In 1990:*

1 whose 431 would have tired FST (to put it mildly)?

2 what noted high-stepper (334 in all) lost his voice?

3 what complement was made to Brilliant?

4 what programme was incongruously trimmed by a Cropper?

5 whose first Home International was won away?

6 what coincidence saw Sinden and Davies get it wrong on 3.x?

7 where were services resumed in an orthodox manner on 14.x?

8 what 'other place' saw *Pavo cristatus* fail to unseat *Accipiter(e)*?

9 who said 'We must certainly remember this was not the Nobel Prize for Economics'?

10 what was the precise moment four seconds before twenty-five minutes to one (pm) on 7th August – or just thirty days earlier in some places?

1991–1992

• 1 • *In 1891 who or what:*

1 first took its bow and proved to be a wow?

2 was taken by a Mr Heath of Wolverhampton?

3 started making tracks for Vladivostok?

4 132,926 received 15,299,004 marks?

5 stone led to an uprising 'Where they'd Lions and Tigers and Camels / And old ale and sandwiches too'?

6 having changed his name from Wade began to cause many a diversion as Prime Minister?

7 did William Fargo use to obtain 50 dollars in Leipzig?

8 constructed a railway for the vast minority?

9 'Icnofalagometrico' was employed by La Plata Police?

10 syndicate punctured Queen Victoria's neck?

• 2 • *Who:*

1 was a Jew?

2 was the youngest of C.20?

3 has his tomb described by Dante in Hell?

4 was rescued by Robert Guiscard?

5 according to the incomparable Max was not remarked upon by his Roman guests – on the morning after?

6 served as a World War I hospital orderly?

7 was Hogsmouth or 'Peter de Porca'?

8 never existed despite her fame?

9 referred to 'Chemins d'Enfer'?

10 was English?

- 3 • *Broadly (etc.) speaking:*
  1 what was due west from the summit?
  2 who used scissors for a sextant?
  3 what was the signal from the lawn?
  4 what was rescued from a chicken coop off Flushing?
  5 where did the pike weigh in at thirty pound and a half?
  6 who answers on Fellside 75?
  7 where was the Geographical Society's Headquarters?
  8 what did young Billy keep in a cigar box?
  9 who kept the *Titmouse* like a new pin?
  10 who wired GUMBOOTS AND OILIES PUT THEM IN FIRST POSSIBLE TRAIN?

- 4 • *Who or what follows:*
  1 first, middle, morning?
  2 Rowe, Eusden, Cibber?
  3 Normandy, Blois, Anjou?
  4 Rutherford, Ostwald, Wallach?
  5 Conversion of St Paul, Purification, Her Majesty's Accession?
  6 Lamb in His Bosom, Now in November, Honey in the Horn?
  7 Methuselah, Salmanazar, Balthazar?
  8 Bradley, Bliss, Maskelyne?
  9 Edgar, Alexander, David?
  10 Nisan, Iyar, Sivan?

- 5 • *Locate:*
  1 Kallenhard, Wipperman, Schwalbenschwanz.
  2 Tamburello, Tosa, Rivazza.
  3 Wakefield Road, Rundle Road.
  4 La Source, Les Combes, Les Fagnes.
  5 Oldfield, De Palma, Joe Weatherly, Campbell.
  6 Variante del Rettifilo, Rettifilo Centro.
  7 Montée du Beau Rivage, Virage Antony Noghes.
  8 Degna, Spoon, Casio Triangle.
  9 Agip, Sachs, Opel.
  10 Byfleet, Members.

• 6 • *Where could you:*

1   start with his heels?
2   find yourself pitted against a man from Spain?
3   have left pedro?
4   cap it with capot?
5   meet Pam?
6   paint?
7   meet Blucher?
8   buck the tiger?
9   find the leader is Vorland?
10 have a round trip?

• 7 • *Whose surname was:*

1   Smintheus?
2   Ultor?
3   Feretrius?
4   Argiva?
5   Acidalia?
6   Upis?
7   Saitis?
8   Mulciber?
9   Moneta?
10 Inachis?

• 8 • *Twitch:*

1   a Scottish ankle.
2   a leaden hammer.
3   piling, protecting the pier of a bridge.
4   the mark of the fourth son.
5   a railway porter at Grand Central.
6   the penultimate outside ring of a target.
7   a tailor's smoothing iron.
8   a pilgrim in a foreign land.
9   a day's work.
10 a show that flops.

• 9 • *In the annals of St Stephen's, who was the first:*

1 to call the commons to be represented?

2 female to be elected?

3 to run a library?

4 as Opposition Leader, to be paid by the state?

5 female to take the Chair?

6 coloured man to take his seat?

7 to offend convention by wearing a deerstalker?

8 to grill a steak?

9 to move a motion live on TV?

10 to inform against the Kitchen Committee for selling alcohol without a licence?

• 10 • *Whose is:*

1 the point of a worm-like addition?

2 deceptive baronial invention?

3 St Vitus' Dance?

4 a hearty quartet?

5 XXY?

6 a very weak VII?

7 the fragmented moon?

8 le main d'accoucheur?

9 the waiter's tip deformity?

10 an occasional alimentary cul-de-sac?

• 11 • *Who was:*

1 the First Lady of MGM?

2 the Baby Vamp?

3 the It Girl?

4 the Sweater Girl?

5 Miss Cheesecake of 1951?

6 Miss Deepfreeze?

7 Divine?

8 the Oomph Girl?

9 the Girl with the Perfect Face?

10 the Funniest Lady in the World?

• 12 • *Decipher:*

1 Tread Head.

2 Bluey.

3 ZULU.

4 Humint.

5 Ulu.

6 BLISS.

7 MRE.

8 Rotor head.

9 Gobbling rods.

10 BAM.

• 13 • *Locate*

1 the county for whom Roger Iddison (from elsewhere!) scored the first century.

2 Glevum.

3 the Bell, only a stage from Leicestershire to London.

4 the largest Roman bath in England.

5 the Cape of the Cats …

6 … and its highest point (by a whisker).

7 Cox's and Gough's.

8 magpie houses oft sitting on salt.

9 a 'drum' tower put on a list in the Civil War.

10 where 'King' Kit Calvert saved the industry.

• 14 • *Who or what:*

1 were born at Clough House?

2 claimed to have taken part in mimic military manoeuvres with Lord Palmerston?

3 paid William Smith Williams to read?

4 wore only silk and took snuff?

5 confederation evolved from 'scribblemania'?

6 both turned down the widower?

7 visited Uncle John Fennell at Woodhouse Grove in 1812?

8 was Tweeny?

9 was chief clerk at Luddenden Foot Railway Station?

10 was Mrs Arthur B Nicholls?

• 15 • *What:*

1   was born at 8 am on 14th November 1963?
2   is the trail of Ta-vwoarts?
3   is the habitat of Tristram's Grackle?
4   did Jove fling on top of Typhon?
5   beat the wolf of the glaciers six short of his target?
6   companion of Olga and Connor is 'where the wind moans always between sunset and dawn'?
7   is Chomolungma?
8   according to Eleanor Roosevelt 'makes our Niagara Falls look like a kitchen faucet'?
9   depression gives rise to Desert Gothic?
10 bridge building was courteously attempted to spare Benandonner wet feet?

• 16 • *Which monarch:*

1   provided Victoria with a line to James Buchanan?
2   undertook the training of wavy stripers on the seafront near Brighton?
3   set up a guild of shipmen and mariners 'to the praise and honour of the most glorious individual Trinity'?
4   had a grandson discovered by the Khedive of Egypt coaling ship at Alexandria?
5   next became Lord High Admiral after James II?
6   had been the last Lord High Admiral afloat?
7   had a Navy commanded by Admiral Sir Samuel Greig?
8   had a lantern in which Mr Pepys kissed five ladies, and a cook who burnt everything?
9   received eight-gun Mary as a present – and a new word for the language?
10 was in the van at Scapa Flow in 1918?

• 17 • *Put two and two together:*

1   Rodolfo's perishing lover.

2   a New Zealand nestor.

3   0-6-6-0 (had it been under steam).

4   one of the charms of West Africa.

5   the nurse who accompanied her charges to Miss Fulsom's Kindergarten School.

6   the granddaughter of Madame Alvarez according to Sidonie Gabrielle.

7   fencing cut not affecting the prospect.

8   Hugo Ball's wayward hobby-horse.

9   a quiz, some 200 years old.

10 a rum sort of cake.

• 18 • *In 1991:*

1   where may women add enchantment?

2   what woman was made first by God?

3   what truth was suppressed on 24th August?

4   who, from Mars, headed roughly in that direction?

5   how were US astronauts Carpenter, Grisson, Glenn, Cooper and Shepard recognised?

6   who having starred 45 years earlier mouldered in enough of the Manor?

7   who prospered at Carmel from an expected Price Increase?

8   where is there no-one to remember the Darling Bids of September?

9   who became an 88-year-old Baby Rat?

10 who turned targets into helianthi?

1992–1993

• 1 • *In 1892:*

1   how old was La Flèche?

2   who was the Dynamitard of Paris?

3   what did Dr James Nasmith devise for beanpoles?

4   How did a Derby winner appear in 'Land and Water'?

5   what did Sir Thomas Beecham's father do for toothpaste?

6   what rules were imposed upon a strong boy from Boston and a gentleman from San Francisco?

7   how did *The Weekly Summary* express itself with feeling?

8   where did Irene make her mark at Blackpool?

9   who paid £100 for Willie Groves?

10   what 27½″ were finally abandoned?

• 2 • *Who or what:*

1   spa was favoured by Edward VII?

2   was John B. and his surname?

3   Congressman fell at Alamo?

4   was du Maurier's Miss O'Farrell?

5   was Mrs Joe Willett before marriage?

6   is the serviceman's golden handshake?

7   was situated-upon-Avon?

8   was Alice Bluebonnet's department-store beau?

9   was Cutty Sark's 'glorious' quarry?

10   was Wren's headmaster at Westminster?

• 3 • *Name the day:*

1   the years started prior to 1752
2   two before Good Friday in Ireland
3   of meat and eggs, preceding Olney's race day
4   for Jenny, stoned in memory of St Stephen
5   women bound up men (and vice versa) demanding payment for release
6   the Champion from 'broad Scrivelsby' rode up Westminster Hall
7   for eating parched peas fried in butter
8   four before Christmas when fold went 'a-gooding'
9   not to survive 'The Farther Adventures......'
10 associated with Hillsborough

• 4 • *Some hand-picked seamers:*

1   why was the Surrey v Kent match abandoned in 1762?
2   how was the Gentlemen of the Hill and the Dale match played at Linstead Park, Kent in 1794?
3   what year saw Wisden record 10 wickets taken by a cricketer in one innings – all bowled?
4   who penned a poem to celebrate his only first-class wicket: WG – caught behind?
5   who made Brighton rock for 90 minutes in 1911 but that was all?
6   what Hockey International hit a Test Match six for England in 1963?
7   who made his first-class debut in 1916 and his last appearance in 1963?
8   who scored well in 208 tests – and for five countries?
9   how did Chris Balderstone interrupt his 1975 hundred v Derbyshire?
10 which county sports three seaxes?

• 5 • *Animate:*

1 oil – a wheel
2 Herbie – the wooden head beating down paving stones
3 clear the throat – cry for sale
4 wot, no paper punchouts!
5 Robert Thompson – Terence Cuneo
6 dashes and dots – slush
7 complaint from a Toytowner – very good in Australia
8 George Washington – Marshal Soult
9 a biscuit – in a paper covering 'Ariel' came first
10 Steiff – a Peruvian stationer

• 6 • *Locate:*

1 the estate of Eburos
2 the crossing of the stags
3 the village with a deer park
4 the cattle farm on the weir
5 the folk who enjoy the art of fisticuffs
6 the colony where the river widens
7 the water-meadow of Bucca's people
8 those who camped on the Soar
9 the territory of the Dumonii
10 Snot's ham

• 7 • *Piece together:*

1 Nellie and Freddie
2 Malcolm and Brenda
3 Charlie and Caroline
4 Sam and Diane
5 Lionel and Jean
6 Tony and Ruth
7 Cliff and Clair
8 Diana and Tom
9 Victor and Margaret
10 William and Adie

• 8 • *Delineate:*

1   fluvially, Szczecin to Zittau

2   divertingly, the cause of Genevieve's victory

3   precipitously, the eastern edge of the old Appalachians

4   frontally, the 'WASHING' sign hung out by Canada's forces

5   papally, 370 miles west of the Cape Verde Islands

6   temporally, Pitt and Chatham erratically ahead of the Rats

7   prominently, the 1169 feet of Ais Gill

8   regimentally, the magazine of the old 93rd Highlanders

9   meanly, the sea level at Newlyn

10   directly, the Appian Way

• 9 • *Interrogate fairly closely:*

1   Sutton's bond with Luton

2   Cromwell's major-general who wrote himself into Marshalsea and Newgate

3   the man to recognise the power of the horse

4   Cobbett on town sprawl

5   the quarry of Matthew Hopkins

6   Black Dick

7   the beauty of Symonds Yat

8   the touchdown of John Gilpin

9   the flier on the goose that flew just one mile

10   New Zealand post-war GP champion

• 10 • *Entitle:*

1   the chemist – Morand

2   the son of Cardinal Mazarin

3   the lady lost to the Vicomte de Bragelonne

4   the wife of Henri of Navarre

5   the motley of Henry III

6   Hélène de Chaverny

7   the pupil of Abbé Faria

8   Prince de Cellemare, Cardinal Alberoni and the Duchesse du Maine

9   the son of the Comte de la Fère

10   ----- ----- Rosa Barlaeensis

• 11 • *Depict:*

1 sea-mat
2 the Hwang-ho
3 a first-class mandarin
4 actors' off-stage sanctum
5 Wild Bill Hickok's horse
6 François Leclerc du Tremblay
7 American St John's Wort
8 fluorspar from Castleton
9 Apatura iris
10 Joe Louis

• 12 • *Cast asunder:*

1 Rhoose Point
2 Keith Inch
3 Cornaglagh
4 Dr Syntax's Head
5 Garbhlach Mhor
6 Porthtaflod
7 Cranfield Point
8 Gallie Craig
9 Pinfold Farm
10 Meg's Dub

• 13 • *Oh, yes, you can recognise:*

1 Robert Fitzooth perchance
2 the Sultan of China's son-in-law
3 the familiar to the Marquis of Carabas
4 the capital coal-merchant (and his collier)
5 the Frampton statue set in Kensington Gardens
6 man's quest to All-Father for wind, rain and genial sun
7 the mariner of York taken by Barbary pirates
8 the lass who fitted *en verre*, not *en vair*
9 Thomas Fleet's Bostonian mother-in-law
10 the Swiss Annenadadeli

• 14 • *What:*

1 inroads were made by Percy Shaw at Drighlington?

2 US Government Surveyor made chilly observations in Labrador, 1912–15?

3 traces the career of Anthony Beavis?

4 optimist had a South Pacific role?

5 thunbergia is alata?

6 is Gotlands' aspect?

7 is a brood of pheasants?

8 secured a shroud end to the chain plate?

9 was Tommy's rotten idea of 'O mihi, beate Martine'?

10 eltsoons followed fillet of fenny snake?

• 15 • *Expressly:*

1 who put the corridor at the side?

2 where did Strasbourg feature in the first departure?

3 what Sachs-Neuzillet revue was presented at the Trianon, 1896?

4 where was there an unscheduled 'buffet stop', 1901?

5 where did 1,500 tons of dynamite shift one million cubic metres of rock by 1906?

6 what world record was established at Tcherkesskeuy Kabakdja, 1929?

7 who was Margaretha-Geertruida Zelle, a frequent passenger?

8 who was King Carol's 'cook' when he left for Switzerland, 1940?

9 who was in charge of the piano?

10 what happened to Mrs S E Ratchett?

• 16 • *At the Central Criminal Court:*

1 how was the first verse of *Ps lii* known?

2 what was likened to grubby Cockney children?

3 what Statesman was tried in 1670 for preaching to an unlawful assembly?

4 who was convicted after laughingly announcing 'Germany calling'?

5 what creature received the death sentence from Mr Justice Hilbery in 1952?

6 how is the December gift of 4½ yards of black cloth known?

7 who gets a bath every August and a gold coat every five years?

8 which octet began demolishments in 1965, to allow for extensions?

9 how many prisoners are held in the cells overnight?

10 what is the gun case?

• 17 • *Porter's burdens:*

1   According to the Kinsey Report
2   when they landed on Plymouth Rock
3   Lithuanians and Letts
4   started painting the town (and)
5   hungry for dinner at eight
6   dined me at the Ritz
7   on fine Finnon Haddie
8   It brings back a sound
9   which repeats and repeats in my ear
10 Unable to lunch today?

• 18 • *In 1992:*

1   what priest came first at CFM?
2   what Mason became a Crusader?
3   where did W Sweeney record 19 as his chosen number?
4   where did the news make the front page on 30th March?
5   what seemingly impossible event was won by K Babb-Sprague?
6   who was checked from a room called Moses by a Carpenter and Joseph?
7   who dropped in, some 350 miles, and late, to a new country?
8   what lady had a ripping time close to Martha's Vineyard?
9   what thimble-carrier spoke on 12th March?
10 where did Gary Lineker score one against Germany?

1993–1994

• 1 • *In 1893:*

1   what destroyers were the first?

2   what did Mr Perky prepare for breakfast?

3   who brought picture politics to the *Westminster Gazette*?

4   whose Black Maria saw the light of day in New Orange?

5   what started on its six-year circuitry north to Parsonage Road?

6   where did St Hilda and, later, St Anne put the ladies on course?

7   who got up to no good in Mr McGregor's garden?

8   what conveyor took on the Mersey beat?

9   what Life Guards came from Britain?

10   what became an open cut?

• 2 • *Suss out:*

1   who had rosbif?

2   what fatal event was published in *Decapolis*?

3   what Sino-Yin comes in 1995?

4   what grunt is a snapper with a grunt?

5   which Empress was 'much too fat' according to Alaric, Duke of Dunstaple?

6   which President advocated liberté and fraternité but qualified égalité?

7   who disliked the ship's name, *Pound of Candles*?

8   what right of common is only exercisable from 25th September to 22nd November?

9   what woman sold crockery?

10   what Danish trotter qualifies for the cross-country?

• 3 • *In what year did:*

1 the Long Island Express travel north?

2 Defoe report on the rise of tile prices – one guinea to £6 per thousand?

3 St Pierre encounter a nuée ardente?

4 a white hurricane signal down the E1?

5 Mrs Margaret Tobin Brown, from Colorado, earn her nickname?

6 Old Father Feather Merchant intrude upon the Empire State Building?

7 Exeter and Ajax see service in Chile?

8 New England have a mackerel year?

9 William Ashcroft start sketching evening skies?

10 the mud angels descend upon Florence?

• 4 • *Who or what:*

1 leads to the everlasting bonfire?

2 links Horsted Keynes and Sheffield Park?

3 stands half as old as time?

4 according to Mrs Montague Barstow was sought both high and low?

5 comes in low from the bowler's end?

6 was Napoleon – from his Elba promise?

7 belle of the Piccaninnies staves off the altar with a hatchet?

8 company incorporating Bass and Guinness went Eiffel towering?

9 are a jobber's speculation?

10 left Violet, Rose and Daisy with a skip?

• 5 • *What:*

1 kind of dog is a chum?

2 was soft gold?

3 is the clam capital of the world?

4 was the Gateway to the Klondike?

5 record 495-pounder was caught near Petersburg?

6 headline was prompted by the contents of George Washington Cormack's suitcase?

7 was Jefferson Randolph Smith's sobriquet?

8 is mother if father is an eagle?

9 was Seward's Folly?

10 are the lower forty-eight?

• 6 • *Identify:*

1 Sitch.

2 Tea-chest.

3 Gin Palace.

4 'Am and Tripe.

5 Jackie's Yacht.

6 The Lord's Own.

7 Billy Ruffian.

8 Great Harry.

9 Niffy Jane.

10 Andy Mack.

• 7 • *Identify:*

1 Betty Perske.

2 Sofia Scicolone.

3 Lucille le Sueur.

4 Vivien Mary Hartley.

5 Margarita Carmen Cansino.

6 Maria Magdalene von Losch.

7 Julia Elizabeth Wells.

8 Harlean Carpentier.

9 Virginia McMath.

10 Camille Javal.

• 8 • *Alight between:*

1 Rosslyn and Farragut West.

2 Opera and Concorde.

3 Vauxhall and Victoria.

4 Barmbek and Borgweg.

5 Benton and Longbenton.

6 Florenc and Mustek.

7 Fulton and Bowling Green.

8 Ordrup and Hellerup.

9 City Hall and Somerset.

10 Gleisdreieck and Hallesches Tor.

• 9 • *Who designed:*

1   Hammersmith Bridge?
2   Waterloo Bridge (Thames)?
3   Conway Road Suspension Bridge?
4   the Bridge of Sighs, St John's College?
5   the Iron Bridge at Ironbridge?
6   the High Level Road Bridge, Newcastle-upon-Tyne?
7   the Royal Albert Bridge (Tamar)?
8   the Forth Railway Bridge?
9   Tower Bridge?
10 London Bridge (Arizona)?

• 10 • *Identify:*

1   a carousel.
2   Old Rowley.
3   a fowl's furcula.
4   the lady who recognised Harry Brown as the lost Bertram.
5   the work wherein Mother Prat (of Brainford) was assailed by Master Brook.
6   the ship that simultaneously shattered a steeple in Calais and sheep on Dover's cliffs.
7   tide-rips in the Pentland Firth.
8   Hugh Stowell Scott.
9   Hanna Glawari.
10 Wakefield.

• 11 • *Identify:*

1   Lol.
2   Slamming Sam.
3   The Crafty Cockney.
4   The Sultan of Swat.
5   The Wizard of Dribble.
6   The Rockhampton Rocket.
7   The Bounding Basque.
8   The Nestor of Golf.
9   The Black Bradman.
10 The Shoe.

• 12 • *Fabricate from:*

1   Zaitun in China.

2   Ankara.

3   Damascus.

4   New York and London.

5   El Fustāt which was once Cairo.

6   a caterpillar or a hairy little dog.

7   the papal town of Avignon.

8   milk and sugar.

9   Nanking.

10   and from Nîmes.

• 13 • *Whodunnit at:*

1   2 Dalton Street?

2   13 Clarendon Road?

3   63 Tollington Park?

4   10 Rillington Place?

5   34 Pembridge Gardens?

6   31 Buckingham Terrace?

7   39 Hilldrop Crescent?

8   105 Onslow Gardens?

9   45 Chester Square?

10   26 Dorset Street?

• 14 • *Who machined:*

1   Ulster and Radial?

2   Red Hunter and Leader?

3   Blue Star and Gold Star?

4   Grey Flash and Black Shadow?

5   Silver Hawk and Silver Arrow?

6   Continental and Flying Flea Rickshaw?

7   Squirrel and Super Squirrel?

8   Slippery Sam and Hurricane?

9   Dominator and Commando?

10   Venom and Thruxton?

• 15 • *Customarily:*

1   what late October fair takes place in Rotherham?

2   how is Lady de Mowbray remembered at Haxey?

3   whose weights are publicly proclaimed in May at High Wycombe?

4   what British Championships are held on Good Friday at Tinsley Green?

5   in what ceremony does a dignitary circulate at Southwold Charter Fair?

6   what mauls take place on Easter Monday at Hallaton … ?

7   … and the following day what buns are enjoyed by the choirboys of St Michael's, Bristol?

8   who play Boxing Day football at Waltham Cross?

9   who are the Coconut Dancers at Bacup?

10   what March ceremony in Lanark dispatches winter?

• 16 • *How might you have fared:*

1   leaping down a passage in Sweden?

2   with the Duke of Exeter's daughter?

3   with your name inscribed on broken pot?

4   with your brass collar a little too tight?

5   moving from yard to yard while the great gun thundered?

6   had you, for not pleading your case, felt pressure from the board?

7   had you encountered Major-General Browne of the Commonwealth?

8   courtesy of Antoine Louis (or a Scottish widow)?

9   prone, doing physical jerks from the beam?

10   detrahatur, suspendatur, devaletur, decapiteur et decolletur?

• 17 • *Try srchng th dctnry fr:*

1   sweet cicely.

2   sandstone with shales.

3   the flood of deadly hate.

4   young salmon in their second year.

5   a flute, architectural but not orchestral.

6   a diminutive crane fighter who climbed Hercules' goblet.

7   a period of the moon – two-foot measure.

8   English militia from times past.

9   Assembly for Athenians.

10   a cattle fair.

• 18 • *In 1993:*

1   who was the six-minute Lion?

2   where were the Viguiers voted from the Valleys?

3   where did Brown and White on Esha Ness get strung along?

4   where was six-year-old Ipec Ensari first through the gates?

5   where did Carly's little pattern, 'Rhythm of the Trees', sell for £295?

6   what Hall made a move from the South Shore to the North Sea?

7   what tigerish footballer hung up his boots after 40 years?

8   what faith and truth has Robert Elderton borne unto you?

9   for what abstract problem has a thorny solution been suggested?

10   whose parting arrangements disrupted departing arrangements?

1994–1995

1. what was Beeman's Pepsin?
2. whence ran a 96-mile-long aqueduct?
3. what now did the law allow on postcards?
4. what entertainment took off after Mona's dress rehearsal?
5. which Napoleon performed for 48 hours non-stop, from memory and without repetition?
6. whose misguided visit to Devil's Island caused Zola to pen his accusation to L'Aurore?
7. what became of the avant-garde reading of the Naughty Nineties?
8. where did the first series of pictorial stamps appear?
9. which Michael and Tom had one price – 1d?
10. who succeeded – the last of his line?

•2• *Who or what:*

1. follows Av and Elul?
2. was once called 'sprout-kale'?
3. month was the October Revolution?
4. is the time of the peridot and the sardonyx?
5. hunt won awards for Cecilia Hall and George Watters?
6. was a favourite subject of Henri de Toulouse-Lautrec d'Albi?
7. was the time of the larkspur and the water-lily?
8. joined Damyan in January's pear-tree?
9. cherries came first from France?
10. follows lokakuu and marraskuu?

• 3 • *How did Lewis Carroll:*

1   remember Longfellow?

2   pass the month of August, 1867?

3   remember Edith Denham and Adelaide Paine?

4   describe a word-puzzle – without using a vowel?

5   name his chess-board game with eight men a-side and nine pieces of card?

6   have 'Mr William Smith, of Yorkshire' pass himself off to attract a larger 'share of public notice'?

7   entitle the tale ending '... afterwards Mrs Cogsby received a couple of wedding cards, with a slice of bride-cake, from "MR AND MRS BYMM"'?

8   proceed after explaining the blamelessness of the *white* kitten whereas the 'wicked' black kitten...?

9   have the tortoise and Achilles each rename the other?

10 amorously pre-empt modern stickers in **A Limerick**?

• 4 • *Connect (no answers in English):*

1   Robin and sparrow.

2   Schwarzenegger and De Vito.

3   nightjar and an island on a horseshoe.

4   forget-me-not and a spiked and knotted whip.

5   Harry Ramsden and a canyon second only to the Grand.

6   lots of bits with chips – but all is lost if switched off.

7   Leo X and his famous 1520 condemnation of Luther.

8   notably, ascends and descends and ascends.

9   St Gerasimus and Androclus.

10 fiddler and hermit.

• 5 • *What colour is:*

1   an eel?

2   a grayling?

3   a sorry horse?

4   a fugitive slave?

5   a Colonel (with – in)?

6   a deer-horn's second tine?

7   a debt collector?

8   an alternative?

9   a cuttlefish?

10 a dock?

• 6 • *Who narrates or narrated:*

1   *Spot?*

2   *Andy Pandy?*

3   *The Clangers?*

4   *Paddington Bear?*

5   *The Magic Roundabout?*

6   *Thomas, the Tank Engine?*

7   *Will o' the Wisp?*

8   *The Mister Men?*

9   *Fireman Sam?*

10   *Madeline?*

• 7 • *How old:*

1   Virginia?

2   Vox stellarum?

3   George Mogridge?

4   Edward Boscowan, Wry-necked Dick?

5   Charles II (and his favourite racehorse)?

6   Robert Paterson, pictured by Sir Walter Scott?

7   Thomas Chamberlain's cordial gin?

8   the drunk on Sinbad's shoulders?

9   Zachary Taylor?

10   87th Foot?

• 8 • *Who was what of:*

1   Zenda?

2   Wantley?

3   Wakefield?

4   the Leopard?

5   Casterbridge?

6   the Western World?

7   the Mohicans?

8   Lammermoor?

9   Property?

10   Raveloe?

• 9 • *Orchestrate:*

1   a pansy.

2   two hogsheads.

3   a slate-trimmer.

4   the sealing ring of a jar.

5   a shuttle in tapestry-weaving.

6   the stave-rims at the end of a cask.

7   a one-time sub-lieutenant.

8   a large strawberry.

9   a kidney bean.

10   a registrar.

• 10 • *Who did for:*

1   Lord Loam?

2   Phileas Fogg?

3   Tommy Handley?

4   Sherlock Holmes?

5   Martin Chuzzlewit?

6   Shelby, St Clare and Legree?

7   Inspector Clousseau?

8   Abraham Slender?

9   Henry Higgins?

10   Jack Benny?

• 11 • *Who or what was or were:*

1   Bör?

2   Gungner?

3   Sleipnir?

4   Geri and Freki?

5   Slidbladnir and Naglfar?

6   Siggë, whose eye is the sun?

7   Hugin and Munin?

8   Hlidskjalf?

9   Draupner?

10   Frigga?

• 12 • *What sea:*

1 is Bahret Lut?
2 is of reeds?
3 was the Pontus Euxinus?
4 is at the east end of the Panama Canal?
5 links Victoria and Marie Byrd?
6 saw the destruction of Lexington?
7 isolates Cornwall, Middlesex and Surrey?
8 is divided by Adventure Bank?
9 is edged with amber?
10 recalls a cricketing hero?

• 13 • *Unearth:*

1 lop.
2 mawk.
3 cowlady.
4 pissimer.
5 twitch-bell.
6 tommy-spinner.
7 forty-leg.
8 attercop.
9 biddy.
10 cleg.

• 14 • *Explain:*

1 Hull cheese.
2 Newgate knocker.
3 Glasgow magistrate.
4 Huntingdon sturgeon.
5 Brummagem screwdriver.
6 Lincolnshire bagpipes.
7 Manchester sunshine.
8 Scarborough warning.
9 Kingston bridge.
10 Worcester weed.

• 15 • *What fighter (or fighters):*

1   was known as Biff?

2   dominated in Bloody April?

3   had humped fairing for its Vickers guns?

4   was produced in the greatest numbers ever?

5   destroyed roughly twice the number of any other in history?

6   was the first from NAA, taking only four months from first drawing to first flight?

7   engine powered the first Messerschmitt 109?

8   was built of balsa sandwiches, spruced up?

9   figured in the 'Fokker Scourge'?

10   were 'Faith, Hope and Charity'?

• 16 • *Who said:*

1   'A little rebellion, now and then, is a good thing'?

2   'Older men declare war. But it is youth that must fight and die'?

3   'No President ever enjoyed himself in the Presidency as much as I did'?

4   'Surely if the United States have a right to make war, they have a right to prevent it'?

5   'People want peace so much that governments had better get out of their way and let them have it'?

6   'No nation on this globe should be more internationally minded than America because it was built by all nations'?

7   'I know only two tunes, one of them is *Yankee Doodle*, and the other isn't'?

8   'Mankind must put an end to war – or war will put an end to mankind'?

9   'Patriotism is no substitute for a sound currency'?

10   'Desperate courage makes One a majority'?

• 17 • *According to IMB:*

1   how ends the maxim 'A stew-boiled ...'?

2   who would take white eggs and soda?

3   how would the bishop and mitre feature at table?

4   how many methods of cookery are commonly spoken of?

5   when are brain fritters and curried lobster a speciality?

6   what carpet problem is solved with hot water, salt and ox-gall?

7   what is the weight of one breakfastcupful of split peas?

8   what should be held in sulphur fumes for cleaning?

9   when are green geese best and cheapest?

10   how long do you boil your cod's head?

• 18 • *In 1994:*

1   what lines are to be trod by Wendy Tomms?

2   where did Nelson Mandela's daughter cast the first vote?

3   what ancient sempstress is celebrating her 300th birthday?

4   what 'scientific civil servant' saw blue skies ahead with Brown?

5   who started whistling to thirty after successfully conducting bands of thirteen?

6   which cricket side has been elected to compete in the Minor Counties Competition in 1995?

7   from where were three oversize kevlon-covered golf-balls driven after 33 years?

8   who went in to eat New Zealand apples for a record 75 days?

9   what 30-year-old bimbo scored a point from a man of action?

10   how, ironically, did Alf Wight suffer from ram-raiders?

1995–1996

• 1 • *In 1895:*

  1   what came to pass at the George Hotel, Huddersfield on 29th August?

  2   how did HJH set pulses racing variously?

  3   how did Miss Lilian Murray qualify to fill a yawning gap?

  4   what trick was played on M. Clerc, the first paid film actor?

  5   what did Mme Bergman Osterberg introduce at her Dartford training college?

  6   why was Don Quixote's Housekeeper's reply 'But Master, you have been knighted', applauded at the Lyceum?

  7   in what was Horace Rawlins putting gutties straight in Newport?

  8   what was the open cut wound on the first-ever news-reel?

  9   who put the Queen's Hall, London, on a sound footing?

10   what King came safely through a close shave?

• 2 • *What is:*

  1   the queer fish of Edvard Eriksen?

  2   the tablecloth design of Cedric Gibbons?

  3   the pinnacle pigeon perch of Edward Hughes Baily?

  4   Mme Tallien's enlightenment of Frédéric Auguste Bartholdi?

  5   the 25′ bronze of Sir Jacob Epstein remembering 14.xi.1940?

  6   the bluff of Gutzon Borglum and his appropriately named son?

  7   the ageless aeronaut of Sir George James Frampton?

  8   the symbol of Christian charity of Alfred Gilbert?

  9   the cycle of Auguste Gustav Vigeland?

10   the moving spirit of Charles Sykes?

• 3 • *What:*

1   footplate was stoker Ray Milland's first flick?
2   was Vivian Ellis's introduction for Paul Temple?
3   was end-of-line for the Midnight Choo Choo from Berlin?
4   artist impressed with steam at the Gare Saint-Lazare?
5   destination had Miss Lloyd in mind when she found herself at Crewe?
6   composer heralded the start of the French Northern and end of the Brighton Belle with *Chant des Chemins de Fer*?
7   cricket lovers were caught out again aboard the Night Train to Munich?
8   racehorse escaped a rail crash on the Drury Lane stage?
9   Astronomical fellow was stationed at Buggleskelly?
10 was Private Godfrey's spectral steamer?

• 4 • *Who or what:*

1   is the longest-lived creature?
2   was Oscar's tribute to *The Longest Day*?
3   wrote the world's shortest/longest piano piece?
4   was the source of E M Forster's title *The Longest Journey*?
5   is the actor longest to hold his speaking part in *The Mouse Trap*?
6   was the longest-reigning World Heavyweight Boxing Champion?
7   is the longest-serving British political party leader?
8   was 'the longest suicide note in history'?
9   is the longest word of Mary Poppins?
10 laughs longest in this life?

• 5 • *Identify:*

1   Plum.
2   Tich.
3   Typhoon.
4   the Demon.
5   the Non-pareil.
6   Johnny Won't Hit Today.
7   the Croucher.
8   Slasher.
9   Gubby.
10 Toey.

• 6 • *What day is or was:*

1   for hansels?

2   Mercury's day?

3   absolutely green?

4   of great significance to Columbus?

5   'Stir Up' welcoming the Christmas school holidays?

6   an unpleasant surprise for those long-irritating Danes?

7   when Judas bargained with the Jewish Sanhedrin?

8   the Day of 'Day by Day'?

9   dies mandati?

10   Kappelhoff?

• 7 • *What:*

1   is the yolk of an egg?

2   is clove-hitched across shrouds?

3   was launched on the waves, 28.iii.1964?

4   results when nuts are cracked in brown sugar?

5   lady was imprisoned thirteen times under the 'Cat and Mouse Act'?

6   would be cross having each arm curved outwards?

7   is composed of German water and Greek oil?

8   British king was 'refinished' by GBS?

9   thistle is also a Scottish hag?

10   is $\frac{1}{12}$?

• 8 • *What Polly:*

1   was unbearably optimistic?

2   was smitten by a strange fancy?

3   might Susanna hear coming from the north?

4   reappeared in a sequel to capture Morano in the WI?

5   advanced from Northern Cyprus but balefully fled back?

6   is rich in sodium bicarbonate and carbon dioxide, flowing freely at Ahr?

7   was chastised for warming her extremities unsuitably?

8   was cyclist, arsonist and pot person?

9   forsook heaven to bring us love?

10   bore the 'Crusader in Pink'?

• 9 • *Toy with these*:

1   whence came Dutch dolls?
2   what results from a marriage?
3   how are Fleischaker and Baum known?
4   who produced an early aural pachyderm?
5   who first turned googlies on a watermelon?
6   in what field did the Jacquet-Droz family excel?
7   what was the inspiration of Rose O'Neill?
8   where is Biedermeier furniture found?
9   for what is Yorkshire cloth used?
10 where is the growler found?

• 10 • *Identify:*

1   Jenny.
2   The Tin Goose.
3   The Spider Crab.
4   The Wooden Wonders.
5   Puff, the Magic Dragon.
6   Faith, Hope and Charity.
7   The Flying Bedstead.
8   The Flying Pencil.
9   The Stringbag.
10 Auntie Ju.

• 11 • *Identify:*

1   Voltaire.
2   the 88th Foot.
3   the spinner in diabolo.
4   the lawyers' pub, No. 2 Fleet Street.
5   St Cuthman's scheme to prevent flooding near Brighton.
6   lines-end steaming from Aberystwyth.
7   the stones of Boroughbridge.
8   the yellow bunting.
9   Cromer Bay.
10 dice.

• 12 • *What:*

1   was Ravel's 'flûte à coulisse'?

2   nationality was Jingling Johnny?

3   fiddle was carried in the pocket?

4   'trumpet' was a single-string violin?

5   bit of 'brass' was a wiggle of wood and leather?

6   was the skeletal rattle in Saint Saëns' *Danse Macabre*?

7   started grinding as the organistrum?

8   harp was a Dutch child's trumpet?

9   was George Formby's instrument?

10   is a licorice stick?

• 13 • *Just peanuts:*

1   who are Belle and Molly?

2   who is Lucy's baby brother?

3   what is the farm at Daisy Hill?

4   what is Charlie Brown's father's job?

5   Snoopy has five brothers – who are they …?

6   … and a Beagle Scout Troop of five – who are they?

7   what was the original name of the strip?

8   who requires a security blanket?

9   who appears in a cloud of dust?

10   who is Charlie's inamorata?

• 14 • *What:*

1   was '¹⁄₄₃rd'?

2   started as 'Mechanics Made Easy'?

3   was made No. 52 with 1″ representing 150″?

4   structural premises started in Binns Road?

5   is the name of the holder of Collector's Licence No. 1?

6   had the Jaguar XK150, Jowett Javelin and Rover 105R in common?

7   was 3–4% Al, 1–2% Cu, 92–96% Zn, and a trace of Mg?

8   world record was set by a 'Bentalls' van?

9   country changed the name to 'Nicky'?

10   was the name of the founder?

• 15 • *Meantime:*

1   who presided for a thousand days?

2   who spent two years before the mast?

3   whose dog inspired a minute of waltztime?

4   who kept Sultan Schahriah at bay for a thousand and one nights?

5   where is Eddie Seaward's year's work trampled underfoot in a fortnight?

6   what happened on the seventeenth day of the second month of the six hundredth year?

7   where may married bliss for a year and a day bring home the bacon?

8   which dam always takes over an hour to cross one way?

9   what is the name of the 445-day year?

10   who mislaid a weekend?

• 16 • *Through the wynds:*

1   what is stationed in Nor' Loch?

2   what was the name of Jock Gray's Terrier?

3   what distance was the city from the castle?

4   what could hurl a quarter of a ton a mile and a half?

5   what burglarious town councillor gave an idea to R L Stevenson?

6   who painted 'large Royal postures' at a rate of one a week for two years?

7   what letters were the goal of debtors chased down Canongate?

8   what prison is marked by a heart in the pavement?

9   where would one be on Nova Scotian soil?

10   what can be seen from the Outlook Tower?

• 17 • *Who or what:*

1   was George R Crane who walked tall?

2   was heard but not seen in High Noon?

3   led the band known as the Drifting Cowboys?

4   Son of the Pioneers teamed up with Dale Evans?

5   national rodeo champion was shot over a hundred times though scarce a shot was heard?

6   appeared with 'William Tell' though Verdi's *Un Ballo in Maschera* might have been more appropriate?

7   according to Bob Hope 'used to ride off into the sunset; now he owns it'?

8   was coached to fame as the Ringo Kid?

9   was the only good guy to wear black?

10   said 'Yup'?

• 18 • *In 1995:*

1   what Long Fellow vacated his seat?

2   how did Jeanne Calment outstay Shigeshiyo Izumi?

3   what two letters appeared in *The Scotsman* on 8th March?

4   what out-of-joint nose went under the hammer for £32,000?

5   what son-of-a-gun had his case taken up belatedly after backing onto a Ford?

6   whar former employer of the Brazilian star, Parker, fetched £34,500?

7   what large family reunion was convened at Barkingside?

8   where did the Scirocco blast Victoria's entrance?

9   where did Michael Nazir-Ali come to see?

10   what came to pass at the Ambassador Hotel, Paris, on 27th August?

1996–1997

- **1** • *In 1896:*

  1   what beehive became number 45?

  2   to whom did William Justus give hearty thanks?

  3   what plat du jour was devised in New York by Li-Hung-Chang's chef?

  4   what, on 4th May, cost the busy man ½d or, maybe, 1d beyond 200 miles from London?

  5   who produced fifty original sketches of guttersnipes and joined a now revitalised periodical?

  6   what opened in New Bond Street following the lead given at Mme Ledouble's Maison de Haute Couture?

  7   who, caught by a cycling PC, was fined 1/- for driving at four times the speed limit?

  8   what was Harvard's J B Connolly's reward for taking three paces?

  9   who (saying 'Good-night' this year) was born Nathan Birnbaum?

  10   what was given by John Rice to Mary Irwin?

- **2** • *Where:*

  1   is K 425 located?

  2   was a lager created in a stone quarry?

  3   did the minstrel discover Leopold V's prisoner?

  4   is the cure attributed to the heaviest of the noble gases?

  5   like Franz Josef, can one still enjoy the hospitality of Zanner?

  6   did Klara bear Alois a son in the Gasthof zum Pommer on 20.4.89?

  7   is the missing item from Maximillian's Innsbruck mausoleum?

  8   have the car numbers been halved on the roundabout?

  9   is the village popularised by Benatzky?

  10   did Marie Vetsera die?

• 3 • *Who or what:*

1   is *Megalaima haemacephala*?

2   was Aaron the Durham mapmaker?

3   mightily has large and sinewy hands?

4   was developed from a hardy French-Tasmanian crab?

5   Ephesian trade unionist owed his livelihood to Diana?

6   wrote of friendship as a disinterested commerce between equals?

7   wrote a diary featuring Lupin's comings and goings?

8   might be described as the father of the key?

9   had it left to him by Wodehouse?

10   was the Aldershot of Natal?

• 4 • *Which encounter:*

1   made the world your debtor?

2   did Handel celebrate with a *Te Deum*?

3   did Harold win centuries before Chelsea?

4   was preceded by the crossing of Twizel Bridge?

5   produced a large round relic for Kaspar's grandson, Peterkin?

6   was attended by the Man of Blood with his long essenced hair?

7   followed both leaders' request for ink and paper?

8   was fought on the day of Crispin Crispian?

9   led to the court-martial of Sackville?

10   in 1916 was won by Germany 14-11?

• 5 • *Where:*

1   is poetry made an art?

2   did we go by way of Beachy Head?

3   did the bells play 'The Brides of Enderby'?

4   did the bells ring sharp and quick all night?

5   found ---- the populous and smokey city is like Hell?

6   are the people urban, squat and packed with guile?

7   did Oldcastle fight a long hour by the clock?

8   were we 76 for 7 with C B Fry in opposition?

9   did precipitation prevent a revisit?

10   -from came a heptagamist?

· 6 · *Who or what:*

1 was Heartwell?

2 climbs to 803 in SD2797?

3 belongs exclusively to Masham?

4 had as blind companion, Slumber-soon?

5 joyous monarch summoned a string trio?

6 lies on the floor of the 'Fox and French Horn'?

7 ancient smithy stands in Pa. and NY?

8 stood on one leg to read Homer?

9 has become of Royal Coburg?

10 was Good Lord Cobham?

· 7 · *Where:*

1 does the Savoyarde hang?

2 does the Lady of Auxerre reside?

3 lie the remains of Sebastian Melmoth?

4 stood gallows that could hang sixty at once?

5 was the Empress replaced by the soldier in 1929?

6 did a toxophilite secure freedom through cholecystectomy?

7 is a regicidal place recalled supersonically?

8 are departing volunteers depicted rudely?

9 does Hugo's classic recall Low Sunday?

10 was a concert recorded by Manet?

· 8 · *Who called what:*

1 Saki?

2 Ruksh?

3 Wallace?

4 Adjidaumo?

5 Swagdagger?

6 Aurunculeia?

7 Modestine?

8 Snowball?

9 Zephir?

10 Lobo?

• 9 • *Where:*

1   is the brewhouse?

2   are undergraduates excluded?

3   is Edward III's second cousin remembered?

4   were Fellows expelled for ejecting a Farmer?

5   are Theology, Medicine, Geometry and Astrology represented?

6   is the Cistercian origin perpetuated by a statue of St Bernard?

7   did Henrietta stay when Charles was in the House?

8   do portraits of Gladstone and twelve others hang?

9   is the tower haunted by a headless man?

10   is *The Light of the World*?

• 10 • *Who:*

1   practised at 4 Palmyra Square NW?

2   was the second son of Lord Clonkilty?

3   circled a fire on the Dyve Burn sands?

4   employed the one-armed Sime as butler?

5   was the senior partner at Paton and Linklater?

6   carved a pipe for Pieter Pienaar in St Helena?

7   was the artillery commander at Chataldja?

8   stood in for Crumpleton at Brattleburn?

9   was the headmistress of Brewton Ashes?

10   was nicknamed Ashie at Cambridge?

• 11 • *Who rhymed, in what:*

1   obey and tea?

2   plain and swain?

3   serene and unseen?

4   inamoratas and garter?

5   these and toasted cheese?

6   Koklophti and scoff'd high?

7   Edinburgh and sorrow?

8   Guzzle and muzzle?

9   Gynt and squint?

10   hern and fern?

• 12 • *What:*

1   is *Minuartia stricta*?

2   are separated by Colwith Force?

3   Florida Fort recalls a Leader's route?

4   Number 2 to the 39th was routed by the 40th?

5   porter is warmed with rum, sugar, cloves, nutmeg and ginger?

6   rival to Lancashire and Cheshire was originally woolly-coated?

7   is only slightly less peripheral than Burnt Oak?

8   did Bassett Lowke convert from 30 to 15?

9   Scar by James Ward hangs in the Tate?

10 is home to North End?

• 13 • *Where, in Douglas, is:*

1   Ava?

2   Armour?

3   Superior?

4   Alexandria?

5   Castle Rock?

6   Douglasville?

7   Waterville?

8   Lawrence?

9   Roseburg?

10 Minden?

• 14 • *Who or what:*

1   is a Gang-gang?

2   is an avian parasite?

3   was Mowgli's ursine friend?

4   is misleading advance publicity?

5   saw 11 deaths and a three-year sentence for Hunt?

6   Little John is 'unchained' by Sheriff of Nottingham?

7   minstrel had a lengthy catalogue?

8   is the witchcraft of Hispaniola?

9   is between the MacNeans?

10 was *that* cat-rabbit?

• 15 • *Wherein:*

1   did Burns write *Scots Wha' Hae?*

2   was Peter Steiler the Elder the landlord?

3   did the Canonry Club hold its dinners in autumn?

4   was one of the three accused of passing counterfeit coins?

5   did partridge and cabbage become a new thing in the eyes of the voyager?

6   during a restless night, did Rupert Brooke write of the preferred Fleur de Lys?

7   did Tom regale himself on the beef-steak and unlimited oyster sauce?

8   did Mrs Gilpin plan to celebrate her China Wedding?

9   did Admiral Leighton entertain three captains?

10   was Mr Jellyband the landlord?

• 16 • *What:*

1   are the rewards if the 'Challenge' is met?

2   was the biggest single order – for the army?

3   was Bradford's *Telegraph and Argus* epitaph headline?

4   city established a record of 11,964 portions on 17th May 1992?

5   do the figures 264,000 and 660,000 and 20,000 mean in Guiseley?

6   was the cost of a portion of fish and chips on 7th July 1952 …?

7   … and on 30th October 1988?

8   namesake nephew played the piano outside on sunny days?

9   was the first overseas restaurant venture?

10   was Harry Ramsden's address during 1963/64?

• 17 • *A last laugh:*

1   was a 1956 Guidry hit,

2   sounding like a bargain,

3   defeat a seed or even two seeds,

4   said to be a Tungusic tribesman …

5   … and his dog (if he hasn't eaten it!)

6   Mrs Mopp's initial banter with that man,

7   won an Academy Award for Red Buttons,

8   got there – with Eric doing the twist,

9   Judge, of Leicester Square,

10   is 2k west of Bordeaux.

• 18 • *In 1996:*

1   who sank 'Deep Blue'?

2   what equine epic was featured on ITV on Dettori's day?

3   what colour were the box-kites making news on 23rd July?

4   where did ex-prisoner No. 466/64 receive eight Honorary Degrees?

5   what was hit upon by batsmen, Altringham (a rasping 45 for Yorks) and Jones (a squeakier 55 for Lancs)?

6   in what sphere were plastic macs offered for sale in the afternoon – an Italian couple opening the business?

7   what too expensive Swiss Army Service was stood down after 70 years?

8   what 'slice of bread between two slices of ham' came off the road?

9   what world title was won vis-à-vis by Gordon Mattinson?

10   whose 'Endeavour' was dextrously named?

1997–1998

• 1 • *In 1897:*

1   what earned Mr Gubbins £5450?

2   who released the Invisible Griffin?

3   what was Sturmy's epic international journey?

4   how did the Adelphi Theatre lose its Lewis Dumont?

5   whose battle with cancer finally failed at Karlgasse 4, Vienna?

6   and what revolutionary creation would, decades later, give Orson Welles a famous ride?

7   where did a sweet endowment bring art instead of convicts?

8   where in IOM did CO account for XIX going down for Pb?

9   what was Mrs Hoodless's foundation?

10   what did anopheles reveal to Ross?

• 2 • *Who or what:*

1   is possession?

2   was Clanroyden's Border home?

3   exceeds the Dollar by thirteen?

4   is Judah, when Moab is my wash-pot?

5   precipitated the Mississippi Bubble?

6   gave up his City job and moved to Piedmont?

7   is as old and as true as the sky?

8   was the Unknown Prime Minister?

9   is administered by a deemster?

10   excludes female succession?

• 3 • *Where:*

1 was Sahgal's Storm?
2 was Mr Hopkins the Collector?
3 did nude cycling get Forbes cashiered?
4 was Nataraj's attic let to a taxidermist?
5 during the siege, did Herncastle steal the diamond?
6 was Cyril Fielding Principal of the Government College?
7 was the Civil Surgeon known as the Dormouse?
8 was Mildred and Barbie's Rose Cottage?
9 was the home of Corbett's Bachelor?
10 was Number 4 Collett Road?

• 4 • *Which schoolmaster:*

1 was nicknamed Hoofer?
2 was Headmaster of Lowood School?
3 was shrivelled up inside like a nut?
4 sailed with David Crawfurd to Durban?
5 was a far truer and deeper Christian than Mr Gordon?
6 had but one eye resembling the fan-light of a street door?
7 was very tall and very old and very well-dressed?
8 always carried a pocket copy of *Odes of Horace*?
9 wrote *Sidelights on Horace*?
10 smelt false Latin?

• 5 • *Where:*

1 Avalanche?
2 Chromite?
3 Dragoon?
4 Galvanic?
5 Iceberg?
6 Jubilee?
7 Musketeer?
8 Shingle?
9 Sutton?
10 Urgent Fury?

• 6 • *Who was the target of:*

1 Jan Kubis?

2 Janusz Walus?

3 Petrus Keleman?

4 Paul Gorgouloff?

5 Prince Felix Yusupov?

6 Nahashon Isaac Njenga Njoroge?

7 Lee Harvey Oswald?

8 Ramon Mercader?

9 Naturan Godse?

10 Yigal Amir?

• 7 • *Who or what:*

1 controlled 007?

2 is Special at breakfast?

3 is the backpacker's beach hut?

4 contains two eyes and a loin bone?

5 Force was nipped in the South China Sea?

6 has a thick skull as empty of brains as a ladle?

7 is essential for seasonable oysters?

8 genetically determines masculinity?

9 features Scully and Mulder?

10 is the affirmative flag?

• 8 • *Who or what:*

1 springs a surprise?

2 combines garlic and mustard?

3 masqueraded as Lord Mortimer?

4 is a cockney's smoked herring?

5 eschewed modesty following a Yuletide digital extraction?

6 needed eight strokes to despatch the vanquished leader from Sedgmoor?

7 was asked to give quip and quidity?

8 with 197, had 27 more than Patsy?

9 started as Kid Blackie?

10 was Jenkin Careaway?

• 9 • *Who or what:*

1   is *Colias crocea?*

2   agent uses *Aedes aegypti?*

3   grinned like a coal-scuttle?

4   describes men of Lincolnshire?

5   sings 'A little bit of bread and no cheese'?

6   misnamed evergreen is found in Alabama and Idaho?

7   was originally found beneath Eleanor Rigby?

8   epithet has been given to the Tiber?

9   separates Shantung from Korea?

10   passes above Jasper?

• 10 • *What is:*

1   a little PC?

2   a form of punctuation?

3   a grey-haired sea captain?

4   an Iberian monarch's snakehead?

5   North British and one hundred-eyed?

6   48x72 in a red and blue mixture?

7   a senior Soviet naval officer?

8   the fuel of hell-fire?

9   pulchritude in SE5?

10   a flying fish?

• 11 • *What first name is shared by these neighbours:*

1   Gamage and Lacy?

2   Bryan and Richard?

3   Rowland and Tracey?

4   Mortimer and Walter?

5   Conyers and Redmayne?

6   Hastings and Mountford?

7   Charles and Udrigle?

8   Burnell and Pigott?

9   Adam and Mackrell?

10   Ferris and Gower?

• 12 • *Who composed:*

1 *Warsaw Concerto?*

2 *Uppsala Rhapsody?*

3 *Liverpool Oratorio?*

4 *Hamburg Ebb and Flow?*

5 *Copenhagen Steam Railway Gallop?*

6 *Johannesburg Festival Overture?*

7 *Leningrad Symphony?*

8 *Chichester Psalms?*

9 *Berlin Sinfonias?*

10 *Linz Symphony?*

• 13 • *Who or what:*

1 are good as gold?

2 is that *Nisi Prius* nuisance?

3 was described as a fleshly poet?

4 was the Duke of Pfennig Halbpfennig?

5 suffered much from spleen and vapours?

6 knows the croaking chorus from the *Frogs* of Aristophanes?

7 is the alternative to *Castle Adamant?*

8 might occasionally say 'Bother it'?

9 was the Vicar of Ploverleigh?

10 is a pudding full of plums?

• 14 • *Which Prime Minister:*

1 was wounded on Putney Heath?

2 served as High Commissioner in Corfu?

3 reputedly and repeatedly knew my father?

4 was the son of his predecessor's father's doctor?

5 got in at Maidstone after four failures at High Wycombe?

6 claimed that most of our people had never had it so good?

7 finished with 'If we must fall, let us fall like men'?

8 signed his letters to Edith – 'Hamish'?

9 was the victim of Bellingham?

10 was Rudyard Kipling's cousin?

• 15 • *Who or what:*

1   Treaty did Sir Henry Pottinger sign in 1842?

2   is stationed between Admiralty and Causeway Bay?

3   animals are associated with Quinella at Happy Valley?

4   met Charlie Townsend at a curio-dealer's off Victoria Road?

5   club was frequented by the Honourable Schoolboy and his friend Craw?

6   typhoon-resistant structure has been designed by Mott MacDonald?

7   vehicle was the meeting place for Suzy Wong and Robert?

8   is struck to reprimand each inmate who's in late?

9   with Lavender, had a Whisky and a Soda?

10   is the SCMP?

• 16 • *Where:*

1   does one alight at Guillemins?

2   does a spring recall Peter the Great?

3   is the Casino graced by the Dead Rat Ball?

4   was Edinburgh's great siege gun forged in 1449?

5   did Arethusa and Cigarette enjoy the hospitality of the Royal Sport Nautique?

6   under the sign of the Golden Compasses, was the *Biblia Regia* printed in five languages?

7   should a Churchillian victory be remembered on 11th July?

8   did the cocks crow and twilight dawn clear?

9   was Mathilda's ring retrieved by a trout?

10   is Belgium encircled by Holland?

• 17 • *According to the Manx Bard:*

1   what has its heather still?

2   whence moans the murdered witches' wail?

3   what is smoky yellow, like old vellum?

4   what are like innumerous-celled revolvers?

5   where, inspired with sacred fury, did Chalse help good Parson Drury?

6   what, of a rule, is just as bad as Liverpool?

7   where do scholars go to learn for clergymen?

8   for whom would he make a water-spaniel?

9   where was the *Hector* bound?

10   what name is supremest?

• 18 • *In 1997:*

1   how did MCC gain a Lords' seat?

2   whose perihelion was on 1st April?

3   what was the vehicle for Cgoise's seven jackals?

4   where was the Cakehole occupied by Muppet and Disco?

5   who could not stay longer, but earned his friends free pints at the Woolpack?

6   what machine failed by seventeen days to equal Phileas Fogg?

7   what baronial inheritance was resolved by DNA testing?

8   how was Swedish valour commemorated by Jackson?

9   in what sphere was Sam's dream realised?

10   who resorted to auricular mastication?

1998–1999

• 1 • *In 1898:*

1   where were 260 Maine men lost?

2   who completed a lone global circumnavigation?

3   who was widowed by the unnatural death of Sissi?

4   who remembered in verse a condemned man in a Berkshire prison?

5   where did French discretion render Marchand's journey futile?

6   who succumbed to Koch's bacillus in the Hotel Cosmopolitan?

7   what element was discovered during work on pitch-blende?

8   what convention secured a new territorial lease?

9   what pugilists were launched by Jane?

10   how did GOMRIP?

• 2 • *Who or what:*

1   is called the Hidden Paw?

2   played the Cincinnati Kid?

3   is at home at Easter Elchies?

4   found jumping jeans in sweet corn?

5   pointed to an appendicular landmark?

6   convalesced at the Kurhaus at Rosensee after slipping into the Tod's Hole?

7   sailed from Benbecula to Portree with Betty Burke?

8   started as Salvatore A Lambino?

9   came from Donaldson's Dairy?

10   was Peck's Rebel General?

• 3 • *What:*

1 is a link with the 45?

2 was popularised by Diego Zamora?

3 was founded in 1827 by J B Lapostelle?

4 is labelled STAT CRUX DUM VOLVITUR ORBIS?

5 did the early settlers produce from *naartjies*?

6 did the Lancet see as an elegant improvement on the *mistura spiritus vini gallici*?

7 is at its flaming best with a floating bean?

8 long-bottled spirit was founded in 1896?

9 is sealed with four mitres?

10 is 'L'Unique'?

• 4 • *Who or what:*

1 found a new identity as Klaus Altman?

2 assumed the identity of Wolfgang Gerhard?

3 had an account with the Reichsbank as Max Helliger?

4 moved to Spain as Robert Steinbacher and founded Die Spinne?

5 escaped from internment at Cham as a Vatican citizen named Ricardo Klement?

6 masqueraded as the one-eyed Heinrich Hizinger when apprehended at Bremervorde?

7 wrote an autobiographical novel entitled *Michael*?

8 posed as Major Schaemmel to Best and Stevens?

9 liaised with Hamilton as Alfred Horn?

10 lived in Damascus as Georg Fischer?

• 5 • *Which lighthouse:*

1   followed Belle Tout?
2   stands nine-legged on the sands?
3   shared its builder with Princetown?
4   stands on the birthplace of an arachnophile?
5   would have resisted the vandalism of Sir Ralph the Rover?
6   is forever associated with the *Forfarshire*?
7   failed the Copenhagen-bound *Invincible*?
8   is nominally gallinaceous?
9   was re-erected on Plymouth Hoe?
10 inspired Virginia Woolf?

• 6 • *Which dictator where:*

1   bequeathed a monarchy?
2   created the Estado Novo?
3   was a family doctor in Harlesden?
4   was national boxing champion for nine years?
5   faced a military tribunal and the firing squad on Christmas Day?
6   received four fatal shots from Rigoberto Lopez Perez?
7   oversaw a regime known as Porfiriato?
8   ruled the Republic of Salo?
9   weathered Desert Storm?
10 was Saloth Sar?

• 7 • *Anyway, who or what:*

1   German white is blue?
2   do oafish louts remember?
3   was the chief prince of Meshech and Tubal?
4   twentieth-century French Premier was executed?
5   is equivalent to one seventeenth of a millilitre?
6   valley houses the brochs of Dun Telve and Dun Troddan?
7   satisfied the serpentine appetite in *Theology*?
8   white animal was likened to the Moor's wife?
9   sang thank you for Benny and Björn?
10 was worth twelve pies?

• 8 • *Who or what:*

1 were the 19th Foot?

2 is distilled at Voiron?

3 is an incomplete juvenile break?

4 began 'For the fatherland of the English race ...'?

5 were reduced from ten to nought by repeated unintentional drops?

6 organisation was the victim of sabotage in Auckland harbour?

7 preceded split cane piscatorially?

8 is the effect of a CO_2 blanket?

9 has a team of Packers?

10 is a yaffle?

• 9 • *Which novel or entertainment features:*

1 a physician in Argentina?

2 a former Communist mayor in Spain?

3 a vacuum-cleaner salesman in Cuba?

4 a fugitive alcoholic priest in Mexico?

5 a foreign correspondent in French Indo-China?

6 a Jewish currant merchant bound for Turkey?

7 a toothpaste inventor in Switzerland?

8 a leprologist in the Belgian Congo?

9 a policeman in West Africa?

10 a hotelier in Haiti?

• 10 • *Which giant:*

1 ape terrorised New York?

2 is *Heracleum mantegazzianum*?

3 was decapitated with his own sword?

4 insects were presented to Gresham College?

5 died in a freshly dug pit on his island home?

6 has a trunk with a thick, soft, fibrous covering?

7 was shown by Mercator with a worldly load?

8 is 180ft tall and carries a 120ft club?

9 was the victim of Great-heart?

10 was nourished by Audhumla?

• 11 • *What topic was first covered by:*
1 H W Horwill in 1935?
2 Gustave Kobbé in 1922?
3 George Bradshaw in 1839?
4 Archibald Cregeen in 1838?
5 William Martindale in 1883?
6 Ebenezer Cobham Brewer in 1884?
7 Leslie Halliwell in 1977?
8 Percy A Scholes in 1938?
9 John Bartlett in 1855?
10 John Wisden in 1864?

• 12 • *Which jazz musician was nicknamed:*
1 Muggsy?
2 Pee-wee?
3 Swee' Pea?
4 Cannonball?
5 Blind Lemon?
6 Tricky Sam?
7 Stalebread?
8 Yardbird?
9 Satchmo?
10 Wingy?

• 13 • *Where:*
1 is home to eleven grasshoppers?
2 was the home of the porter Joseph Zimmer?
3 were the sulphur springs called Aquae Helvetiae?
4 did the mountain claim four out of seven at its 1865 conquest?
5 does the cathedral suggest an equine association with Doncaster?
6 had Holmes planned to spend the night of 4th May?
7 did the Council enable Amadeus to become Felix?
8 does Byronic graffiti adorn the third pillar?
9 was the birthplace of Gessler's assassin?
10 are the platforms of Cornavin?

• 14 • *Who or what:*

1   is a green drake?

2   hangs like a blue thread?

3   did Ali liken his buoyancy to?

4   has smaller ones that on him prey?

5   wild creature cried 'Six weeks to frost'?

6   is urged to return to a burning deserted home?

7   shared with Crun, Bloodnok and Thynne?

8   share a similar taste to Ariel?

9   came in droves from Wolfsburg?

10   makes Barton broad?

• 15 • *Which vessel:*

1   kept Billy Budd hanging about?

2   was called *Joan d'Arc* prior to her easy purchase?

3   went aground at the Rue with Nelly Quine on board?

4   took Rachel Vinrace on her voyage out to South America?

5   sailed from Queen's Ferry with the kidnapped David Balfour?

6   was owned by a Chinaman, chartered by an Arab and commanded by a sort of renegade New South Wales German?

7   brought Davies and Carruthers together at Flensburg?

8   was engaged by Fogg for the voyage from Hong Kong?

9   accidentally sailed to Flushing?

10   received Sir Joseph Porter KCB?

• 16 • *Which American Indian:*

1   died of Smallpox at Gravesend?

2   led the tribes at Little Bighorn?

3   received a medal from President Washington?

4   invented, over twelve years, the Cherokee alphabet?

5   greeted the Pilgrims landing at Cape Cod with 'Welcome Englishmen'?

6   deferred the execution of Miantonomo to his brother?

7   claimed to have cut out Tom Custer's heart?

8   dictated his autobiography to Barrett?

9   besieged Detroit for five months?

10   slew Big Mouth?

• 17 • *Who wrote of whose death:*

1 'His landmark is a kopje-crest
    That breaks the veldt around'?

2 'For though his body's under hatches
    His soul is gone aloft'?

3 'When lilacs last in the dooryard bloom'd'?

4 'Weep no more woeful shepherds, weep no more'?

5 'Her fist of a face died clenched on a round pain'?

6 'The bright brain is dulled in Death's slumber
    The stage is for others to fill'?

7 'Farewell, too little and too lately known'?

8 'Alas! My treasure's gone, why do I stay?

9 'He would not do as he was told'?

10 'Let the Irish vessel lie
    Emptied of its poetry'?

• 18 • *In 1998:*

1 who lost her head for the second time at 84?

2 who settled for individual equality in Peshawar?

3 what activity betrayed 'Quo Fas et Gloria Ducunt'?

4 what made 100 in its 50-year pursuit of insular supremacy?

5 what birthday allowed sixty white mice free at the ballet class?

6 what grammatical split has gained lexicographical acceptance?

7 who proved to be a traffic hazard under solar power?

8 from which ceremony were Alexei and Maria absent?

9 what fundamental bruiser was finally outlawed?

10 which team won trophies with bothy barrels?

1999–2000

• 1 • *In 1899:*

   1   whose burner was extinguished?

   2   whose perpetual motion was stilled?

   3   where was a chain put to the test on 1st June?

   4   which international gathering was instigated by Muravyov?

   5   who set the various idiosyncrasies of his friends to music?

   6   which Wigan weaver's widow established a library in his memory?

   7   where did Labour enjoy its first brief taste of government?

   8   which ice-bound vessel made an explosive escape?

   9   what was patented by Felix Hoffman?

  10   who modelled the Lord Protector?

• 2 • *During which century in the current millennium did which British monarch:*

   1   die with a cardiac engraving?

   2   pacify the peasants at Smithfield?

   3   lend his name to an insular academy?

   4   become the last to take the field of battle?

   5   suffer incarceration on the banks of the Danube?

   6   enjoy a postponed coronation owing to appendicitis?

   7   offer his realm in exchange for a quadruped?

   8   experience irreversible cervical division?

   9   make a costly tidal miscalculation?

  10   marry a previous incumbent's widow?

• 3 • *Complete these notices of Hatch, Match and Dispatch:*

1 On 25th February at Boulevard Sainte-Catherine, Limoges, to Marguerite (née Merlet) and Léonard _____ , a son _____-Auguste.

2 On 12th May in Firenze, to Fanny and William _____, a daughter _____, a sister for Parthenope.

3 On 26th May at Mr Hewer's house in Clapham in his 71st year, _____ _____ BA JP FRS (President   1684–86), Freeman of the City of London. The burial will take place at St Olave's, Hart Street.

4 On 22nd June at Sint-Annaparochie, near Leeuwarden, _____ Harmenszoon van _____ to Saskia van Uylenburgh.

5 On 28th July in Leipzig, _____ _____ _____, Cantor of St Thomas's School, aged 65, devoted husband of Anna Magdalena and a much loved father and grandfather. The funeral will take place at St John's Church, Leipzig.

6 On 6th September in Christiania, _____, son of Baldur and Adelaide _____ to Eva, daughter of the late Michael and Maren Sars.

7 On 12th December at Severin, Mecklenburg, Paul _____, youngest son of Friedrich and Katharina _____ to Maria Magdalena Quandt, daughter of Dr Ritschel and Frau Friedländer.

8 On 19th December at the Parsonage, Haworth, _____ Jane _____ after a long illness, aged 30, daughter of the Rev Patrick and dear sister of Charlotte and Anne.

9 On 25th December at Bellagio, to Marie d'Agoult (née de Flavigny) and _____ _____, a Daughter Cosima.

10 On 30th December at the Esplanade, Bombay, to Alice (née Macdonald) and John Lockwood _____, a son _____.

• 4 • *Complete the trio:*

1 1189, 1377, _____

2 Clegg, Foggy, _____

3 M'Turk, Beetle, _____

4 Worrell, Weekes, _____

5 Melchior, Caspar, _____

6 Götaland, Svealand, _____

7 Holland, Lindsey, _____

8 Incus, Malleus, _____

9 Harris, George, _____

10 Sidon, Tyre, _____

• 5 •　*What repetitious word is or was:*

1　a dwarf antelope?

2　a soft-nosed missile?

3　a contemporary car-ferry?

4　a small rum-soaked sponge cake?

5　a result of severe Vitamin B deficiency?

6　a Correctional Facility in New York State?

7　a type of North African semolina?

8　a Siamese three-wheeled taxi?

9　an up and down spinner?

10　dead in comparison?

• 6 •　*Which variety of gem:*

1　fixed Oswald?

2　suggests a fingernail?

3　is associated with January?

4　is distilled from a 1761 recipe?

5　does the clown compare to Orsini's mind?

6　was first contested on the Thames in 1844?

7　was an unsafe haven for *Arizona*?

8　was stolen by Col. Herncastle?

9　created a Yangtze Incident?

10　was Hitchcock's?

• 7 •　*What tale begins:*

1　'I was born in 1632, in the city of York'?

2　'There was no possibility of taking a walk that day'?

3　'I had a farm in Africa, at the foot of the Ngong hill'?

4　'The First Lord of the Admiralty was unpopular at Pin Mill'?

5　'The schoolmaster was leaving the village, and everybody seemed sorry'?

6　'Mr Jones, of the Manor Farm, had locked the hen-house for the night, but was too drunk to shut the pop-holes'?

7　'I wonder when in the world you're going to do something Rudolf'?

8　'A week had passed since the funeral of my poor boy Harry'?

9　'The oranges were more plentiful than usual that year'?

10　'It was the best of times, it was the worst of times'?

• 8 • *Who called what:*

1 Mor?
2 Kehaar?
3 Jezebel?
4 Chetowaik?
5 Daughter Dell?
6 Old Brown?
7 Seekonk?
8 Redruff?
9 Moses?
10 Ie?

• 9 • *Who:*

1 gave unlimited credit?
2 was nursed by Mrs Chippy Hackee?
3 rowed away from the *Pound of Candles*?
4 felt rather sick and went to look for some parsley?
5 gave his guests roasted grasshopper with ladybird sauce?
6 declined to sing, apologetically, because of tooth-ache?
7 provided a laundry service from her home on Cat Bells?
8 was rescued by Kep and two fox-hound puppies?
9 was punished by caudal avulsion?
10 was an unwilling bee-keeper?

• 10 • *Who or what:*

1 was viler?
2 is 'For Gallantry'?
3 was formerly Stabroek?
4 squarely links Charlotte and St Andrew?
5 did not, despite Cowper's prediction, float again?
6 made affectionate gestures resulting in lacrimation?
7 believed himself incapable of mendacity?
8 saw no limit to his TT skills?
9 was Mary Ann Evans?
10 created Svengali?

• 11 • *Who or what:*

1   drops out of Skene?

2   was Alison Uttley's heroine?

3   loan was requested of Tom Pearse?

4   oriental beverage is flavoured with bergamot?

5   New World import competes with *Sciurus vulgaris*?

6   churchyard was home for fourteen years for the grieving Bobby?

7   fawning animal was Bolingbroke likened to?

8   enjoyed a reginal interlude of nine days?

9   area is occupied by Betz cells?

10 were the 21st Foot?

• 12 • *In which city:*

1   is Charlemagne's octagon?

2   did Böttger develop hard-paste?

3   did Gutenberg set up his press?

4   did Sally sing at the Lady Windermere?

5   was minor abduction the sequel to vermin extermination?

6   did the London *Clarion* have offices at Kaiser Wilhelmstrasse 33?

7   is the painter's tombstone inscribed 'emigravit'?

8   did J inadvertently steal a bicycle?

9   did Perkeo guard the great vat?

10 does one embark at St Pauli?

• 13 • *Which river:*

1   still ga'ed singin' past?

2   was Cotton's beloved nymph?

3   is spacious, spreading like a sea?

4   separates Men of Kent from Kentish Men?

5   lingers in the hills and holds a hundred little towns of stone?

6   had Sam Oglethorpe's joinery business on its bank?

7   spreads like some earth-born Giant?

8   is crossed at Bablock Hythe?

9   is lovelier than the Arno?

10 fills twice a day?

• 14 • *Who or what:*

1 was Minnehaha?
2 is an object of ridicule?
3 appears to be an avian donkey?
4 is a spotted African hunchback?
5 brings merriment to Manchester Square?
6 is a scaly outcrop of Superior humour?
7 was Stan and Ollie's brown sauce?
8 caught the world's great hands?
9 was there in Conrad's sneer?
10 is Nitrous Oxide?

• 15 • *Who was famously (or infamously) associated with:*

1 Héloïse?
2 Geli Raubal?
3 Emma Hamilton?
4 Christine Keeler?
5 Beatrice Portinari?
6 Clementina Walkinshaw?
7 Mary Jo Kopechne?
8 Marie Walewska?
9 Clara Petacci?
10 Delilah?

• 16 • *Locate:*

1 Wyle Kop
2 Broomielaw
3 Mann Island
4 Priestpopple
5 Friars Vennel
6 North Bar Within
7 Great Dockray
8 Petty France
9 Petty Cury
10 Tombland

• 17 • *During the first millennium AD:*

1   who was betrayed by Ganelon?

2   which poet was banished to Tomi?

3   to whom did the Angel Gabriel appear on Mount Hira?

4   whose transfer to the choir was delayed by continuous summer rain?

5   whose burial place was destined to be covered by platform 8 at King's Cross?

6   whose indifferent performance in Somerset would have disappointed Mr Kipling?

7   which three kings are remembered by baldness, obesity and simplicity?

8   who lost his brother at Aylsford after success at Ebbsfleet?

9   what destroyed Herculaneum and Pompeii?

10   who was the victim of Boleslav?

• 18 • *In 1999:*

1   whose 10-74 recalled whose 10-53?

2   where was the passing of their Mwalimi mourned?

3   for whom did Arianna sing *Erbarme, dich, mein Gott*?

4   which Bunny has completed his life's, often chilly, adventure?

5   how did a time of 2 min 23 sec make Riminicu Vilcea pre-eminent?

6   what received an accidental direct hit following imperial and metric confusion?

7   how was defeat in Catalonia received with disbelief in Bavaria?

8   what discovery recalled the answer 'Because it's there'?

9   what newly sited ocular phenomenon is sightless?

10   where did Ibbeson bring me sunshine?

2000–2001

• 1 • *During the year 1900:*

1   who fell to Angelo Bresci?

2   who launched Hickory, Hunk and Zeke?

3   what was first aired over Friedrichshafen?

4   who was the railroad hero of Vaughan Miss.?

5   who made his final journey from Brantwood to Coniston?

6   where was the Doctor dismissed, uniquely, by Conan Doyle?

7   who declared 'I am dying beyond my means'?

8   whose theory explained black body emission?

9   which product of Holland was not Dutch?

10   what put Bond Street in the red?

• 2 •

1   what jingle precedes a debt of 1¼d?

2   what lays its eggs on the Cuckoo Flower?

3   what is black and made from young downy leaves?

4   where did three deaths follow attempted tenpin desegregation?

5   in which of his cases did Holmes incriminate the Ku Klux Klan?

6   with what did a Venetian playwright inspire a Russian composer?

7   what infamous herbicide had teratogenic effects in Indo-China?

8   what was founded at James Sloan's Inn at Loughgall?

9   what divides the land of the Nama people?

10   what was Burgess's mechanical device?

• 3 • *Who or what:*

1 was Awdry's No. 5?
2 was a murdered by Robert Ford?
3 published some unreliable memoirs?
4 earned the title Matamore at Clavijo?
5 described events of 16th June 1904 in the Irish capital?
6 advised parents against a solo descent to the urban limit?
7 has Hannah and Rupert as subsidiaries?
8 failed to complete his *Ivory Tower*?
9 married Maria Beatrice d'Este?
10 is Phyllis Dorothy White?

• 4 • *Who or what:*

1 is 4722?
2 introduced the Delmonico?
3 is chalked up on Windover Hill?
4 was the subject of a Copland fanfare?
5 is the predicted spouse with seven plum stones?
6 results from a confinement west of the Medway?
7 was commissioned as HMS *Cadaceus* in 1941?
8 was resurrected by McDonald Fraser?
9 is a Middle Eastern interpreter?
10 is a sinister wrong'n?

• 5 • *Identify these jazzmen:*

1 Oran Thaddeus
2 Thomas Wright
3 Charlie Melvin
4 Theodore Walter
5 Ferdinand Joseph La Menthe
6 Hezekiah Leroy Gordon
7 Irving Milfred
8 Edward Kennedy
9 Leon Bismarck
10 John Birks

• 6 • *Which capital city was formerly:*

1 Ledra?

2 Bytown?

3 Triaditsa?

4 Philadelphia?

5 Port Nicholson?

6 Christopolis?

7 Christiania?

8 Batavia?

9 Revel?

10 Urga?

• 7 • *In which sports are the following contested:*

1 Iroquois Cup?

2 Bermuda Bowl?

3 Camanachd Cup?

4 Leonard Trophy?

5 MacRobertson Shield?

6 Doggett's Coat and Badge?

7 St Bride's Vase?

8 Strathcona Cup?

9 Lugano Trophy?

10 Kinnaird Cup?

• 8 • *On the small screen, which production was associated with:*

1 52 Acacia Drive?

2 368 Mandela House?

3 17 Railway Terrace?

4 23 Railway Cuttings?

5 24 Sebastopol Crescent?

6 1 and 2 Copse Cottage?

7 46 Peacock Crescent?

8 66 Sycamore Street?

9 30 Kelsall Street?

10 165 Eaton Place?

• 9 • *What is:*

1 a form of humbug?

2 *Bucephala clangula?*

3 a very wide-angle lens?

4 like the ever-changing moon?

5 Marks and Barfield's revolver?

6 amblyopic from neglected strabismus?

7 a beast of a name, ain't it?

8 an Aboriginal walkabout?

9 periorbital ecchymosis?

10 Inis Mac Neasain?

• 10 • *What title described:*

1 Amina?

2 Angelina?

3 John of Leyden?

4 Sandor Barinkay?

5 Lady Harriet Durham?

6 Don Eugenio de Zuniga?

7 Leonora di Gusmann?

8 Violetta Valery?

9 Cio-Cio-San?

10 Marenka?

• 11 • *Which rhyming words describe:*

1 a stupid boy?

2 diversionary nonsense?

3 a floral embroidery stitch?

4 highly qualified emigration?

5 an old-fashioned pompous person?

6 wealthy, fashionable globetrotters?

7 language intended to confuse?

8 whether you like it or not?

9 a traveller's tummy upset?

10 a barrel organ?

• 12 • *Who, in disguise, was:*

1 Morgan?

2 Cambio?

3 Cesario?

4 Balthasar?

5 Lodowick?

6 Mother Prat?

7 Ganymede?

8 Sebastian?

9 a pilgrim?

10 Caius?

• 13 • *Where:*

1 *Arctic* and *Vesta*?

2 *Mont Blanc* and *Imo*?

3 *Victoria* and *Camperdown*?

4 *Andrea Doria* and *Stockholm*?

5 *Empress of Ireland* and *Storstad*?

6 *Aegean Captain* and *Atlantic Empress*?

7 *City of Lisbon* and *Douglas*?

8 *Marchioness* and *Bowbelle*?

9 *Doña Paz* and *Vector*?

10 *Utopia* and *Anson*?

• 14 • *Which makers used:*

1 a hare?

2 a snipe?

3 a sphinx?

4 a greyhound?

5 a viking's head?

6 the goddess of speed?

7 a flying stork?

8 an elephant?

9 Icarus?

10 a lion?

• 15 • *On which island:*

1   was Daedalus imprisoned?

2   did Theseus abandon Ariadne?

3   did burning Sappho love and sing?

4   did Durrell place Prospero's Cell?

5   did an Old Rugbeian poet die on St George's Day?

6   is there a natal association with the hypotenuse?

7   was the Colossus dislodged by an earthquake?

8   was Jesus Christ revealed to John?

9   was the father of medicine born?

10   did Penelope await her husband?

• 16 • *What:*

1   was Nag?

2   is Tweed's last feeder?

3   was the purchase of my Yucutan aunt?

4   on revision must have been next Wednesday?

5   agent caused Caesarion's bereavement after Actium?

6   creature's dietary advice was an eye-opener?

7   South American is the greatest of all?

8   is the place where 57 peaks at 512?

9   is an alternative to Mr Bean?

10   is *Natrix natrix*?

• 17 • *Which President:*

1   was Old Hickory?

2   served only 31 days?

3   was impeached and acquitted?

4   declared 'All men are created equal'?

5   lost when representing the Bull Moose Party?

6   was 'always honest, often great, but sometimes mad'?

7   was airborne when he took the oath of office?

8   was shot by a self-styled Stalwart?

9   announced Fourteen Points?

10   served three terms?

• 18 • *In the year 2000:*

1   who has emulated Emmanuel Laskar?
2   for whom was the instruction 'Senz'aglio'?
3   what event united Cleopatra and Mary Poppins?
4   who was placed fourth after Don, Garry and Jack?
5   in what did ignorance of Jason prove a costly pilot error?
6   which Victorian partner can now be found in Bangkok's Pariwas Temple?
7   whose successful round trip recalled the ill-fated *Örnen*?
8   who celebrated 100 with 100 when who was 100?
9   whose ignominy recalled defeat at Paardeberg?
10   which third secret has been revealed?

2001–2002

· 1 · *In 1901:*

1   who fell to a Buffalo shot?

2   by whom were the blades blunted?

3   who was at home to Washington in Washington?

4   what made its debut between Shepherd's Bush and Kew?

5   which line was completed despite carnivorous interruptions?

6   where, in spite of paternal familiarity, did he have to dress up as a copper?

7   who opened a concert hall next door to his showrooms?

8   who became the first on the first of the first?

9   which King created a revolutionary blade?

10   who revealed the apian story?

· 2 · *In which tale:*

1   was the villain twice resurrected?

2   were callops on the menu at the Cage?

3   did Toddy secure Gray's head for Richardson?

4   did the hijacked *Good Hope* founder on the sands?

5   did the narrator ride from Clackmannan Pool to Inverary?

6   was the heroine the colour of a mouse, with a kindly eye and a determined under-jaw?

7   were the travellers cheated by one named Carnival?

8   was the skeleton of Allardyce left as a pointer?

9   did Sir Danvers Carew meet a violent death?

10   did a father sentence his son to death?

QUESTIONS

• 3 • *Using all the same letters, create:*

1 Marie-Henri Beyle and the venue for Up-Helly-Aa.
2 a test venue and the infinitive of dividing equally into two.
3 Pasternak's heroine and the much-reduced recipient of Oxus.
4 the elected chamber of Tynwald Court and the island home of Talisker.
5 a week which, unlike its founder, is not dead, and the murderess of Scarpia.
6 a mediaeval university hall and, according to Swift, what every man desires to do.
7 Bolivar's native city and a purgative derived from the bark of buckthorn.
8 a motorcycle carnival and a small, dispersed, amount of something.
9 a frame with a hinged pin and the setting for *Buddenbrooks*.
10 small table mats and an unwilling imbiber of hemlock.

• 4 • *Complete:*

1 ………. i Rana
2 ………. il Bahar
3 ………. sur Alzette
4 ………. en Famenne
5 ………. de Barrameda
6 ………. ob de Tauber
7 ………. la Gaillarde
8 ………. del Grappa
9 ………. de Fonds
10 ………. op Zoom

• 5 • *What infectious disease was associated with:*

1 Eyam?
2 Stratford?
3 North Tawton?
4 Gruinard Island?
5 The Isle of Sheppey?
6 the barque *Hecla* at Swansea?
7 Cambridge Assizes?
8 a pump in EC2?
9 Rochdale?
10 Worksop?

• 6 • *Which Nobel laureate:*

1   shared with his son?

2   felt it was Best to share?

3   experimented with maize?

4   received two awards for Chemistry?

5   immediately followed another laureate as Master?

6   investigated the antibacterial properties of carpet dyes?

7   carried out cardiac self-catheterisation?

8   started as Manya Sklodowska?

9   studied canine salivation?

10   studied sticklebacks?

• 7 • *Beneath the surface, what is:*

1   a rod?

2   a weapon?

3   good on ice?

4   a light touch?

5   the one and only?

6   one of Burton's best?

7   a pintle partner?

8   a dusty digit?

9   a butterfly?

10   a cleaner?

• 8 • *Who or what:*

1   was stabbed by Felton?

2   repealed the Stamp Act?

3   revealed the Babington Plot?

4   is renowned for bikes, boots and players?

5   are northern representatives of *Bos Taurus*?

6   plain-woven cotton fabric is typically checked?

7   was purchased from Mr Spencer Cowper?

8   hybrids are reared at Maple Tree Farm?

9   created Albert Campion?

10   shot the Prime Minister?

• 9 • *Who or what:*

1 was Jonathan Buttall?

2 is the Lone Star's flower?

3 brought scholarship to Horsham?

4 did Mrs Peterson find in a goose's crop?

5 is Derbyshire's rare form of Calcium Fluoride?

6 executed George Dixon, only for him to be resurrected on the small screen?

7 links Sheffield Park and East Grinstead?

8 was developed by Diebach in 1704?

9 signals impending departure?

10 recalls Sultan Ahmet I?

• 10 • *What is:*

1 Duroc?

2 Marans?

3 Kuvasz?

4 Chianina?

5 Percheron?

6 Beltsville?

7 Loaghtan?

8 Embden?

9 Saanen?

10 Pekin?

• 11 •

1 who produces *La Gitana*?

2 with what was Findlater's *Dry Fly* illustrated?

3 who, rather tactlessly, remind their hosts of 1588?

4 what accompanies post-prandial jollity in Barataria?

5 which pale dry creation can be interpreted as Uncle Joe?

6 who obtains *Pata de Gallina* from the almacenista Jaranda?

7 what are Macharnudo, Carrascal, Balbaina and Anina?

8 which great house was founded by Patrick Murphy?

9 whose amontillado recalls Florizel and Perdita?

10 what is abbreviated as PX?

- 12 • *Who or what:*

  1 is self-fertile?

  2 comes from Sebastopol booty?

  3 has produced an aviation manual?

  4 was Freeman's great African traverse?

  5 started as *Deutschland* and finished as *Hansa*?

  6 accommodated female compositors in Great Coram Street?

  7 found the cathedral cold, dreary and dingy?

  8 was celebrated this year on 21st May?

  9 failed, tragically, to reach Larne?

  10 began as Gomez Cima?

- 13 • *Uncover:*

  1 Tate

  2 Hero

  3 Garbo

  4 Cicero

  5 Tramp

  6 Tricycle

  7 Sniper

  8 Artist

  9 Sonia

  10 Snow

- 14 • *Which Old Testament Book:*

  1 is *The Preacher*?

  2 inspired Browning?

  3 cost Robert Blake a fine of £300?

  4 other than *Genesis*, inspired Marriott Edgar?

  5 was the last in the 1988 Tyndale House *Paraphrase*?

  6 inspired the 6th Baron Byron to a lupine comparison?

  7 confused reptile and mammal in a 1950 publication?

  8 has an identical chapter in *II Kings 19*?

  9 possesses the longest verse?

  10 ends with a curse?

QUESTIONS

• 15 • *Where:*

1. is Tacca's *Porcellino*?
2. do slow toads creep out in damp corners?
3. did principle discovery precede a nudist's dash?
4. does the town sit in the heat amid the mulberry trees?
5. did a massacre start with the call to evensong on Easter Monday?
6. does the Basilica honour the resurrection of three butchered and pickled boys?
7. did Alessandro and Luigi produce a spicy wormwood concoction?
8. was the subjugation completed with 'Kiss me Kate'?
9. was the jester the victim of Monterone's curse?
10. did the Fifth go ashore on the ninth?

• 16 • *Which twins:*

1. were called Dioscuri?
2. catalogued the extremes?
3. confusingly, employed twin brothers?
4. came to live with Mr Crisparkle at Cloisterham?
5. were left as babies in a foundling basket at a convent in Lima?
6. born to the same mother by different fathers, were confronted by serpents in infancy?
7. were unaware that their father was Fergus Crampton?
8. were the children of John Brooke and Meg March?
9. were nourished by a woodpecker?
10. fixed Jack 'The Hat'?

• 17 • *Which mutiny:*

1   was led by Cinque?

2   provided Joost Hartgers with a best-seller?

3   resulted from inadequate safety regulations?

4   was followed by suspension of the Gold Standard?

5   saw Barney Greenwald secure the acquittal of the mutineers?

6   was pre-empted by Capt. Mackenzie, who was later court-martialled?

7   was achieved with the assistance of convict passengers?

8   followed the collection of *Artocarpus altilis*?

9   was a rebellion against Capt. Hugh Pigot?

10   was due to maggot-infested meat?

• 18 • *In 2001*:

1   how did IOW become HW?

2   to what was Zalyotin the last visitor?

3   who has confirmed the limitations of banana movement?

4   which waterway has been 'blinkered' by a revolutionary palpebra?

5   where might pupils have found Mrs Beeton a safer option than the Internet?

6   which processed bovine organ seemed to be indistinguishable from its ovine equivalent?

7   whose bagman compounded indifferent arithmetic with excessive somnolence?

8   where would declining standards have saddened Robert Wodelarke?

9   where did Sabbath reflections cause a derailment?

10   who faced up to Baltic bolshevism?

2002–2003

• 1 • *In 1902:*

1. what damaged Sansovino's loggetta?
2. who was enthroned on his sixteenth birthday?
3. how did we learn about solitary feline ambulation?
4. what tragedy preceded a similar disaster by 69 years?
5. whose legacy provided fresh opportunities for German further education?
6. whose representation of a warrior queen was unveiled on Westminster Bridge?
7. how was Golders Green able to reduce Woking's fuel consumption?
8. from which Terror to Evil-doers were males excluded?
9. how did the tenancy of No. 10 remain in the family?
10. which club paid a record £500 for Common?

• 2 • *In which town or city:*

1. does the sun also rise?
2. did Jean Botin start business in 1725?
3. did a Slad lad find it hard as its syllables?
4. is the cathedral incorporated into the mosque?
5. did the university publish the first polyglot bible?
6. did Leporello enumerate his master's amorous adventures?
7. did Philip's beard receive unsolicited attention?
8. did a blind composer set his guitar concerto?
9. did we leave him alone in his glory?
10. did a painter from Candia excel?

- 3 • *Who lost:*
  1   a pre-war ear at Havana?
  2   his hair, while asleep on his lover's knees?
  3   his nose, in a duel, and made a silver prosthesis?
  4   his tail, prior to escaping through the attic window?
  5   both legs, but returned heroically and was downed at Béthune?
  6   his head, after criticising the tetrarch for marrying his sister-in-law?
  7   his leg, in his country's service, under the immortal Hawke?
  8   his head after making a donation of six guineas?
  9   an eye, in the naval battle of Kolberg roads?
  10   his right arm at Santa Cruz de Tenerife?

- 4 • *Who:*
  1   rode Roos?
  2   died on Black Auster?
  3   rode the highway on Black Bess?
  4   rode Topper as William Boyd?
  5   rode Gulltoppr to Balder's funeral?
  6   tamed Pommer, the yellow Horse of Crooksbury?
  7   was the comical owner of Capulet?
  8   offered Harkaway for 45 guineas?
  9   rode Rocinante?
  10   created Thunderhead?

- 5 •
  1   who is a bewitched girl?
  2   to be what is it absolutely scrumptious?
  3   who was said to be lovely as Peer Gynt?
  4   to what extent could Indian Army officers read?
  5   where did love come to Mrs Wentworth-Brewster?
  6   where can you hear the yells of woe-begone bourgeoisie?
  7   what did Cyril scream prior to debagging himself?
  8   how long does it take Government Whips?
  9   where must the heat and smell be hell?
  10   what is a flower that is free?

• 6 • *Numerically, what or where:*

1   is Vermuden's?

2   is a megalithic tomb?

3   includes a mediaeval clapper?

4   appears to be a Salopian conurbation?

5   will the mountainy goats be wagging their chins?

6   apart from Armagh, Augher and Clogher, should presbyters and piddlers pray for me?

7   does Angus receive hospital treatment?

8   is the grave of the *Torrey Canyon*?

9   witnessed a 1692 bloodbath?

10   is Crocketford?

• 7 • *Which Archbishop of Canterbury:*

1   advertised?

2   visited the prisoner of Dürnstein?

3   attended a belated coronation at Bath?

4   provided a venue for the Encaenia Ceremony?

5   was banished by the King, but later translated to St Andrews?

6   had his detached head replaced on London Bridge by that of a revolting peasant?

7   opposed the Deceased Wife's Sister Marriage Act?

8   held Canterbury in plurality with Winchester?

9   died on the same day as his sovereign?

10   shared a natal origin with St Paul?

• 8 • *Who depicted himself:*

1   as St Paul?

2   with Isabella Brandt?

3   bearded and wearing a bowler hat?

4   in a bandage, following auricular self-harm?

5   among the Officers and Subalterns of the St George Militia Company?

6   in military attire, in the year of his death in a powder magazine explosion?

7   overlooked by *The Spirit of the Dead Watching*?

8   with *Eryngium*, a symbol of fidelity?

9   with Doctor Arietta?

10   in a burial scene?

• 9 • *What*:

1 is made in reverse?

2 is nettle-wrapped in Cornwall?

3 originates from the valley of the Ure?

4 matures in the limestone caves of Combalou?

5 is prepared in tsaudières in the Valle d'Aosta?

6 is wrapped in chestnut leaves and tied with raffia?

7 in its antiquity, can be found off Fleet Street?

8 is still served with plum bread at the Bell?

9 is made from the second milking?

10 is holey Norwegian?

• 10 • *With whom did the following share his majesty's bedchamber:*

1 Jane Shore?

2 Marie Mancini?

3 Dorothea Jordan?

4 Elizabeth Blount?

5 Marquise de Pompadour?

6 Amalie Sophie Marianne von Wendt?

7 Anna Sophie Reventlow?

8 Maria Fitzherbert?

9 Barbara Palmer?

10 Alice Perrers?

• 11 • *Ossify:*

1 yoke

2 hooked

3 shallow dish

4 small key

5 clasp

6 sieve

7 u-shaped

8 crescent-shaped

9 pea-shaped

10 anvil

• 12 •

1 who left a doll's house?

2 who tried to fill his gap?

3 whose name escaped him?

4 whose ways were doubly wicked?

5 who, amongst other things, was gruesome?

6 for whom was the apple sauce produced too late?

7 who admitted to a Russian debt of $2000?

8 who described a solo tango?

9 who loitered with intent?

10 who is the eternal male?

• 13 •

1 where is the Tickly Tap?

2 who was Nutkin's brother?

3 what is right before Signpost?

4 who escaped to Jackson's Island?

5 who made it to number one with *My Ding-A-Ling*?

6 what accompanied a pound of Rice and a hive of Silvery bees?

7 what is lined with a fawn tartan?

8 what was an artificial harbour?

9 who was Verges's partner?

10 which fields are forever?

• 14 • *What:*

1 SW preceded VW's NE?

2 brings a Saharan dust-up to Senegal?

3 may regularly put the wind up Baghdad?

4 caused great loss of life in Valetta in 1555?

5 ruffles the feathers of the Camargue's flamingos?

6 Egyptian phenomenon has a fifty-day periodicity?

7 brings gales from the Andes to Buenos Aires?

8 speeds Tarifa Bay's windsurfers westward?

9 can bring winter warmth to Colorado?

10 breezes in late at the WACA?

• 15 • *Where, in Europe, is:*

1   the Zähringen?

2   Duqesnoy's wee man?

3   Wallgren's Havis Amanda?

4   Guet's representation of the planets?

5   Oceanus drawn by two sea-horses and two tritons?

6   the god of fertility, the recent victim of brachial trauma?

7   Bundgaard's representation of insular creation?

8   Abraham's Cantonese imitation?

9   Labenwolf's goose man?

10   Milles's Poseidon?

• 16 • *At what time:*

1   was the train to Yuma?

2   did the clock signal murine descent?

3   was high tide at Bradgate on 15th June?

4   in Bangkok, do they foam at the mouth and run?

5   stood Grantchester's church clock as remembered in Berlin?

6   had Ratchett's watch stopped in the snowbound train west of Vincovici?

7   did Erzberger's Compiègne agreement come into force?

8   did Alcock and Brown land in Connemara?

9   did Fogg's train leave Charing Cross?

10   does the second dogwatch finish?

• 17 • *Where:*

1   is Milton's mulberry tree?

2   does one enter by the chimney?

3   was the founder a Bedford bicycle salesman?

4   does the apostrophe distinguish it from somewhere in the other place?

5   is the chapel the first of two built by the Savilian Professor of Astronomy?

6   was a library bequeathed by a former King's Secretary for Admiralty Affairs?

7   is George Gordon represented by a Danish sculptor in the library?

8   did the Lord Protector's head finally come to rest?

9   does Humility lead to Virtue and Honour?

10   are there three gloomy courts?

• 18 • *In 2002:*

1   for whom is it now really all over?

2   who escaped capital punishment in East Berkshire?

3   whose decapitation was a protest against global capitalism?

4   why might melliferous activity have been reduced in Co. Durham?

5   which self-styled refuse collector's son has come to the end of the line?

6   which great redeemer ended his pilgrimage when which land became too barren?

7   where did 45 Commando go ashore following a map-reading error?

8   where did Adam collapse with a comminuted fracture of his leg?

9   which insular admiral caused damage in Nottingham?

10   what has made Preston even prouder?

2003–2004

• 1 • *In 1903:*

1 who founded the WSPU?

2 what speed limit was imposed on motor cars?

3 who was the Sublime Paralytic, who died of cholera?

4 whose weekly journal began to publicise atrocities in the Congo Free State?

5 whose residence at Holly Lodge was commemorated by the first blue plaque?

6 whose hand-written catalogue described works for sale at their Peckham residence?

7 who was hounded by the Governor of Ceylon to suicide in a Parisian hotel?

8 which Franco-Peruvian reached his journey's end on Fatu Iwa?

9 in what was the Chimney-Sweep the first victor?

10 how was Giuseppe Sarto renamed?

• 2 • *Which pioneer:*

1 was the Oldham egg-collector?

2 experimented with family planning in Hispaniola?

3 achieved whole-hearted substitution in the 'great barn'?

4 discovered the anaesthetic and analgesic properties of laughing gas?

5 devised a system of raised point writing at the Institution des Jeunes Aveugles?

6 is now credited with the discovery of the retrovirus which compromises immunity?

7 combined a surgical approach to Schizophrenia with Portuguese diplomacy?

8 described his invention in *Traité de l'auscultation médiate*?

9 discovered in soil, an agent to counter Koch's bacillus?

10 worked out inheritance in Moravia?

• 3 •   *Who painted:*

1   the church of Auvers?
2   the church of St Séverin?
3   a 404ft spire with a rainbow?
4   the church of St Jacques near the Quai Duquesne?
5   a Notre Dame lookalike in a 'pretty' town by the Seine?
6   a Norman cathedral, more than 20 times, from above the draper's shop?
7   the Confessor's building with a procession of KCBs?
8   Mariakerk, with Buurkerk and the cathedral?
9   the old church in Sundborn?
10 the church at Blainville?

• 4 •   *Who composed:*

1   'Alligator Hop'?
2   'Maple Leaf Rag'?
3   'Stevedore Stomp'?
4   'Riverboat Shuffle'?
5   'Bourbon Street Parade'?
6   'Shim-me-sha-Wabble'?
7   'One O'Clock Jump'?
8   'Muskrat Ramble'?
9   'Milneburg Joys'?
10 'St Louis Blues'?

• 5 •   *What culinary delicacy misleadingly suggests:*

1   sugary loaves?
2   Maharashtrian poultry?
3   a citrus dairy product?
4   a North British gamebird?
5   a bunny from the Principality?
6   tarts filled with ground ungulate flesh?
7   a partly concealed amphibian?
8   a lizard from Banffshire?
9   a dachshund in season?
10 satanic riders?

• 6 • *What:*

1   is 3.14159?

2   is back to back clothing?

3   represents one millionth of a metre?

4   was the timely creation of Louis Brandt?

5   fraction of serum contains the antigen opposition?

6   cerebral activity consists of oscillations with a frequency of 8–13 hertz?

7   is the destination of the posterior fontanelle?

8   blockade was investigated by Black?

9   project was devised by van Veen?

10   is a minimal amount?

• 7 • *In which town:*

1   was Ryan's bridge too far?

2   does a modern bridge recall Gerritszoon?

3   did Mesdag create his suburban panorama?

4   did Freeling's Piet advance to Commisaris?

5   was silence doubly assured by Balthazar Gerard?

6   did Gerard and Anton establish the Incandescent Lamp Works?

7   did the peacemakers cede Gibraltar to Britain?

8   did van Aeken adopt his natal city's name?

9   does the Elfstedentocht start and finish?

10   did the *Goblin* arrive by mistake?

• 8 • *Who or what:*

1   was Tashunka Witco?

2   is 4400 foot pounds per second?

3   was devised by Nils and Janne Olsson?

4   supplied St Pancras vestry with eight acres for a cemetery?

5   is a cocktail of ginger ale, brandy and a twist of lemon?

6   was the apparatus instrumental in the escape from a Silesian POW camp?

7   stands where the Alaska and Klondike highways meet?

8   has two daughters crying 'Give, give'?

9   nebula is adjacent to Zeta Orionis?

10   was Sir Anthony Meyer?

· 9 · *In which city might one wait at:*

1 Sants?

2 Saint-Jean?

3 Santa Justa?

4 Santa Lucia?

5 San Giovanni?

6 Santa Apolónia?

7 Saint-Charles?

8 Sint Pieters?

9 Saint-Loud?

10 São Benito?

· 10 · *What:*

1 bleeds at St Brynach's?

2 is tallest of all at the Hermitage?

3 is Coleridge's Lady of the Woods?

4 did the Jews hang their harps upon in Mesopotamia?

5 Christmas bloomer came from Joseph's staff on Wearyall?

6 was the HQ of the Kentish smugglers Quested and Ransley?

7 provided a perch for the Royal fugitive after Worcester?

8 conundrum was introduced by Archibald Menzies?

9 is St Lawrence's unique feature?

10 shelters the village smithy?

· 11 · *Who or what:*

1 was the Pontus Axeinus?

2 was that young Mars of men?

3 sticker was succeeded by brown in 41?

4 was Billy's ante-mortem gift from the blind beggar?

5 name was on the lid of a box to be left with Barkis till called for?

6 was acquitted in Mogador on the evidence of Lady Cicely Waynflete?

7 had a particular wish to turn down Moultrassie Avenue?

8 blemish arises from the oxidation of sebum?

9 is Leicester's troglodyte cannibal?

10 is *Dendroapsis polylepis*?

• 12 • *Identify titularly:*

   1   Sauron

   2   Heartwell

   3   James Durie

   4   Thorkell Mylrea

   5   Francisco Scaramanga

   6   Zafrillah bin Ismail bin Said

   7   Sir Edward Manley

   8   Harvey Birch

   9   Alec Leamas

  10   Gabilan

• 13 • *Who:*

   1   was Levi, the taxman?

   2   was executed at Achaia?

   3   is associated with *Pecten maximus*?

   4   was the second martyr after Stephen?

   5   was accompanied by his wife on his missionary travels?

   6   financed the purchase of the Field of Blood with his reward?

   7   may, or may not, have been the Patmos seer?

   8   is remembered annually with Simon?

   9   was the twin, who needed proof?

  10   came on as a substitute?

• 14 • *Translate further, to the popular English name:*

   1   harvester

   2   little plum

   3   farm-worker

   4   little brother

   5   green-footed chicken

   6   grass widow on Ithaca

   7   swift immerser

   8   softest body

   9   goat-milker

  10   watchman

• 15 • *Complete:*

1   Angela, Saphir, Ella, ...

2   apples, cherries, hops, ...

3   ...., Nuoro, Oristano, Sassari

4   Rheingold, Walkure, Siegfried, ...

5   Mildred Harris, Lita Grey, Paulette Goddard, ...

6   ...., Norbert Brainin, Siegmund Nissel, Martin Lovett

7   Burnt Norton, East Coker, ..., Little Gidding

8   de Morville, de Tracy, ..., Brito

9   Justine, Balthazar, ..., Clea

10   market, home, ..., none

• 16 • *Which waterfall:*

1   is Ireland's highest?

2   embraces three county boundaries?

3   is adjacent to a succession of three bridges?

4   is traversed by Lord Tweedmouth's iron bridge?

5   according to Borrow, resembled thin, beautiful threads?

6   saw the Buggane come to grief through a cut apron string?

7   is eddying and whisking and spouting and frisking?

8   can be seen through More's eyes on the Mound?

9   witnessed the death of a sleep-walker?

10   is Skene's overflow?

• 17 • *Who:*

1   is Ingvar Kamprad?

2   showed that $k=A \exp(-E/RT)$?

3   was represented by Verdi as Renato?

4   was the 'curator of the secrets of 82 nations'?

5   successfully absorbed nitroglycerin in kieselguhr?

6   beat Floyd, but was felled by him the following year?

7   marched his invading army across the frozen sea?

8   was tutored in philosophy by Descartes?

9   wrote about an anserine passenger?

10   devised a binomial flora?

• 18 • *In 2003:*

1   who did 42.195 x 7 in 7/365?

2   who was stitched up after a managerial tantrum?

3   what took Baumgartner 12 minutes and 3 seconds?

4   who scored three golden ducks and one short of a ton?

5   who was tempted to recommend Schultz as a concentration camp commandant?

6   who, sadly, can no longer advise us to eat the hamburger and throw away the bun?

7   who got in through St George's after a quick change in the Highlander?

8   whose failure to avoid dying has ruined his career?

9   which diary has given way to capital espionage?

10   how did Sweden score 56-42?

2004–2005

In the year 1904, who or what:

1   insular reef was struck by Capt. Gundal's vessel?

2   was uncovered by Gustafsson beside Slagenbekken?

3   designed Tea Rooms opened in 'The Alley of the Willows'?

4   began a reign which, with one slight hiatus, was to last 55 years?

5   made a post-mortem journey from Badenweiler to the Novodeviche Monastery?

6   after a fiasco in Milan, received seven curtain calls in Brescia three months later?

7   celebrated its centenary with the opening of new HQ in Vincent Square?

8   city followed Paris and was itself followed in 1908 by London?

9   tragedy befell the Knickerbocker Steamboat Company?

10   Midland Railway initiative took place on 15th June?

• 2 •

1 who was the albino Vicar of Altarnum?

2 which zealous High Churchman gained preferment?

3 who was joined on the footplate by the Bishop for the run to Mallingford?

4 which Rector of Hunsford was a conceited, pompous, narrow-minded, silly man?

5 which Minister gave the appearance of having a good deal of train oil in his system?

6 who was the Vicar of Tredannick Wollas, with whom Mr Mortimer Tregennis lodged?

7 which black marble clergyman classed Consistency as the first of Christian duties?

8 who was the Vicar of Ploverleigh who favoured three spoons to the teapot?

9 who preached about racial equality in the Free Kirk at Kirkcaple?

10 who was the perpetual Curate of Hoggleswick?

• 3 •

1 where does Molly display her long legs?

2 who lived at the fictitious 30 Kelsall Street?

3 who are represented by Murphy in Church Street?

4 what replicates a memorial in Edinburgh to the Keeper of the Signet?

5 who created two ornithological oddities and was later interned on the Isle of Man?

6 what link between James Street and Hamilton Square was opened by the Prince of Wales?

7 who was the American Consul who lodged at Mrs Blodget's at 153 Duke Street?

8 where, miserably, did Priestley buy himself a good cigar?

9 where did 25 perish beneath the collapsed tower?

10 where was Fix fixed with a right and left?

• 4 • *Who poisoned:*

1 John Russell with phosphorus at Windy Nook?
2 his wife Cora with hyoscine at 39 Hilltop Crescent?
3 Jane Taylor with antimony at 22 Royal Crescent, Glasgow?
4 Matilda Clover with strychnine at 27 Lambeth Palace Road?
5 his wife Margery with arsenic at Milford Sanatorium, Godalming?
6 aided by Anne Turner, Sir Thomas Overbury with an enema of mercury sublimate in the Tower of London?
7 Percy John with aconitine at Blenheim School, Wimbledon?
8 Frederick Biggs with thallium at Bovington, Hertfordshire?
9 his son Terence with quinalbarbitone at Portsmouth?
10 his wife Katie with morphine at Hay-on-Wye?

• 5 • *What was damaged by:*

1 *Merle?*
2 *Tayjack?*
3 *Christiana?*
4 *Marlborough?*
5 *James & Jessie?*
6 *Port Royal Park?*
7 *Prince Leopold?*
8 *Foudroyant?*
9 *Ovenbeg?*
10 *Europa?*

• 6 • *What is the connection between:*

1 Sälen and Mora?
2 Zermatt and St Moritz?
3 Chepstow and Prestatyn?
4 Edale and Kirk Yetholm?
5 Page's Park and Stonehenge?
6 Vohwinkel and Oberbarmen?
7 Shannon and St Petersburg?
8 Wallsend and Bowness?
9 Cheriton and Sangatte?
10 Horta and Cornella?

• 7 • *Which reigning or future English sovereign was married to whom in:*

1   Norway?

2   a two-letter town?

3   a Hampshire Abbey?

4   a Northamptonshire village?

5   the Queen's Closet at York Place?

6   the Monasterio de Santa Maria la Real?

7   the Cypriot Chapel of St George?

8   a south coast Naval Base?

9   the Palace of Kew?

10 York Minster?

• 8 • *Who or what:*

1   slew Gessler?

2   would have chosen to be Henry IX?

3   was originally known as Middle Plantation?

4   in a work dedicated 'Absit Oman', discovered the National Debt?

5   fishery research trawler was renamed and launched to combat whaling?

6   stretch of water received 257,000 barrels of North Slope Crude on Good Friday?

7   formerly feared that incessant inversion might cause cerebral injury?

8   was Miss Lamburn's posthumous publication?

9   may have been felled by Walter Tirel?

10 is *Dianthus barbatus*?

• 9 •

1   what is in the affirmative?

2   what has a shady glen on its steep steep side?

3   what, far to the eastward, rises in pearl-grey air?

4   where, in summertime, do the bells sound so clear?

5   on what summit does the Oratory recall the navigator saint?

6   from what shaggy side do three streams in three directions glide?

7   where does a Bristol merchant's folly take it to 1000 feet?

8   what dread name is derived from church and storms?

9   under what bare head is Drumcliff churchyard?

10 where did twelve fair counties see the blaze?

• 10 • *Who:*

1 did a Mass for JFK?

2 did nudes for the BMA?

3 introduced waterproof mascara?

4 related his story to Capt Robert Walton?

5 took receipt of Devereux's halberd at Eger?

6 developed his early theories in the Patent Office in Berne?

7 was credited with the best film ever made?

8 established a grand factory in 1856?

9 had Knewstub as a middle name?

10 launched Winter Gale?

• 11 • *Which conflagration:*

1 was depicted in *A Rake's Progress*?

2 coincided with the confinement of Olympias?

3 has been dubiously attributed to imperial arson?

4 led to the decapitation of Marinus van der Lubbe?

5 coincided with the performance of an interesting play by Pinero?

6 obliged the proprietor to write to customers that '… in the consequence of the above premises being burnt down, your orders will be delayed in the execution a day or two.'

7 was followed by Kaiser-assisted rebuilding in Jugendstil?

8 saw the debut of Braithwaite's steam fire engine?

9 prompted a fatal confession from Robert Hubert?

10 began in Patrick O'Leary's cowbarn?

• 12 • *Who achieved, superlatively:*

1 18.29 m?

2 16 min 19 sec?

3 68 – 27 – 90 – 19?

4 66-68-69-64 – 267?

5 38 – 26 – 12 – 0 – 73 – 26 – 90?

6 1,315 – 61,237 – 106–316* – 50.65?

7 1-6, 7-5, 6-3, 6-7 (16-18), 8-6?

8 2 hr 15 min 25 sec?

9 3 min 59.4 sec?

10 127.68 mph?

• 13 • *What on 198:*

1   is also Antifer?

2   embraces Man?

3   is Mendelssohnian?

4   acknowledges 21st October?

5   replaced an exchange for Zanzibar?

6   is a two-masted Dutch fishing vessel?

7   is a surgical textbook with Love?

8   recalls Mutt and Jeff?

9   is Puffin Island?

10   recalls *Beagle*?

• 14 • *Who or what:*

1   is *Thecla betulae*?

2   is topped by Abdon Burf?

3   was the small curé from Cobhole?

4   condiment can be parliamentary or paternal?

5   was not enamoured of the Dean of Christ Church?

6   was opened by members of Byron's staff in the year of Victoria's accession?

7   was hanged at Charlestown after Harper's Ferry?

8   began at Calle Nuño de Cañas in 1919?

9   was *Single-handed* in the States?

10   were the Sturmabteilung?

• 15 •

1   what is Georgia?

2   where did the moon stand still for Gene Autrey?

3   what part is played by the third party at a lovers' tryst?

4   the eastward deviation of what was decreed by Teburoro Tito?

5   what is the translucent legacy of a Cornish barber with premises in Gerrard Street?

6   which President overlapped the premierships of Lisulu, Mundia and Musokotwane?

7   who rode on the Great Wheel at the Prater with Rollo Martins?

8   what is a hydraulic crane with a terminal railed platform?

9   who produced his first number on 17th July 1841?

10   who managed Jardine's bodyliners?

• 16 • *Which first name is shared by these neighbours:*

1 Leer and Rouse?

2 Abbots and Grey?

3 Bohune and Bruce?

4 Dayrell and Lovell?

5 Bowdler and Carbonel?

6 Beauchamp and Harcourt?

7 Cheriton and Newton?

8 Bishop and Butler?

9 Priors and Hersey?

10 Abbas and Stoke?

• 17 •

1 what comes before golf?

2 who was Zinneman's Jackal?

3 who was Colin Roy Campbell of Glenure?

4 which athlete features in a 33-letter pangram?

5 which of Aesop's fables encourages pre-saltation inspection?

6 what was the subject of a 1785 account by a Birmingham physician?

7 whose foundation appeared to be an amiable association?

8 what was Seton's tale of maternal devotion?

9 who designed an airborne rugby team?

10 what is Te Morka o Tuawe?

• 18 • *In 2004:*

1 who reached Hill's Antwerp summit?

2 where did 100 x 824 occupy 9 hours 15 minutes?

3 what flightless new species recalls *Pyrrhocorax* in its colouring?

4 what centurion has continued to advocate knowing where to look?

5 who, uniquely, included Count, Dave, Jabba, Bomb, Polar Bear and Jughead?

6 whose passing recalled defeat for the All Blacks and brought sadness to many former schoolboy all-blacks?

7 who, having started on Christmas Day, broke all records in getting to 102?

8 what statistical compendium omitted to include the Principality?

9 what preceded Frances and Ivan on their trip to the Peninsula?

10 who was trailed rapturously after Betsy?

2005–2006

• 1 • *During the year 1905:*

1   what opened with *Blue Bell*?

2   what little red flower appeared in a new guise?

3   whose election recalled that of his Uncle Wilhelm?

4   whose big cat got into the wild beasts' show in Paris?

5   whose discovery of mycobacteria took him to prize-giving on 10th December?

6   which organisation was formed to alleviate excessive constabulary restrictions?

7   what was the result of arthropod larvae appearing en route for Tendra?

8   under what title was a long letter to Bosie published?

9   what collapse interrupted a theatre's rebuilding?

10   what brought jollity to Vienna?

• 2 •

1   whose clandestine marriage thwarted Robinson?

2   who enjoyed mince and quince at their wedding breakfast?

3   at whose wedding was the unknown groom accused of magic by his rival?

4   at which event were the affianced first represented by Nancy and Francesco?

5   whose hasty marriage was prompted by knowledge of Fra Filippo's departure for the continent?

6   after whose wedding did the bride send slices of cake to her companions in the pork-dressing business?

7   at whose quiet wedding were Traddles and Sophy, and Doctor and Mrs Strong the only guests?

8   at whose quiet wedding were 'he and I, the parson and clerk, alone present'?

9   which miserable object was accused of treachery by his bride?

10   at whose wedding feast did they eat sturgeon and pike?

• 3 • *Who wrote about the Isle of Man with the following words:*

1 'The coast runs level to the Point of Ayre
    A waste of sand, sea-holly and wild thyme'?

2 'He strides through the tamarisks down to the ocean
    Beyond the lush curraghs of sylvan Lezayre'?

3 'Oh, what do Manx fairies think of claret in Sulby Glen?
    Alas, where are the fairies now?'?

4 '... also a memorial pillar dedicated to one Governor Smelt with a flat top for a statue, and no statue standing on it'?

5 'But the old pile soon rose before him, serene, and sternly still, amid the sleeping ocean. The banner, which indicated that the Lord of Man held residence, hung motionless by the ensign staff.'?

6 '... they visited a copper-mine by the side of the Head, and filled their pockets with bits of quartz or red shining spar ...'?

7 'The day was calm and beautiful. Old Barrule wore his yellow skull-cap of flowering gorse ...'?

8 'The glowing orb of the sun was already soft enough to look at almost directly, bisected in the middle by some strange Celtic tower on the top of the cliff, that from the distance had the look of a giant key.'?

9 '... the Calf of Man, on which are no habitations, but only a cottage or two lately built'?

10 'Where ancient trees this convent-pile enclose,
    In ruin beautiful ...'?

• 4 • *Which Book inspired:*

1 whose oratorio about the Hasmoneans?

2 whose oratorio about a loyal daughter-in-law?

3 which Lancastrian's rendering of the writing on the wall?

4 which Etonian's oratorio about a major owner of livestock?

5 whose oratorio for the Pietà, in which the heroine is a murderess?

6 which Londoner's serenata, comprising a dialogue between He and She?

7 a mysterium, which preceded whose appointment as professor?

8 which Tudor favourite's representation of grieving verses?

9 which Nazi exile's oratorio involving a bovine effigy?

10 which Tivoli organist's marine oratorio?

• 5 • *What:*

1 is a bibionid?

2 grows in fairy rings?

3 provides quality duvets?

4 might be translated as redskin?

5 was described by the English Hippocrates?

6 is now worn on 5th, although formerly on 24th?

7 is luminous, and witnessed by seamen?

8 are equidistant from Whitekirk?

9 is the gourmet's bivalve?

10 is single-bloomed?

• 6 • *Of what figures of speech or rhetorical devices are the following examples:*

1 The town was starving?

2 I can't find it any blooming where?

3 Faith unfaithful kept him falsely true?

4 For gold his sword the hireling ruffian draws
   For gold the hireling judge distorts the laws?

5 Not to mention their unpaid debts of several millions?

6 There was an atmosphere of gloom and despondency?

7 Love's fire heats water, water cools not love?

8 The low last edge of the long low land?

9 If you don't do as I say I'll …?

10 A citizen of no mean city?

• 7 • *In which tale:*

1 was there solar/lunar confusion?

2 were multiple embraces terminated at 86?

3 was the hero confronted by rodent *paskontrol*?

4 did a cervical arthrodesis prevent an arranged marriage?

5 was postmaturity managed patiently beneath the leaves of *Arctium*?

6 was a transformation preceded by exsanguination and glossectomy?

7 did the heroine die from hypothermia on New Year's Eve?

8 were there three cases of canine macrophthalmia?

9 was insomnia due to a deeply hidden pulse?

10 was there syncope in Santa Croce?

• 8 • *Evaluate*:

1 Tarrant's County Seat.

2 Devonshire's Derbyshire home.

3 Lancaster's successful 10 cent store.

4 St Custard's most celebrated alumnus.

5 the location of White Surrey's final saddling.

6 the breed of Malmesbury's notorious escapees.

7 the location of Wilfrid Fox's tree garden.

8 a visitor to the Wye valley on 13/7/98.

9 the site of an Edwardian resignation.

10 the creator of Quirk as narrator.

• 9 • *What*:

1 vessel could fill 25 Salmanazars?

2 comes, appropriately, in a clear bottle?

3 regional addition caused anger in Marne?

4 house took over the crypt of St Niçaise Abbey?

5 was the important creation of Holden and Colonet?

6 at their first dinner, did James and Tiffany drink with caviar?

7 venerable house first used ice to remove the lees?

8 can be found at 5 Place du Général Gouraud?

9 museum houses the world's largest cask?

10 vessel recalls a great Babylonian feast?

• 10 • *Which town is associated with*:

1 glazed carrots?

2 whipped cream with sugar and vanilla?

3 baked offal and calf's feet with Calvados and cider?

4 deep fried amphibian limbs garnished with fried parsley?

5 scalloped puff pastry filled with an almond and rum mixture?

6 a liquid mixture of carrots, onions and leeks with rice and crème frâiche?

7 fish stock, white wine, freshwater crustaceans and cream?

8 fillets of anchovy, eggs, lettuce, tuna and black olives?

9 sweet and sour onion salad with raisins?

10 sweet mutton pies?

• 11 • *Which, of Peter's successors:*

1   was a troglodyte?

2   was attacked with a kris by a surrealist painter?

3   was saved from strangulation by an eclipse of the sun?

4   narrowly avoided the fate of an authority on ocular disease?

5   underwent exhumation, re-clothing, re-enthronement and trial?

6   was vilified by Petrarch as an ecclesiastical Dionysius with his infamous artifices?

7   claimed that his office was god-given and should be enjoyed?

8   finally succumbed on the disappearance of a celestial body?

9   allegedly died through a satanic blow to the head?

10   was depicted protecting a Lilliputian Siena?

• 12 • *Which thriller features:*

1   *Aigion?*

2   *Napoli?*

3   *Matapan?*

4   *Nantesville?*

5   *Morning Star?*

6   *Fort Ticonderoga?*

7   *Morning Rose?*

8   *Marianne?*

9   *Canton?*

10   *Vectra?*

• 13 • *Extract homophones from the following oblique hints:*

1   rabbit pie

2   54 and 100

3   pelvic viscus

4   needled and cultured

5   washerwoman and bargewoman

6   connects between bear and twins

7   twelve for Mr Badger

8   cherry hangs limply

9   line up a pot

10   sandstone

1   of what plight was a certain motorcycle devoid?

2   complete '.......... engineering contraptions'

3   what motorcycle was built like a structure to cross a river?

4   what motorcycle was *all right* and had a Ptolemaic predecessor?

5   what motorcycle failed to win a TT, while displaying *1066 and all that* on its tank?

6   what had a *big* exhaust and should not have been passed on an anticlockwise circuit?

7   what motorcycle proclaimed that a son was better than his father?

8   what nickname indicated the use of another maker's spares?

9   what fruit flew to a lowly finish in the 1921 Junior TT?

10   what missile was made like its firing mechanism?

• 15 • *Wombling free, what destination:*

1   is partly algebraic?

2   implies inept play at whist?

3   should be good for woodcock?

4   features Pegasus and Agnus Dei?

5   commemorates the Calabrian defeat of Reynier?

6   recalls an arboreal disaster in the year of the Regent's promotion?

7   is derived from Falkes de Breauté?

8   suggests olive trees in Tuscany?

9   was formerly Tyburn Gate?

10   was originally worth 6/8?

• 16 • *Who or what:*

2   was Colin Campbell of Glenure?

3   'cocktail' uses methylated spirits?

4   do Salopians know as Bessie Brantail?

5   was the site of Maria Marten's murder at Polstead?

6   first appeared to Darsie's friend, Alan, in a green gown?

7   asked 'What's the French for fiddle-de-dee?'

8   is, alternatively, *Turf and Towers*?

9   was snared on Stormy Mountain?

10   suffered lupine deception?

• 17 • *Who:*

1   were tea brokers in Mincing Lane?

2   was a pawnbroker in Saxe-Coburg Square?

3   was the well-known Curzon Street money-lender?

4   was set up in medical practice at 403 Brook Street?

5   imported the red wines of Bordeaux in Fenchurch Street?

6   had rooms in Montagu Street, close to the British Museum?

7   were the solicitors in practice at 426 Gresham Building?

8   was the fictitious practitioner at 369 Half Moon Street?

9   were funeral directors in the Kennington Road?

10   was a poulterer at 117 Brixton Road?

• 18 • *During 2005:*

1   where did the Jolly Farmer fall in?

2   which twelve have been reduced by one to eight?

3   where has a Saxon phoenix been restored to normality?

4   how has severe weather affected Kent boundary regulations?

5   what inherited dermatological disorder has benefited from a wader's determination?

6   where has a heart specialist taken over to treat a dictatorial disease afflicting the nation?

7   which sometime *Beagle* passenger has recently celebrated her birthday?

8   where did a Walk in the Park lack sufficient motivation?

9   whose final embrace has been worthily remembered?

10   which Gentleman is now Up in the Clouds?

2006–2007

• 1 • *In the year 1906:*

1   which *bedstefar* was mourned multinationally?

2   which fruity concoction rivalled the first all-big-gun ship?

3   who benefited, through his far eastern mediation, from a Nordic inventor's bequest?

4   who emerged for a journey, which would eventually take him to join the Iron Age dead?

5   which emasculated beverage received 1,3,7 trimethylxanthine as an alternative stimulant?

6   what named vehicle, having set off from Paris, arrived victoriously on the North York Moors?

7   what addition to the English language was introduced by a popular daily on 10th January?

8   which vessel paid the ultimate penalty for cutting the corner off the coast of Murcia?

9   who was reinstated and decorated following the annulment of his guilty verdict?

10   which association agreed on a downsizing to 13?

• 2 • *Who is or was*:

1 the guy, who went for his entire bundle on Apparition?

2 the clubman, found at Blimp's when game is in season?

3 the foundling, whose amorous adventures finally led him to Wisdom?

4 the actress, having a familial connection with Douglas and parts of Kirkmichael?

5 the painter, who introduced *The Sleeping Beauty* into a country house salon with the aid of four thorny scenes?

6 the player, who started, but later terminally departed from, a Sisyphian project, which proverbially failed to accumulate?

7 the clothmaker's son, who built a barn, and an eating house which was later the scene of a public execution?

8 the very stout, portly man, credited by the *Standard* with energy and sagacity?

9 the diarist, for whom consumption was a matter of daily concern

10 the composer, who wrote an opera eponymously featuring one of the above, but made himself ineligible to appear here?

• 3 • *Chronologically:*

1 which man in holy orders had a first edition of his own revolutionary theory of the heavens presented to him on his deathbed?

2 whose seventeenth-century *sidereal herald* did Rome find unwelcome?

3 whose Jovian satellite timekeeping led him to a measurement of the ultimate speed?

4 who gained posthumous and eponymous recognition for his prediction of a return visit?

5 whose puzzlement at nineteenth-century darkness was explained by a twentieth-century American stargazer?

6 which Anglo-French duo helped find a heavenly incarnation of a sea-god?

7 which apparently unreliable wanderer made two crossings within the space of eight years during the nineteenth century, none at all in the twentieth, but is expected to complete another two in the twenty-first?

8 in which year did a seven-part wartime composition become incomplete?

9 which two telephonists were at first irritated, but later gratified by the background noise from an explosion?

10 which gravitational phenomenon has recently provided a focus on new worlds?

• 4 • *What:*

1   is the drain?

2   is a mighty good road?

3   has restricted loads for 130 years?

4   might a dentist see in copper poisoning?

5   was the third and better known name of Wilhelmine Dorothea?

6   embraces Cheshire, Kent, Lancashire and Oxfordshire under three legs?

7   generated a false sense of Gallic security?

8   separated the free and the enslaved?

9   secures a non-slip loop?

10 was breached by Haig?

• 5 • *Where:*

1   did scissors counter subsidence?

2   does a phoenix oversee my rising again?

3   is a divorcee's grave marked with pomegranates?

4   do the lines 'Repentance is the Station then
                 Where Passengers are taken in' appear?

5   did Sue frequently attend the fictionalised Cathedral-church?

6   does a surrealist's creation depict praise with various instruments?

7   does he remain, unspoken to, for days and days and days?

8   is a cross-legged gnome found among the angels?

9   might eider ducks have joined the pilgrims?

10 was she called to praise and pray …
     while the choir sang Stanford in A?

• 6 • *Where:*

1   is there a through-otherness?

2   does a cold old black wind blow?

3   did Napper receive his death sentence?

4   do the donkeys equate to the unpaid flunkeys?

5   have the fair maids left, in a body, their woebegone swains?

6   should the lost comet be visible at sunset like a glimmer of haws and rose hips?

7   was the dredger grumbling all night in the harbour?

8   do the sons defy Pope, traitor or defender?

9   was the town famed for lovely Kitty?

10 did feline combat end in a draw?

• 7 • *Which:*

1   first was a loathsome Lackwit?

2   second is sans everything?

3   third is also first?

4   fourth would be breached by Aurora?

5   fifth suffered episcopal impugnment of his pedigree?

6   sixth involved the location of China in Snowdonia?

7   seventh enters the aqueductus fallopii?

8   eighth is wholly philatelic?

9   ninth was for Victoire?

10   tenth was Too?

• 8 •

1   who saw the light?

2   what folds to make 36 pages?

3   what might be described as *florless*?

4   who was a noble duke, in nature as in name?

5   who, in modern parlance, was a hideous giant all horrible and high?

6   what did Conrad describe as an Arab steed in a string of carthorses?

7   in which city did Signorelli depict the Last Judgement?

8   to which city did the Chaste transfer his court?

9   what was formerly Urbis Tellus?

10   who was the voice?

• 9 • *Where:*

1   did the ass-cart fail to turn up?

2   was Sixpenny warned to keep down the blind?

3   did Lady Diana give Prince Séliman a last kiss?

4   was a fat fool called Bhansi Lall the stationmaster?

5   did I get a luncheon-basket, which I shared with the fat woman?

6   did a line of stiff sedate men in black broadcloth and women in black veils wait along the platform?

7   did the narrator buy a pocket ordnance map of Friesland?

8   was 'native rabbit' later described as 'jungle rabbit'?

9   is the stationmaster greeted with feline elation?

10   did the narrator accidentally steal a bicycle?

• 10 • *Which decorative plant owes its name to:*

1 an Essex rector?

2 King James I's physician?

3 a Royal Commissioner in Santo Domingo?

4 a Quaker Professor of Anatomy, albeit misspelt?

5 Linnaeus's honouring of which Moravian Jesuit missionary?

6 the recognition by a Danish botanist of the gardener to a Hanoverian King?

7 a Spanish abbot's memorial to which Swedish botanist?

8 a pioneer, who discovered the lymphatic system?

9 his country's first round-the-world sailor?

10 an ophthalmic anatomist?

• 11 •

1 who found the breath of Jupiter sulphurous?

2 who had more of gravy than of grave about him?

3 what Indian souvenir brought £200 and a fatal industrial accident?

4 what had particular qualities of silence, power and trustworthiness?

5 which invited dinner guest returned the invitation before guiding his host to Hell?

6 who, following a terminal fever, now offers shellfish from streets of varied dimensions?

7 who appeared as a gaunt vision, with icy glare and stern relentless brow?

8 who broke his arm, wrestling with a slippery, oozy, horrible thing?

9 what grey, now ghastly white, appears in cold, windy weather?

10 who do the sentries confuse with Alec James?

• 12 • *What:*

1   was mark'd with permanent ink?

2   shared its fate with an auld body astride of a gate?

3   was produced as evidence of Wallace's impromptu meal?

4   provided nesting opportunities for the rodents of Lower Saxony?

5   was worn by the woman with the slender jewelled hand when greeting the narrator in Constantinople?

6   was the receptacle in which the narrator placed a stone, following a meal of Bologna sausage and chocolate, washed down with neat brandy?

7   Amazonian apparel was worn with brown shirts and blue knickerbockers?

8   did Mr Alexander Holder take as security for a £50,000 loan?

9   do the simple creatures hope to see impaled upon a tree?

10   are in contrast to a stiff upper lip?

• 13 • *Who or what:*

1   is Hydrargyrum?

2   lost out to *Bubo* at Castle Frank?

3   was formerly farmed by Sigewulf?

4   is the bristletail of the kitchen cupboard?

5   are seen as a harvest mouse goes scampering by?

6   was rusticated for painting the Dean's house red?

7   did I catch when moths were on the wing?

8   was commemorated with a £1 blue?

9   was frustratingly unwheedlable?

10   was Harry Heegan's reward?

• 14 •

1   who imposed a levy on beards?

2   who described a multinidal growth?

3   whose father had pigmented dentition?

4   what is also identified by Jack's midday bedtime?

5   which bearded and bright-eyed old tar delayed a wedding guest?

6   who suffered his beard to grow until it was about a quarter of a yard long?

7   what indignity did Hunan inflict on the suspected spies?

8   how did an old Grenadier address his statistician?

9   who had a beard of burnt-up black?

10   what was ignobly done by Regan?

• 15 • *Who:*

1   claimed to eat cow dung for salads?

2   was offered a pigeon dish by the clown's father?

3   was described as the sweet marjoram of the salad?

4   had a bill amounting to 2s. 6d. for a capon and sauce?

5   threatened his daughter's suitor with a diet of bivalves?

6   asked the quarrelsome captain to eat the emblem on his cap?

7   urged against eating certain bulbs to avoid halitosis?

8   expounded on the virtues of pancakes and mustard?

9   required crocus stamens to flavour the pear pies?

10   indicated a preference for conserve of beef?

• 16 • *Which manufacturer's product is:*

1   waxed?

2   a whorl of petals?

3   a Brahmin genealogist?

4   a pendulant tropical climber?

5   surely of very limited horsepower?

6   a blessed lottery of beauty, wisdom and modesty?

7   an American jazz saxophonist?

8   by the same token *msupial?*

9   an absurd pretence?

10   palindromic?

• 17 • *Who:*

1   was nicknamed Toddy?

2   had a bottled Arabian dormouse in his holster?

3   gave Clara a pair of sunglasses from Gruber's?

4   was accused of improper behaviour during a cave trip?

5   had never heard of Bernard Shaw, but supposed he was a Methodist preacher?

6   was mollified with a donation of a lightweight aluminium collapsible garden chair?

7   used astrology to choose a favourable time for treatment?

8   was brought to safety by Murray on a packhorse?

9   threatened to cut the throat of a Welsh parson?

10   assisted Clarice in her search for Gumb?

• 18 • *During 2006:*

1   who won at 16 despite losing a 9 at 7?

2   which Voice in the Wilderness is now silent?

3   what has been dwarfed through orbital overlapping?

4   where was the result decided by glass balls ringing bells?

5   whose suggestion of a golden handshake was speedily revealed?

6   which exceptionally hardy annual has finally been gathered after 27 years?

7   who pronounced herself ready for Mr Prescott at Scunthorpe?

8   where was the theft of an Elizabethan reticule enacted?

9   where was revealed a Day to remember at 1450?

10   whose anniversary recalled a sixties hit?

2007–2008

• 1 • *During the year 1907:*

1   what became the 46th?

2   what theft denied Castletown his investiture?

3   what revolutionary washing product came from Düsseldorf?

4   who brought bulls, wolves, curlews and ravens to Poole Harbour?

5   who, despite his inferiority to his *bhisti,* gained the highest award in his field?

6   what 'vile and inhuman story told in the foulest language' precipitated riots in the capital?

7   who was the first to receive a death sentence at the Old Bailey for murder?

8   which unique seven-master came to grief on Hellweather's Reef?

9   whose return for 1st June was 31.1 – 14 – 48 – 17?

10   what started on Tuesday 28th May at 10 am?

• 2 • *Which fictitious school:*

1   was convenient for the Cockchafer at Maltby?

2   lay in a cradle of fog and fog-bound pestilence?

3   stressed the four D's: Dramatics, Dance, Debating and Dating?

4   was a long and cold-looking house, one story high, with a few straggling outbuildings behind, and a barn and stable adjoining?

5   was founded in the eighth century by a Saxon saint and was the abode of monks until the Dissolution of the Monasteries?

6   had been partially endowed in the middle of the nineteenth century by the wealthy widow of a bookbinder, who had been an admirer of Garibaldi before she died?

7   boasted an observatory to study worms, the fortifications to pot at gamekeepers and that round thing which hav no use at all?

8   towered behind the crumbling fragment of a picturesque fort, which rose high above the beach?

9   allowed students to bring an owl OR a cat OR a toad?

10   accommodated The Fat Owl of the Remove?

• 3 •

1   who 'discovered' *Vortigern*?

2   which Old Borstalian was unmasked by Oberhuber?

3   which epistle, allegedly from Grigori, helped Stanley to defeat Ramsay?

4   who created documents covering an 11-year period, supposedly found in a hayloft in the DDR?

5   who produced a group of physicians to prove his innocence, but laid himself open to alternative charges?

6   who was able, through his own work, to convince experts that the painter Martini was also a sculptor?

7   which self-styled Japanese heathen described an island where broiled serpents were a favourite dish?

8   in what was the mandible of *pygmaeus* equipped with the dentition of *troglodytes*?

9   who palmed off depictions of a Brighton suburb, but later owned up?

10   who provided Lübeck with an anachronistic fowl?

• 4 •

1   after which action were eleven decorated for valour?

2   where did the Tidy Pachyderm start his journey to the Limpopo?

3   who was described by James Arcoll as a sort of black Napoleon?

4   who replaced Cartwright and caused a quarter of a century's isolation?

5   who acquainted the Tswana people with the confusing story of Egeon's twin sons?

6   who loved honey with a passion that we, with a sweet-shop on every corner, cannot hope to understand?

7   who regretted lack of achievement, with so large an outstanding agenda?

8   who was the victim of a tapeworm's instruction to a schizophrenic?

9   which flagship was accompanied by *Reijger* and *Goede Hoope*?

10   where was government conducted from a railway siding?

• 5 •

1   what is Penwith?

2   whence 19/20 at Manchester?

3   wherein – two legless paupers confined to dustbins?

4   whose work on crop rotation earned him a derogatory nickname?

5   which tragic tale ended 'I'm too tired and old to learn to love, leave me alone for ever'?

6   where did the congregation consist of an old marsh-donkey and a wet yoke-weary bullock?

7   where did Jack spend ½d on a roll and ½d on some cheese at a Chandler's Shop?

8   where were pigs' teeth stuck into the trunk of a wych-elm?

9   what began as a settlement on the Prittle Brook?

10   what overlooks Sprinkling Tarn?

• 6 •

1   whose papal audience proved fatal?

2   who is remembered for his petrol bomb?

3   who introduced us to an uncle and three sisters?

4   who, during 14 years of generous subsidies, never met his benefactor?

5   which monarch outscored his English counterpart in his marital arrangements?

6   whose complicity in the murder of his lover's spouse insured the imperatricial succession?

7   which spitefully insulted cuckold was fatally wounded by his brother-in-law?

8   whose predictions were acknowledged in the naming of number 101?

9   who shared the Prix Galabert with Glenn?

10   who investigated canine salivation?

• 7 •

1   for whom did Zaretski act as second?

2   which contestants were slain with the same envenomed point?

3   who died in the Brecknock Arms following a duel with his brother-in-law?

4   who was challenged to a duel by a Gibraltarian, whose patriotism had been impugned?

5   who allowed his opponent to leave a message for Patterson beneath his silver cigarette case?

6   whose performance against the three-handed marvel was described by the Princess as 'unique'?

7   who was killed by his father in single combat as the sun sparkled on the Oxus stream?

8   whose second was accused of surreptitiously stabbing his opponent in Hyde Park?

9   which cuckold was mortally wounded at Barn Elms on 16th January?

10   who fell to a frontal blow and then completely lost his head?

• 8 • *Which pirate:*

1 inspired Sir Walter Scott?

2 had a terminal encounter with a crocodile?

3 masqueraded as Sir Charles Ewan, Governor of St Kitts?

4 was terminated off Ramsey when the Marine Offence Act became law?

5 together with her colleague Mary, pleaded pregnancy and escaped the gallows?

6 had a high, old, tottering voice that seemed to have been tuned and broken in the capstan bars?

7 was placed in his apprenticeship through a mishearing of the word *pilot*?

8 was hacked to pieces and roasted limb by limb in the Gulf of Darien?

9 tended his geraniums in his window box in Bridgewater?

10 hated man too much to feel remorse?

• 9 •

1 where warn't there nobody but just me and pap left?

2 where did Willingdon Beauty die peacefully in his sleep?

3 where, in the Frome valley, did Angel, the pupil farmer, fall in love?

4 where does Bessie, smelling like a cowshed, snore bass and gruff in a loft?

5 where did the farmer find his gin sprung with three toes of a lutrine paw lying in a red spatter about it?

6 from its fulicine origins, and after periodic encounters with *thymallus*, what was the tributary's ultimate landmark?

7 which farm was successively demolished by Edward VI, William & Mary, George II and George IV?

8 from which farm did Martin, the young gander, depart with his passenger?

9 which farm of some 500 acres was Dickson's retirement home?

10 to which farm, Jurby way, was Tommy sent to work?

• 10 •

1. what is a WLAR?
2. where is there peace and holy quiet?
3. who was the master of Thornfield Hall?
4. which club did Race leave to manage A C Monza?
5. who wrote of his hero's Innocence, Wisdom and Incredulity?
6. whose twentieth-century lymantrid emulated a seventeenth-century cervid?
7. what name was given to the Belgic town – Calleva?
8. what coat typically boasts a velvet collar?
9. where was Dr Arabin appointed Dean?
10. where do 11 U's unite?

• 11 •

1. what is a VSD?
2. in which tale did Ticki end it with Evipan?
3. what featured a doomed octet of D'Ascoynes?
4. what combines Dexamphetamine with Amylobarbitone?
5. in what did Marlow describe the corrupt but charismatic Kurtz?
6. what, obliquely, was once milk-white, now purple with love's wound?
7. what was the ultimate destination of the phthisical Leithen?
8. in what serial did Dr Kate succumb to Leukaemia?
9. who indiscriminately demanded decapitation?
10. what marks the site of the Tolbooth?

• 12 • *Which words are particularly associated with these small towns and villages:*

1. Repton
2. Thaxted
3. Wolvercote
4. Rockingham
5. Down Ampney
6. Cwm Rhondda
7. Abbots Leigh
8. St Clement
9. Monkland
10. Cranham

• 13 •

1 who had a Lonely Hearts Club Band?
2 who was hoodwinked by Sir Percy at Laragne?
3 who liked gramophone records to be played at speed 61?
4 whose Concert Party duet with Lofty Sugden got to No. 1?
5 who had bestowed upon him the high-sounding title of Governor of La Merced?
6 who shot tiny field mice every night with huge bullets from the .45 he had stolen from the dead man?
7 who could quote historical fights between 490 BC and 1815 AD?
8 whose favourite game would end with the command 'Change at Löhne!'?
9 which lepidopterist claimed to have taken Lungtungpen?
10 who related how he lost his ear in Venice?

• 14 • *Who or what:*

1 began as Crocetti?
2 shared his cloak with a beggar at Amiens?
3 device is used to limit equine cervical extension?
4 is a female calf, rendered infertile by its twin male calf?
5 island witnessed the most lethal volcanic eruption of the twentieth century?
6 was produced by Wallace, Walter, Edwin and Charles in a disused soap factory in Southall?
7 shares the same choice of accommodation as Merops and Alcedo?
8 built a palace inspired by Garnier, next to Sandeman's?
9 might be regarded as the pharmacist's bible?
10 travelled to America with Mark Tapley?

• 15 •

1 who stood in for Sam Bideford?
2 whose guilt was confirmed by Dick's flash?
3 what did the doctor's son set adrift to protect No. 7?
4 what prehistoric creature accessed *Speedy* with splatchers?
5 which vessel was lost through monkeying around with a cigar?
6 what species' addition to the Jemmerling Collection was thwarted?
7 where did they leave a new halfpenny in a round brass box?
8 what viral infection placed three families in quarantine?
9 where was the Baltic home of the barque *Pommern*?
10 who turned out not to be an armadillo?

• 16 • *Which University*

1 has a caprine clock tower?
2 boasts a 406-year-old laburnum?
3 was founded by King Gustav II Adolf?
4 displays *vítores*, originally painted in bulls' blood?
5 thrived on the proceeds from tobacco and chocolate?
6 was transferred to the new national capital following a conflagration?
7 has a contemporary edifice, likened to a typewriter?
8 stands on the site of an inn 'at the sign of the ox'?
9 was founded by King George II?
10 incorporates Botany Bay?

• 17 •

1 what terminus is ursine?
2 where does the canal lack the grandeur of its namesake?
3 who would appear to have places at Smithfield and the Strand?
4 which district derives its name from the appearance of St Mary Matfelon?
5 where might an obelisk be perceived as a memorial to a North African seamstress?
6 which establishment, in the interest of political rectitude, discarded its Bavarian name for that of a Gaelic province?
7 what former hostelry was not the residence of a former Foreign Secretary?
8 where do frequent delays recall a famous late arrival over 200 years ago?
9 from what corner of London is it possible to see Copenhagen?
10 whence the ill-fated Liza Kemp?

• 18 • *In 2007*:

1 what form of confectionery bothered Zaheer?
2 which ensemble rubbished *Pomp and Circumstance*?
3 who reluctantly accepted the rust-proof qualities of bronze?
4 where did hyoid misrepresentation cause multinational distress?
5 which herb has withered leaving memories of a north London diet?
6 whose investiture has recalled a previous recognition of bovine excellence?
7 where has a noontide run eclipsed Cecil's eighty-year-old record?
8 who spoke of unrivalled love of life, laughter, fun and folly?
9 which piscine Mandarin scholar has become the 26th?
10 who has progressed from KGB via MI5 to CMG?

2008–2009

• 1 • *During the year 1908:*

1   who announced T?

2   who finished at 59 with 15 and 25?

3   what confectionary was inspired by Shaw?

4   who gained her second first at an old east coast fort?

5   where did the Thomas Flyer arrive on the Asiatic mainland?

6   whose birthday present was cut into nine pieces for the family headdress and other equipment?

7   whose resignation pre-empted his demise by just 16 days?

8   which tale launched a nouveau riche boy-racer?

9   for whom was Lord Hugh Best Man?

10 what event elevated Manuel?

• 2 • *Who began what by:*

1   recalling unusual citrous abundance?

2   describing his subject's physiognomy with a succession of v's?

3   justifying the creation of a short palindromic nickname for 'himself'?

4   describing the emergence at dawn of a moustached little man with bow-legs?

5   recalling melancholy inspiration from early evening sights and sounds in a rural churchyard?

6   suggesting that it was generally accepted that a well-heeled loner must be looking for a lady?

7   describing a studio filled with the scents of roses, lilac and pink-flowered thorn?

8   describing his hero facing execution and recalling the discovery of ice?

9   recalling a send-off from family and friends at Charing Cross?

10 providing an alibi for the white kitten?

• 3 •

1   whose ground-breaking effort quoted *Numbers XXIII, 23*?

2   who wired who confirming worst fears and requesting gumboots?

3   whose telegram caused Dew to hasten westward on the *Laurentic*?

4   who, on sighting the enemy, urgently requested a firearm and 300 bullets?

5   whose expression of delight was accompanied by a request for a patent oil cooking stove?

6   with what single word did the defeated Governor allegedly advise cancellation of the papal travel arrangements?

7   who described a suave, Bohemian, elderly storekeeper in the Commercial Road?

8   which repetitious message prompted the query 'Does that mean Yes?'

9   who discovered a crumpled telegram *'Suivez à Bokhare Saronov'*?

10   on what occasion was the Royal wrath not expressed in code?

• 4 •

1   what is the Island of Sheep?

2   where did the sea cave inspire Op. 26?

3   where was Magnus Erlendsson executed?

4   what was David's gift to the Berkshire monks?

5   where did an amputated digit earn its owner the right to build a monastery?

6   where did the great grandson of King John III make his first British landfall?

7   where is the unique mutton derived from a diet of *Laminaria*?

8   where was quarantine enforced for 48 years?

9   to what was Meg's deafness compared?

10   where was Andie Dale the Prefect?

• 5 • *Travelling from Nordic lands, try unravelling:*

1   the eponymous traitor,
2   then Merrill's famed fisherman partner
3   and a misplaced cygnet,
4   contrasting with a little anser,
5   thousands of whose elders visit a Waddenzee barrier island,
6   while in Belgium, memories of Ursula are awakened by a Flemish Primitive,
7   and in the Amblève, or perhaps the Lesse, one might confusingly make geometry a sport
8   and try to catch a little trout
9   or even its seemingly lepidopteran relative
10   before celebrating in Germany with Piesport's speciality

• 6 • *Who:*

1   was Foolish?
2   was Rodrigo de Borja y Borja?
3   invested Henry Sinclair as Earl of Orkney?
4   had a half-sister sired by his father's physician?
5   founded a Siamese school, which was later named in his honour?
6   was born on the 34th anniversary of the death of his great-grandfather and the 17th of that of his great-aunt?
7   was the offspring of parents sharing the same grandmother?
8   was the 36th and last in a line started in 1299?
9   was blinded by his mother Irene?
10   was tripartite?

• 7 •

1 which language was developed by a Polish ophthalmologist?
2 which language of the Romance group has a definite article suffix?
3 of which European language is the origin unknown, even to the experts?
4 which geographically Scandinavian language is not linguistically Scandinavian?
5 which European language is the only survivor of its branch of the Indo-European group?
6 which Slavonic language is spoken in a country whose national language is not Slavonic?
7 which European language is spoken by about 1% of the population of Switzerland?
8 which European language has a past tense form which looks like a future?
9 which Slavonic language has done away with the case forms of nouns?
10 which European national language still retains the dual number?

• 8 • *What:*

1 is also a game using 28 marbles?
2 formed part of a linear horticultural decoration?
3 are typically preserved in seasoned butter in Lancashire?
4 when released in America, suggested involvement with Christine Keeler?
5 are geographically confusing names of what is neither one thing nor the other?
6 pelecypod was perhaps familiar to the pupils (and their successors) of Rev. Thomas Langhorne?
7 did the man from the Borough regard as the invariable accompaniment of poverty?
8 legs are found in unbaled water together with tangled lines?
9 nominally, has blue representatives in another kingdom?
10 when baked too brown, must sugar his hair?

• 9 • *Journeying on what, between which termini, might one's thoughts turn to:*

1 sleepwalking?
2 elliptical orbits?
3 the quintessential libertine?
4 a soldier without a passport?
5 the founding father of the EU?
6 the royal prisoner of Sönderborg?
7 Judith and three mute wives?
8 clothed and naked versions?
9 the mount of Bellerophon?
10 melting clocks?

• 10 • *Which river:*

1 received the defeated Aunus?
2 floats laden barges by banks of myosote?
3 was central to the non-payment of a mayoral debt?
4 was identified without doubt by the discovery of the initials AD?
5 saw Captain Schenk acquire an engineer to replace the deceased Walter?
6 despite being in flood, could be crossed dry-shod following clerical plantar immersion?
7 provided drinks for kine, and horses, and little humorous donkeys?
8 along with Cairo was passed unnoticed by the raft in the fog?
9 was a source of shelly snails and green lettuces?
10 witnessed a case of unwitting filicide?

• 11 • *Who or what:*

1 had instinct?
2 reds started as Villa?
3 uniquely, got three in whose match?
4 claimed continuing labial adhesiveness?
5 was formerly William and succeeded Louis?
6 in repetitive utterances, anticipated Glyn Daniel et al?
7 described a small arm accident on 17/6/15?
8 was executed at Bolton after Worcester?
9 was targeted by Nat and Dermot?
10 was presumptuous?

• 12 • *Where:*

1 was the mistress leguminous?

2 were the Harmonic Meetings regularly held?

3 was Rogue resuscitated after his prolonged immersion?

4 did the circus manager point out that 'People must be amuthed'?

5 did the curate speak for one hour and twenty-five minutes at an anti-slavery meeting?

6 did a little, yellow high-shouldered man, with a fixed grim smile, tell about a queer client?

7 did the landlord report that Phil was so drunk that a boy might take him?

8 did the Yorkshire schoolmaster interview tutors and pupils?

9 did the strange man stir his rum-and-water with a file?

10 did the hangman bind the old man to his chair?

• 13 •

1 who remained a bachelor?

2 who had been ADC to Mad Anthony?

3 who was described as a withered little apple-john?

4 whose nickname was perfect for a slogan of approval?

5 who enlisted as a private, but came out as a brevet major?

6 who maintained that silence ensured no need for repetition?

7 who, in his youth, admitted to cutting down a cherry tree?

8 who compared his strength to that of a male cervid?

9 who is remembered, nominally, in West Africa?

10 which two died on the same day?

QUESTIONS

• 14 • *Within the capital of which member state of the United Nations will you find:*

1 calluna?

2 3.14159?

3 that its alright?

4 a Windermere resident?

5 a West Country watercourse?

6 a pudding distinguished by ladies' fingers?

7 a simian representative?

8 a Tibetan monk?

9 a semi-metal?

10 nothing?

• 15 • *Who:*

1 was morally pure in EC2?

2 shot Buffalo Bill at Belvedere, Ohio?

3 went to the wrong church for her wedding?

4 believed, erroneously, that Byron murdered Ezra Chater?

5 killed Lord Frederick in a duel, following his return from Belgium?

6 possessed nothing but the contents of his wallet, the clothes he stood up in, the hare-lip, the automatic he should have left behind?

7 was as little interested in love as in the habits of Trematodes?

8 wore white for her immolation on 27th October?

9 advocated unlimited slaughter of bluejays?

10 posed as Doctor Copernicus?

• 16 • *Following my leader, who or what:*

1 is a Hampshire jewel?

2 decorated Findlater's label?

3 is meteorologically striking?

4 houses Colum Cille's shrine?

5 could be wild duck washed down with Ch. Latour?

6 might refer to poor Sarah's biliary obstruction?

7 is absolutely necessary to a ram?

8 was Anastasia's great aunt?

9 could have been a crusader?

10 is a musteline appendage?

• 17 • *In which town*:

1. did prisoner 24601 steal the episcopal silver?
2. did Lady de Winter poison the novice at the convent?
3. was the Cathedral like a vast boudoir prepared for Emma?
4. did Jake, dining alone, drink a bottle of Ch. Margaux for company?
5. did Duhamel ask that the crayfish should be very lightly boiled – just seized?
6. did la Baronne de la Chalonnière encounter Alexander Duggan at the Hôtel du Cerf?
7. did Holmes spend some months in a research into coal-tar derivatives?
8. were plum-coloured shoes removed to expose red stockings?
9. did Harry urge his uncle to enter and fortify the town?
10. did Hannay receive hellish news from Laidlaw?

• 18 • *During 2008:*

1. which gartered kiwi was laid to rest?
2. which fine food has gained PGS in Leicestershire?
3. who, following 2nd at 2K with 3 others, got 1st at 3K alone?
4. which sometime bulbous plant would seem to be involved with 'arthrology'?
5. who made successive day trips to Abergele, Fountains Abbey and Mugdock?
6. where has the pancake bell ceased to signal the start of a race owing to health and safety issues?
7. where did a giant arachnid briefly invade an apparently coleopteran habitat?
8. what legendary diamond fell to the successors of the fictitious Misson?
9. who got six months for dishonesty at White Plains?
10. whose job-centre manager fetched £17.2 million?

2009–2010

• 1 • *During 1909:*

1   what hidden addiction was revealed in Munich?

2   what was founded at the southern tip of Kinneret?

3   who filed a patent for a hermetically sealed burial casket?

4   which youngsters received numbered anklets by the Aberdeenshire seaside?

5   who, contrary to generally accepted opinion, may have reached where after Cook?

6   whose gallinaceous offering was held up by the censors and emerged posthumously?

7   who was rewarded for lofty idealism, vivid imagination and spiritual perception?

8   which Portuguese island colonies lost their Quaker customers?

9   whose unscheduled dip in La Manche cost him a grand?

10   which negative logarithm came from Carlsberg?

• 2 • *Which politician:*

1 was brought down by arachnoid largesse?

2 was expelled as Speaker following bribery by the Corporation?

3 in a constituency renowned for its RHS Show, succumbed to *Campanula vestimenta alba*?

4 enriched himself as PMG and provided a suitable surname for one of Disraeli's fictional characters?

5 was impeached, but not convicted, for allegedly accepting a bribe of 5000 guineas from the East India Company?

6 continued to draw an annual income of £25,000 from moneys which were not his, for 15 years after resigning as PMG?

7 transferred his non-transferable vouchers for his wife to travel from Glamorgan on the Great Western Railway?

8 similarly provided, inappropriately, first-class tickets for his mistress to travel to Yorkshire?

9 was impeached on bribery charges shortly after his elevation to a viscountcy?

10 used a Guest List for awarding Orders and other honours?

• 3 • *In which city:*

1 did Dizzy Mabel get drunk on gin?

2 did George confuse the words for cushion and kiss?

3 did Peregrinus bring Christmas presents to the poor bookbinder's family?

4 did the enormous Olga address her guest, inappropriately, as her little turtle-dove?

5 was the Cardinal encouraged to forsake celibacy in favour of a Lutheran union to solve a financial crisis?

6 did the dinner guests of the extended family include poet, physician, broker, wine-merchant, lumber-merchant and pastor?

7 did the disguised head groom cause a fire to reduce 42 houses to rubble and ashes?

8 was the annual subscription for the Blue Diamond 175 (in pre-euro money)?

9 was the bearer of a pound of Raven mixture expected at 9.34 pm?

10 did the people proclaim their Mayor a noddy?

• 4 • *In the finals of the A E L T & C C's championships:*

1 which runner-up won 29 games?

2 which match was decided after 12 games?

3 who required 40 games for his 3-set victory?

4 which two-set match was decided after 46 games?

5 which champion is now remembered for his predatory reptile motif?

6 in which match did the runner-up win as many games and sets as the victor?

7 which titled finalist was imprisoned by the Gestapo?

8 what was the role of Brooke's grandfather?

9 who was the only victor to lose a set 0-6?

10 who defeated his brother three times?

• 5 •

1 where did 13 go to the scaffold on Friday 13th?

2 who carried out the last public execution in Britain?

3 whose controversial execution by firing squad was alluded to by Voltaire?

4 which tailor, under sentence of death, was reprieved and elevated to Headsman?

5 which sexagenarian was chased around the scaffold and needed eleven blows with the axe?

6 which teenager was hanged for rape and murder, but revived while being prepared for dissection in Surgeons' Hall?

7 who was burned alive, without prior garrotting, owing to bungling by the executioner?

8 which trooper's swollen purple throat and stark and staring eyes were mocked?

9 how was the poisoner cook from John Fisher's household executed?

10 who survived three attempts at hanging at Exeter?

• 6 •   *Who or what:*

1   are endocrine?

2   invested in the Goat?

3   is overlooked by Calum's Hill?

4   is repetitious (and inspiring) at Cardiff?

5   is neither brightly coloured nor feathered?

6   were placed in 774 pots, 39 tubs and 24 boxes?

7   nickname has been applied to the Ukraine?

8   emphasises enthusiasm for a new idea?

9   is flavoured with cloves?

10   is palindromic?

• 7 •   *Who or what:*

1   was watched at eye level?

2   found room at one end for Victoria?

3   is not trusted for the way he parts his hair?

4   tale was found among the papers of the late Diedrich Knickerbocker?

5   painted an ecclesiastical decoration for a Flanders-based Florentine banker?

6   under a changed name, was allegedly instructed to include all facial blemishes?

7   turned to architecture following a relapse and provocation of the wife?

8   took his name from the city of Sint-Janskathedraal?

9   had a costly wetting in the Barry Burn?

10   revealed lives by invitation?

• 8 • *Who or what:*

1 is tragelaphine?

2 is also a hummingbird?

3 was considered better than best?

4 has a contrary reaction to that of litmus?

5 reverted to its former name following caprine slaughter?

6 retained his virtuosity despite accidental conversion to syndactyly?

7 had a facial expression likened to a fireside utensil?

8 is garnished with eggs and crustaceans?

9 is black and fork-tailed?

10 stepped out from BA?

• 9 • *Where does the brewer:*

1 recall 4468?

2 produce a preserved gamebird?

3 start his product with a silent 'P'?

4 provide a label for a hirsute cage bird?

5 remember the birthplace of 007's adventures?

6 remind us of a battle with a heptacephalic rodent?

7 produce evidence of canine appreciation?

8 commemorate Joanna Maria Lind?

9 appear to condone avian greed?

10 recognise a recurved bill?

• 10 •

1 who did Paul much evil?

2 who extended his realm into the Irish Sea?

3 who attributed the cold winter wind to the Almighty?

4 who confused *rubrum* and *notatum* when making his epic discovery?

5 who shot himself following annihilation of the Second Army by the Eighth?

6 who, following his death, may have re-emerged as a hermit, living for a further 39 years?

7 which monarch was shot, together with the French Foreign Minister?

8 who perceived his life as a protracted period of infirmity?

9 who was challenged by Gray over his patent?

10 who was mistaken for a match?

• 11 • *Which ordinal:*

1   is metronomic?

2   is liable to neuralgia?

3   was secured by MacArthur?

4   may forecast persistent precipitation?

5   was applied to Sarto, the village postman's son?

6   recalls tearful memories of the Tigris and Euphrates?

7   is associated with an annual brainteaser?

8   was used by Wraysford in his *Diary*?

9   signalled a peaceful trio?

10   was applied to Lime?

• 12 • *Which Queen of England or Great Britain:*

1   battled for Lancaster?

2   was the first to be kissed by Pepys?

3   was the consort of two Kings of England?

4   made a posthumous journey to London leaving her viscera at Lincoln?

5   numbered two archbishops and one bishop among her maternal uncles?

6   on first meeting her future spouse had prompted him to order a glass of brandy?

7   escaped in a hurry from a Cambridge Hall, before it was burned down?

8   died following surgery for an umbilical hernia?

9   regretted the jettisoning of *this* for *that*?

10   corresponded with Mrs Freeman?

• 13 • *Which historic English cathedral:*

1   is built on the highest ground?

2   has both a Bishop and a Dean with a glass eye?

3   contains a mediaeval lectern representing a large water bird?

4   has accommodated a pilgrim and his family annually since 2002?

5   achieved its current lofty status through meteorological intervention in 1584?

6   has a gallinaceous motif commemorating the founder of a Cambridge College?

7   possesses a plurality of plumbous receptacles for baptismal water?

8   houses the tomb of the founder, in 1264, of an Oxford College?

9   has a pulpit accessed by an intramural staircase?

10   houses the only equestrian statue?

• 14 • *Name the venue and the activity:*

1 Royal flood-plain.
2 A half of cuckoo pint.
3 The headsman's victim.
4 Simmonite, lacking a vowel.
5 A *glorious* shire relocated *by the sea.*
6 A shortened and outdated underground carriage.
7 The chiropteran hang-out of the eccentric.
8 Milne's joey by the river.
9 Calverley's alternative.
10 An ox cart perhaps.

• 15 • *Who or what:*

1 is perifoveal?
2 is bridged by a memorial to Pepi?
3 was a notoriously cruel Wallachian prince?
4 overlooks the burial ground of Anne, Catherine and Jane?
5 was thought, through its bite, to cause an extreme impulse to dance?
6 was a probable tuberculous infection, so named after a breeding sow?
7 is an abnormal passage connecting two epithelial surfaces?
8 broken bone is associated with an unspoken wish?
9 was Linné's name for the sea parrot?
10 is the Hill of the Fords?

• 16 • *Having got into the red, complete:*

1 B-dul Carol – .... – B-dul Eroiler
2 Holmens Kanal – .... – Torvegade
3 Robinson Road – Shenton Way – ....
4 Sancová ulica – Vajnorská ulica – ....
5 Strandvägen – Kungsträdgårdsgatan – ....
6 .... – Boulevard Malesherbes – Avenue Henri-Martin
7 Plaza Urquinaona – .... – Ronda San Pedro
8 .... – Tartu maantee – Pärnu maantee
9 .... – Capel Street – Henry Street
10 Lönnrotinkatu – .... – Simonkatu

• 17 • *What eponymous word owes its origin to:*

1   F René?

2   J D Scotus?

3   H P Mitchell?

4   Gerhard Kremer?

5   Charles de Rohan?

6   R V Shepherd and H J Turpin?

7   John Montague?

8   Haile Selassie?

9   C Cardoni?

10   M Tracy?

• 18 • *During 2009:*

1   who mischievously rocked the boat?

2   whose victory in Bavaria has recalled *I Samuel XVII*?

3   which Hat-maker has become the first female to be so honoured?

4   what left Lavender Hill intact but sustained a rupture at Langhorn Drive?

5   who, in disgrace, became Steward and Bailiff of the Manor of Northstead?

6   which vessel's sinking with the loss of all 36 lives has been recognised philatelically?

7   what non-event at Fort Collins recalled a fictional disaster in the Chilterns?

8   who has provided extremely interesting reading matter for rail travel?

9   who will never stir again, however much he is shaken?

10   what, according to Unesco, has risen from the dead?

2010–2011

• 1 • *In the year 1910:*

1   who was the victim of al-Wardani?

2   who began with Helen's letters to her sister?

3   what activity, where, was banned as a potential cause of delays?

4   which vessels were involved in a collision in la Manche costing 27 lives?

5   who ordered a large quantity of a muscarine antagonist from a shop at 2 Bucknall Street?

6   whose death in the stationmaster's house led to the station taking his name some years later?

7   who, having ruled which principality for fifty years, declared himself King?

8   whose memorial was placed behind the National Portrait Gallery?

9   which two unaccountable freaks went out together?

10   what was set alight on the Parisian stage?

• 2 • *Who or what:*

1   blew hot and cool?

2   was Mad Jack's spouse?

3   was the stuff that Smith was made of?

4   is an expression of surprise or indignation?

5   did the Emperor reward with the Yellow Jacket?

6   started as the 100th, but became the 92nd and was later joined by the 75th?

7   is marked by the rarest dish in all the land?

8   did a wartime treble on a solar vehicle?

9   was Raymond's creation?

10   merged with Osborne?

• 3 • *Going out, what (numerically), where suggests:*

  1   a clutch of curlew's eggs?

  2   a beverage 'Faithful to the original'?

  3   an encounter on 13th September 1882?

  4   an annual event initiated by James Stanley?

  5   an earlier connection with the Morning Post?

And coming in:

  6   is there a geographical misplacement from South Uist?

  7   sounds like a resident of Puddleby-on-the-Marsh?

  8   is an apparent refuge for the bald?

  9   follows Calamity?

10   finishes on time?

• 4 •

  1   who demonstrated phonetic pronunciation?

  2   whose notes were worth one hundred crowns?

  3   who footed it in Italy, Spain, Japan and Holland?

  4   who sold Estonia and took a Baltic Island instead?

  5   who was first to cross the North-West Passage by dog-sled?

  6   who died during the wedding celebrations of Tove and Gythe?

  7   who was decorated for valour following the Amiens push?

  8   whose tale about a sixth daughter inspired Eriksen?

  9   who is especially associated with a supernova?

10   who was cuckolded by the Royal physician?

· 5 · *Which independent school:*

1 started in the Depot?

2 favours Malvolian hosiery?

3 is approached by the Hundred?

4 sold the site to Merchant Taylors'?

5 possesses a relic of an epic crossing of the Scotia Sea?

6 had in its statutes a cryptic acknowledgement of the final chapter of St John's Gospel?

7 owes its foundation to *Salmonella typhi*?

8 has a boomer in the chapel tower?

9 was pictured by a little canal?

10 replaced a lofty hermitage?

· 6 ·

1 what was updated by H G Wells?

2 what might be perceived as an apiary?

3 which island is doubly recognised on 198?

4 who left great designs in the Gulf and New South Wales?

5 who, aided by wizardry, cuckolded his rival by impersonating him?

6 who, being the son of Suzanne, changed his name through the benevolence of her friend Miguel?

7 what did hateful and rough weeds lose apart from beauty?

8 what was the native city of a unique pontiff?

9 what can be used instead of mahogany?

10 who recruited Hare for Dad's Army?

· 7 ·

1 who began with 7-43?

2 what excluded Hall in 1856?

3 what did Virginia adopt instead of Jones?

4 who gained valuable experience from Gillespie?

5 who knocked out Jackie to become undisputed flyweight champion?

6 who looked into the disappearance of his West African GP's daughter?

7 what was judged to be a considerable distance from the Strand?

8 which minstrel finished with Danny Boy?

9 where is St James the highest of all?

10 what is a funny five-liner?

• 8 • *Who or whose:*

1   benefited from projectile vomiting?

2   likened the messenger to fullers' soap?

3   was a fruiterer specialising in *Ficus sycomorus*?

4   placed the caterpillar at the end of the food chain?

5   wife, a lady of ill-repute, bore him two sons and a daughter?

6   narratives both start during the second year of the monarch's reign?

7   dreamed of a bear-like beast with three ribs between its teeth?

8   broken yoke was replaced by one made of iron?

9   alluded twice to Leo becoming a vegetarian?

10   found himself in an open-air ossuary?

• 9 • *Who or what:*

1   is Hazel's cousin?

2   was crowned in Dublin Cathedral?

3   eponymous water bird has long been bedded down?

4   gained the GC for heroism on the Ely–Newmarket line?

5   died in legal captivity of coronary thrombosis on 16th November 1952?

6   wrote a risqué novel, which saw him tried but acquitted for irreligion and immorality?

7   carried on with George, regardless of Caroline, and later Frances?

8   put his name to a Top Secret Management Handbook?

9   tragically completed his fourth, but not his eighth?

10   created William and Maudie?

• 10 • *Which musician might have been:*

1   in SW3?

2   a mongrel?

3   an ottoman?

4   a hurried exit?

5   a plumbous abdomen?

6   more specifically, Atropos?

7   emulsified by bile?

8   a fit of pique?

9   coniferous?

10   lignified?

• 11 •

1   what was izzard?

2   when did Neptune begin?

3   what gave way to 18 in 83?

4   what is a feature of aerial punctuation?

5   which food substance can adversely affect the embryo?

6   what convinced Benedict of the suitability of the Florentine master?

7   where did Jane lodge for 2 guineas a week?

8   what, symbolically, melts at 3410°C?

9   who is a sharp know-all?

10   what is a zoonotic?

• 12 •

1   what is perhaps the equal of roly-poly?

2   what epidemic was survived by Sarah and Emily?

3   what is made from hog's lard, mutton suet and quicksilver?

4   upon whom had the captain's steward poured boiling jam juice?

5   which ancient bibulous Dane with pale red-rimmed eyes, was presented with a case of Priorato?

6   where, more than once, was a dead orphan child brought back for dissection and kept in a cupboard?

7   where did the small apothecary display the skeleton of an aardvark in his window?

8   translate 'Les bouts-dehors des bonnettes du petit perroquet'.

9   what was the ultimate fate of the Armenian polyglot?

10   who found a Frenchman's ring finger in his bowl?

• 13 •

1   who rescued John Galt?

2   who was No. 1, of No. 1 Company of the XIVth Army?

3   what entitles Mrs Magnusson to add R af E after her name?

4   who chased Ran Bagha and caused a bridge of boats over the Jumna to collapse?

5   whose son had served the Indian Government in every way for forty-seven years?

6   who was the favourite, and the only one of the 37, to survive the conflict with Scipio?

7   who, being the gift of a Mesopotamian ruler, was to perish on Lüneburger Heide?

8   who was presented to a Habsburg Prince by the King of Portugal?

9   who was presented to a Pope by the King of Portugal?

10   who set off for their honeymoon in a yellow balloon?

• 14 •   *Which elevated conduit:*

1   rotates for tall vessels?

2   might suggest marzipan?

3   is suspended from two open-web ribs?

4   is well seen 20 minutes after leaving Piccadilly?

5   features at the V & A, without its taller and younger companion?

6   although a few weeks younger than Holmes, proved greatly more durable?

7   took its name from the Honourable Member for Berkshire?

8   bears the inscription 'To Public Prosperity'?

9   provides an outlet for Trevor?

10   straddles Watling Street?

• 15 • *Where*:

1   does one come off the rails?

2   might there be a quarryman's shelter?

3   does the hairpin recall Loch and his successors?

4   must one look in vain for Noble's Peel and Derby?

5   does a dwelling at barely 30m seem seriously misplaced?

6   might one be excused for wrongly supposing a link with Camilla's great-grandmother?

7   is there a possible source for the winner's garland?

8   did a party from Grange Hill cause a disturbance?

9   is there a suggestion of a subterranean spirit?

10   is there a fraction over the glass?

• 16 • *Where:*

1   did Robinson settle for the elder sister?

2   was the master tailor interrupted in his reading of *The Divine Comedy*?

3   did apparent Benedictine hatred change, with assistance from friends, to love?

4   did the seemingly simple sister of the Hungarian Captain end up marrying his landlord?

5   did the beloved offspring of opposing feuding families commit suicide following the Friar's ruse?

6   did a Sicilian knight defeat the Duke in a duel and learn from the Saracen that his loved one was innocent?

7   did the rejected hunchback reveal the identity of his wife's real lover to the troupe leader?

8   did the dragoon gain the innkeeper's daughter in spite of a diabolical intrusion?

9   did the accursed jester unexpectedly find that his daughter had been bagged?

10   did the General's wife stab herself after being ravished by the Prince?

• 17 • *Which author concluded what with these words:*

1 'Assist'?

2 'All the papers on the subject are there in my safe'?

3 'As soon as they had strength they arose, joined hands again, and went on'?

4 'At any moment, it seemed, there could be surprises, huge upsets, even the end of small lizard worlds'?

5 'The sun dipped down from the great tower on to the upturned face, and his eyes were glistening through their tears'?

6 'He remembered how Marie had said he was a man whom women loved easily, and he felt uncomfortable at being reminded of her'?

7 'I can't reconcile my mind to their taking up with kanakas, and I'd like to know where I'm to find them whites'?

8 'And I began to curse and swear under my breath, because I'd left my shoes in the Mayni Tunnel'?

9 'Very lightly she slipped up into bed, and very soon she was asleep'?

10 '"Steer north," said he'?

• 18 • *During 2010:*

1 where did Joy uncover Fletch?

2 which city honoured a 1945 hero with its Große Siegel?

3 which Wizard Rose wilted towards the end of summer?

4 who finally achieved a victory by 417 days over Sinclair?

5 who was finally ousted by a Scottish philosopher and economist on 30ᵗʰ June?

6 which joint, showing a philatelic fracture, required a proper replacement before release?

7 where did Schadow's figure receive a multicoloured multiplication?

8 which leo-aquiline promoter missed out on afternoon tea?

9 who found that three coppers did not fool two coppers?

10 where did the tallest last the longest?

Answers

1981–1982

• 1 •

1 Wales XV (Blackheath)
2 Sir George Colley
3 Uranus
4 President Garfield
5 Kemal Ataturk
6 Isle of Man
7 Sam Goldwyn
8 France
9 Roumania
10 Chile

• 2 •

1 George IV and Mrs Robinson
2 Humphrey Bogart and Lauren Bacall
3 Caesar and Cleopatra
4 Bonnie and Clyde
5 John Lennon and Yoko Ono
6 Abelard and Eloise
7 Shelley and Mary Wollstonecraft
8 Pierre and Marie Curie
9 Dr Crippen and Ethel Le Neve
10 David and Bathsheba

• 3 •

1 Pyromancy
2 Oneiromancy
3 Necromancy
4 Rhabdomancy
5 Spodomancy
6 Hydromancy (or Lecanomancy)
7 Ceromancy
8 Belomancy
9 Chiromancy
10 Coscinomancy

• 4 •

1 Robert Louis Stevenson
2 Dickens
3 Jane Austen
4 Henry James
5 Mrs Gaskell
6 Thackeray
7 Raymond Chandler
8 Charlotte Brontë
9 Flann O'Brien
10 Macaulay

• 5 •

1 Antiochus IV
2 Pippin IV
3 Murad IV
4 Pope Adrian IV
5 Henri IV of France
6 Henry IV of England
7 Michael IV of Byzantium
8 Charles IV of Spain
9 Amenhotep IV
10 Ivan IV, the Terrible

• 6 •

1 Del Shannon
2 Delamere forest
3 Tierra del Fuego
4 Delta
5 Della Cruscan School
6 De la Rue
7 Delaware
8 Delphi
9 Delilah
10 Delectable Mountain

• 7 •

1 Jack Horner
2 Jack O'Lantern
3 Pelorus Jack
4 Jack Nicklaus
5 Gorging Jack
6 Jack Sprat
7 Jack Robinson
8 Jack Ketch
9 Jack Cade
10 Jack the Ripper

• 8 •

1 Charles II
2 Philip III
3 Louis VI
4 Philip V
5 Charles VI or Louis XIV
6 Charles VII
7 John I
8 Pepin
9 Charles III
10 Louis II

• 9 •

1 'The Lady is a Tramp'
2 'The Battle of New Orleans'
3 'My Favourite Things'
4 'A Fine Romance'
5 'In the Cool, Cool, Cool of the Evening'
6 'We Wish You a Merry Christmas'
7 'Thanks for the Memory'
8 'The Nightmare Song' from *Iolanthe*
9 'Tea for Two'
10 'You're the Tops'

• 10 •

1 Sirhan Sirhan
2 Charlotte Corday
3 Gavrilo Princip
4 Leon Csolgosz
5 Balthasar Gerard
6 Jacob Johann Anckarström
7 David Chapman
8 James Earl Ray
9 'Jacson'
10 Nathuram Godse

• 11 •

1 Walking
2 Badminton
3 Bridge
4 Ladies' Table Tennis
5 Public Schools' Football
6 Crime Writing
7 Magic
8 N. American Ice Hockey
9 Flower Arrangement
10 Seaplane Racing

• 12 •

1 *Headlong Hall*
2 *Wuthering Heights*
3 *Huntingtower*
4 *Jamaica Inn*
5 *Northanger Abbey*
6 *The House of Seven Gables*
7 *Bleak House*
8 *The Castle of Otranto*
9 *Uncle Tom's Cabin*
10 *Howard's End*

• 13 •

1 turkey
2 Cleopatra's Needle
3 whalebone
4 rice paper
5 The Isle of Portland
6 galvanised iron
7 Jerusalem Artichoke
8 German Silver
9 Meerschaum
10 Cor Anglais

• 14 •

1 Bhutan
2 Albania
3 India
4 Taiwan
5 Algeria
6 Ellice Islands
7 Georgia SSR
8 Republic of Cyprus
9 South Korea
10 United Arab Emirates

• 15 •

1 Pittsburgh
2 Marilyn Monroe
3 KGB
4 The Norway
5 Elektra
6 J F Kennedy Airport

7 O' Connell Street, Dublin
8 Marlene Dietrich
9 Oslo
10 Kinshasa

• 16 •

1 Charlie Parsons
2 John Smeaton
3 James Watt
4 Henry Maudslay
5 William Murdoch
6 John Wilkinson
7 Richard Trevithick
8 Isambard Brunel
9 Thomas Bouch
10 George Stephenson

• 17 •

1 Lord Clive
2 George II
3 William Henry, Duke of Gloucester
4 Duke of Wellington
5 Isaac Newton
6 Samuel Johnson
7 Henry II
8 George III
9 Patrick Henry
10 Palmerston

• 18 •

1 20th January (hostages and inauguration)
2 HMS *Edinburgh*
3 Polish Independence Day
4 Engine 752
5 Ronald Biggs
6 Space Shuttle
7 Miss Zara Phillips
8 Guillotine abolition
9 Ben Abruzzo and Larry Newman
10 Frank Adamson

1982–1983

• 1 •

1 Swan Electric Lamp (first used as shop light)
2 Frozen mutton from New Zealand
3 Quagga became extinct
4 Franklyn Delano Roosevelt
5 Treasure Island
6 The Ashes – the urn
7 Judo NOT Ju-jitsu (devised by Dr Kano)
8 Corinthian Football Club (first game)
9 H W Seeley (invented electric iron)
10 Sir James Douglass and Eddystone Rocks Lighthouse

• 2 •

1 Witch of Endor
2 Wizard of the North
3 The Witchfinder (C17)
4 Witch-hazel
5 Wizard Prang/Show
6 Wizard of Menlo Park
7 Witchcraft (wrote *Discoverie of W*)
8 Witch of Atlas (Shelley)
9 Wizard of Oz
10 *Which* magazine

• 3 •   *All C S Forester*

1 *Death to the French*
2 *The Captain from Connecticut*
3 *The African Queen*
4 *The Good Shepherd*
5 *The Gun*
6 *Flying Colours*
7 *The Ship*
8 *The Commodore*
9 *Hornblower and the Atropos*
10 *The Happy Return*

• 4 •

1 (Lakes of) Kashmir
2 Turkey
3 Israel
4 India/Pakistan/Bangladesh (hill stations)
5 Japan
6 Yucatan/Mexico
7 USA (W Prairies)
8 Malta
9 Sicily
10 Finland/Lapland

• 5 •

1 Phobos and Deimos
2 Castor and Pollux (Polydeuces)
3 Danaus and Aegytus
4 Hercules and Iphicles
5 Romulus and Remus
6 Jacob and Esau
7 Elvis and Jesse Presley
8 The Shah and Princess Ashrof (Persia)
9 Hamnet and Judith Shakespeare
10 Ross and Norris McWhirter

• 6 •

1 Arnold Bennett
2 Daventry
3 Napoleon
4 Charles I
5 Ferdinand (of Naples – *The Tempest*)
6 Nonconformist ministers
7 James I
8 The Five Boroughs (Derby, Leicester, Lincoln, Nottingham and Stamford)
9 Magpies
10 Sherlock Holmes

• 7 • *Bibles*

1 Terror (1535)
2 Murmurers (1801)
3 Princes (1702)
4 Sin no (more) (1716)
5 Forgiven (1638)
6 String (1746)
7 Vineyard (1717)
8 Life (1810)
9 Cause (1820)
10 Damsels (1823)

• 8 •

1 A A Milne
2 von Richthofen
3 Matisse
4 Hans Andersen
5 Fennimore Cooper
6 Giuseppe Garibaldi
7 Hewlett Johnson
8 *The Desert Song*
9 Eric, the Red
10 Winnipeg

• 9 •

1 The First Gentleman of Europe
2 The Second Mrs Tanqueray
3 The Third Man
4 The Fourth Horseman (of the Apocalypse)
5 Henry, the Fifth
6 James, the Sixth of Scotland
7 The Seventh from Adam
8 The Eighth President of the USA
9 The Ninth in Succession (to the Throne)
10 The Tenth Muse

• 10 •

1 Vernon and Irene Castle
2 Jaikie Galt
3 Ruddigore
4 Carlisle Castle
5 Castle Cornet (Guernsey)
6 Colditz
7 Château de Steen (Rubens)
8 Pepys and Windsor Castle
9 J Austen and Lesley Castle
10 Barbara (Anne) Castle

• 11 •

1 Ring ye Bells at Whitechapel
(Earliest version of 'Oranges and
Lemons')
2 Ni sit bissextus, februus minor, esto
duobus (pre 1612 *Thirty days hath
September ...*)
3 Have you any feathers loose? (alt)
4 Barcelona, bona, strike (New York
version of 'Eena, meena, mina, mo')
5 'I' says the Quarterly (Byron)
6 A popingo-aye (peacock) (C19
Scots)
7 Your mammie's gane to Seaton
(Scots version of 'Bye, baby
Bunting')
8 Had a doubtful strife, Sir
(Congreve's 'Tinker, Tailor ...' from
Love for Love 1695)
9 Die ist Zerbrochen ('London Bridge
is broken down')
10 Am now in my Castle (C17 Scots
version of 'I'm the King of the
Castle')

• 12 •

1 Irish rebels (1798)
2 Pied Piper
3 Mary, Queen of Scots
4 Bunker Hill
5 Irish Kings
6 Sheridan (Civil War)
7 National Exhibition Centre
(Birmingham)
8 Gravelly Hill (Spaghetti Junction)
9 Bredon Hill (A E Housman)
10 Brigadoon

• 13 •

1 Alto-Sax (Marshal Royal for Count
Basie)
2 John Barton King (US swerve
bowler – probably finest in the world
at that time)
3 'Duke' Edward Kennedy Ellington
4 John Wayne

5 Cyril Lord (carpets)
6 Nosmo King
7 Peer Gynt (Hall of the Mountain
King)
8 (Count of) 10 (boxing)
9 Ruff/fish (fish club)
10 King Cotton (US Senate 1858)

• 14 •

1 The Shimmy
2 The Piccolino
3 Balling the Jack
4 Lobster Quadrille
5 The Clog
6 The Tango
7 The Bolero
8 The Java Jive
9 The Hootchie-Kootchie
10 The Varsity Drag

• 15 •

1 Miss Lemon
2 Date
3 Gooseberry
4 Cherry (Nissan/Datsun)
5 Prof. Plum (*Cluedo*)
6 Quince
7 Nut (ridge on fiddle finger-board
and bow-tightener)
8 Strawberry (*Watership Down*)
9 Mrs Orange
10 Raspberry

• 16 •

1 Evelyn Waugh and Belle
2 Thomas Hardy and Michael Mail
3 Parson Woodforde
4 Solzhenitsyn (*The First Circle*)
5 George R Sims
6 Shakespeare and *Love's Labour's Lost*
7 George and Weedon Grossmith and
Diary of a Nobody
8 Addison and Sir Roger
9 Queen Victoria and Her Diary
10 Charles Dickens and *A Christmas
Carol*

• 17 • *Ditties by Marriott Edgar:*

1 Tuppence per person per trip ('Runcorn Ferry')
2 Three ha'pence a foot (Noah's Ark in 'Three ha'pence a foot')
3 The tinker's moke ('Marksman Sam')
4 Cold dripping toast ('Albert and the 'Eadsman')
5 Todmorden Swifts ('Goalkeeper Joe')
6 An egg for his tea ('Gunner Joe')
7 Elephant and the one at the back ('Little Aggie')
8 And you! ('The Battle of Hastings')
9 Eighteen pence a therm ('The Jubilee Sov'rin')
10 Wallace ('Albert and the Lion')

• 18 •

1 De Lorean cars
2 Alan Wells and Mike MacFarlane (200m Commonwealth Games)
3 Lech Walesa (his own words)
4 Panda cubs (Madrid Zoo)
5 Craig Stadler
6 Joseph B Walker ('Zoom' lens)
7 Arthur Askey
8 Tog Mor (crane that raised *Mary Rose* under the direction of Mgt. Rule)
9 *Admiral De Ruyter* (Queen Beatrix's visit)
10 *Manxman*

1983–1984

• 1 •

1 Liberty (Statue of)
2 Galvanised dustbin (portable)
3 Winners of the first league cricket cup (Heavy, Woollen)
4 Special Branch (CID)
5 First Children's Lending Library (Nottingham)

6 Krakatoa (caused Blue Moon over Ceylon)
7 (Acceptance of) Time Zones in Whole Hours (from Greenwich)
8 Rugby 'Seven-a-Sides'
9 Floodlit Baseball
10 GPO (Parcel Post)

• 2 •

1 Sand
2 Stones
3 Thieves/Highwaymen
4 Cobbler's Tools
5 A Cave in Lough Derg
6 Halter/Gibbet
7 Poverty/Impecuniosity
8 Ox
9 August Bank Holiday
10 Never

• 3 •

1 Ravens (two)
2 Petrel (as St Peter)
3 Woodpecker
4 Wren (*Troglodytes troglodytes*)
5 Swallow
6 Stork
7 Roc
8 Pelican
9 Phoenix
10 Crow

• 4 •

1 Pear's Soap
2 Palmolive Soap
3 Toni
4 Beecham's Pills
5 Sloan's Backache and Kidney Oils
6 Dr William's
7 Knight's Family Health Soap
8 Amami
9 Listerine
10 Lifebuoy

• 5 •

1 Oliver Goldsmith
2 Sir Walter Scott

3 Robert S Surtees
4 Washington Irving
5 James Agate
6 Walter de la Mare
7 Henry Fielding
8 John Galsworthy
9 Wm. Makepeace Thackeray
10 Laurence Stone

• 6 •

1 A Swiss
2 A Frenchman
3 A French Canadian
4 An American
5 A Dutchman
6 A German
7 An Australian
8 A Scandinavian
9 An Englishman
10 A Chinaman

• 7 •

1 Mr Bruff (*The Moonstone*)
2 Sydney Carton (*A Tale of Two Cities*)
3 Markby, Markby and Markby (*The Importance of Being Earnest*)
4 Pooh-Bah (*The Mikado*)
5 Mr Murbles (*Unpleasantness at the Ballona Club*)
6 Sir Robert Morton (*The Winslow Boy*)
7 Mr Briggs (*South Riding*)
8 Serjeant Buzfuz (*The Pickwick Papers*)
9 Soames Forsyte (*A Man of Property*)
10 Richard Rich (*A Man for All Seasons*)

• 8 •

1 First German railway (Wilson was driver of *Der Adler*)
2 First travelling Post Office
3 First monarch to travel by rail (Queen Victoria)
4 First mile-a-minute run
5 First murder on a British train (Müller/Briggs)
6 First train over first Tay Bridge

7 First (and only) railway to the top of a volcano (Thomas Cook/Vesuvius)
8 First Orient Express
9 First World War Armistice signing
10 First container Japan to Great Britain on Trans-Siberian Railway

• 9 •

1 Mull of Kintyre
2 White Cliffs of Dover
3 Scarborough Fair
4 America (*West Side Story*)
5 Swanee River
6 Le Pont d'Avignon
7 Argentina
8 Blue Ridge Mountains of Virginia
9 The Moon (*Fly me to the …*)
10 Ilkley (Ilkla) Moor

• 10 •

1 Henry VII (Elizabeth of York on playing cards)
2 William III (I, Ireland; II, Scotland; III, England; IV, Normandy)
3 Edward VII (1909 Derby)
4 George V (Princess May became Queen Mary)
5 George I
6 Elizabeth II
7 Victoria
8 Richard I
9 Edward VIII
10 Charles I (lost his head by one vote)

• 11 • *All British films with American titles*

1 *Brighton Rock*
2 *Whisky Galore*
3 *Dear Octopus*
4 *The Guinea Pig*
5 *Pimpernel Smith*
6 *The 49ᵗʰ Parallel*
7 *The Maggie*
8 *Albert RN*
9 *Dangerous Moonlight*
10 *The Quatermass Experiment*

• 12 •

1 MAN (not 'Isle of Man')
2 AMEN
3 MANSE
4 LE MANS
5 LAST MEN
6 SALT MINE
7 LAMINATES
8 ASSAILMENT
9 SAINT ANSELM (Not St Anselm)
10 STALIN'S NAMES (*exactly* those words)

• 13 •

1 Bay Area Rapid Transit (System)
2 The Pony Express
3 Telephone Area Code
4 Cable Car (1869)
5 Lombard Street
6 Baseball
7 Alcatraz
8 New York City
9 His Heart
10 San Francisco

• 14 •

1 MO (Little Mo)
2 PO
3 NO
4 IO
5 HO
6 JO
7 GO
8 ZO
9 LO (L'eau)
10 BO ('10')

• 15 •

1 Near Gale (Beaufort)
2 First dog (watch)
3 Shaft with leather (oar)
4 Man overboard (MOQ)
5 Vice Admiral of the White
6 Lima (International code JLN)
7 Tropic of Capricorn

8 A piece of white linen canvas (leadmarks 10.15. 20 fathoms)
9 Parcelling (worming a rope)
10 . . . . . (Morse 1. 5. 9)

• 16 •

1 *Redgauntlet* (Scott)
2 *The Egoist* (Meredith)
3 *The Tenant of Wildfell Hall* (A Brontë)
4 *Little Lord Fauntleroy* (Burnett)
5 *The Prince and the Pauper* (Twain)
6 *The Mayor of Casterbridge* (Hardy)
7 *Soldiers Three* (Kipling)
8 *The Woman in White* (Collins)
9 *The Vicar of Wakefield* (Goldsmith)
10 *The Spy* (J F Cooper)

• 17 • *All Ambrose Bierce*

1 Future
2 Bore
3 Coward
4 Patience
5 Cannon
6 Pride
7 Peace
8 Egotist
9 Riot
10 Past

• 18 •

1 £1 coin (Latin motto on edge)
2 Lady Mary Donaldson (first Lady Lord Mayor of London)
3 Calvin Smith *AND* Evelyn Ashford (2 x 100m. World Records)
4 Wakers – Sir Wavell Wakefield's death
5 Thames Flood Barrier (stamps)
6 Space/orbit (first US woman)
7 to correct EXACT time (seven pips at 01.00 1ˢᵗ July)
8 Lord's cricket paintings (Colman)
9 Bernard Weatherill (Speaker)
10 *Liberty* (America's Cup)

1984–1985

• 1 •

1 *Oxford English Dictionary*
2 P O Telephone Call Boxes
3 Fabergé
4 Gaudi (Barcelona)
5 Arthur Ransome
6 New Guinea
7 Wisden (J Wisden died)
8 Gordon (Khartoum)
9 Grover Cleveland
10 First pedestal water closet

• 2 •

1 schooner
2 gig
3 cruiser
4 galley
5 windjammer
6 junk
7 dingy
8 pontoon
9 ice-breaker
10 sloop

• 3 •

1 *Twelfth Night* (Smetana)
2 *Much Ado About Nothing* (Berlioz)
3 *Henry IV, Parts I and II* (Orson Welles)
4 *Romeo and Juliet* (Bernstein/Laurents)
5 *Coriolanus* (John Osborne)
6 *The Merry Wives of Windsor* (Vaughan Williams)
7 *Macbeth* (Kurosawa – *The Castle of the Spider's Web*)
8 *The Comedy of Errors* (Rodgers and Hart)
9 *Romeo and Juliet* (Bellini)
10 *The Taming of the Shrew* (Cole Porter/S and B Spewack)

• 4 •

1 curling
2 angling (coarse)
3 tennis (real)
4 surfing
5 shove-halfpenny
6 boules
7 lacrosse
8 Australian Rules football
9 trampolining
10 dwile flunking

• 5 •

1 Leonard Bernstein
2 Verdi
3 Rossini
4 Liszt
5 Schoenberg
6 Bruneau
7 Kurt Weill
8 Richard Rodney Bennett
9 Benjamin Britten
10 Handel

• 6 •

1 Lobelia
2 Red feathers ands a hula-hula skirt
3 Adelaide (*Guys and Dolls*)
4 Conakry
5 Sweeney Todd
6 Pearl S Buck
7 Troilus
8 Pearl Bailey
9 Margaret Clitherow
10 Jerry Gray (for Glenn Miller)

• 7 •

1 U.20 (*Lusitania*)
2 D.8
3 A-1 (satellite)
4 R 101
5 X 10 (*Tirpitz*)
6 A 4 (*Mallard*)
7 K.2 (Mount Godwin-Austen)
8 U-2 (Eisenhower-Krushchev)
9 M 6
10 K 9

• 8 •

1 Trilby
2 Pinafore
3 Garibaldi
4 Sou'Wester
5 Leotard
6 Jeans
7 Tam O'Shanter
8 Bikini (Ralik Chain)
9 Panama
10 Cardigan

• 9 •

1 Chatham
2 General Wolfe
3 Mozart
4 Nelson
5 Sardanapalus
6 Procris
7 Queen Elizabeth
8 a miner
9 Rubens
10 Socrates

• 10 •

1 Tokyo/Osaka
2 Paris/Bordeaux
3 Chicago/St Paul
4 London/Paris
5 Sydney/Perth
6 Hook van Holland/Cologne
7 San Francisco/Los Angeles
8 Rome/Milan
9 Port Augusta/Alice Springs
10 London/Brighton

• 11 •

1 Captain Queeg
2 Captain Briggs (*Marie Celeste*)
3 Captain Bligh
4 Captain Boycott
5 Captain Cook
6 Captain Vanderdecken
7 Captain Orton
8 Captain Gilpin (John)

9 Captain Bayonet
10 Captain Kidd (E A Poe)

• 12 •

1 Viola (*Twelfth Night*)
2 Overlord
3 Purpure
4 Sepia
5 Orange (House)
6 Black (Olympic Links)
7 Yellowhammer (Alabama)
8 Magenta
9 Gamboge
10 Green and yellow (electric wiring)

• 13 •

1 *The Turn of the Screw*
2 *Rebecca*
3 *Gone with the Wind*
4 *Beau Geste*
5 *Little Lord Fauntleroy*
6 *Pride and Prejudice*
7 *The Man of Property*
8 *Poldark*
9 *Guy Mannering*
10 *Woodstock*

• 14 •

1 Edward (J M D P) Dunsany
2 James (A A) Joyce
3 Ezra (L) Pound
4 Evelyn (A StJ) Waugh
5 Thomas (H H) Caine
6 Rupert (C) Brooke
7 Joseph (H P) Belloc
8 John (R R) Tolkien
9 Dylan (M) Thomas
10 Oscar (F O'F W) Wilde

• 15 •

1 Chicago (1871)
2 Reichstag (1933)
3 Greek Fire
4 Portland (Cumberland-Maine, 1866)
5 St Elmo's Fire

6 Troy (C II, BC)
7 The Firefly
8 Oslo (1624)
9 Rome (64)
10 London (1666)

• 16 •

1 Terrazzo
2 Mezzanine
3 Lazzarone
4 Lipizzaner
5 Embezzle
6 Mozzarella
7 Muezzin
8 Mezzotint
9 Morbidezzi
10 Pizza

• 17 •

1 F D Roosevelt
2 D D Eisenhower
3 Theodore Roosevelt
4 Grover Cleveland
5 Andrew Jackson
6 J F Kennedy
7 R M Nixon
8 W H Taft
9 R B Haynes
10 James Buchanan

• 18 •

1 Cambridge University Boat
2 Princess Margaret
3 Donald Duck
4 Last village in England to receive mains water
5 Daley Thompson and Sebastian Coe (Lowe won 800m in 1924 and 1928)
6 Harold Macmillan
7 17 (Chesterfield bi-election)
8 Independence Day (repairs to Statue of Liberty)
9 Pete Marsh (B C Man)
10 Winston Smith (Orwell)

1985–1986

• 1 •

1 Salisbury (3rd Marquis)
2 Serbo-Bulgarian War
3 (First) Touring-Caravan ('Wanderer' built by Dr G Stables)
4 Banff National Park
5 House of Commons
6 Blackpool (Trams)
7 Rover
8 Chicago (First Skyscraper – Home Insurance Building)
9 William Jacob
10 Canadian Pacific Railway

• 2 •

1 A high breaking wave
2 Drinking from rum-filled coconuts (brought on board illegally)
3 A boatswain's mate (piping orders)
4 A tube (straw) for pinching liquor
5 Waking a sleeping sailor (with a bucketful of cold water)
6 Decoying a ship ashore (with false lights)
7 A straw mattress
8 A food stain on clothing
9 Sleeping on deck
10 No warning at all

• 3 •

1 Appletreewick
2 Slaithwaite
3 Fowey
4 Edensor
5 Weobley
6 Hawick
7 Mousehole
8 Laugharne
9 Staithes
10 Borrowstounness

• 4 • *All stamps*

1 Barbados (1906)
2 Belgium (1849)
3 Sicily (1859)
4 Western Australia (1854)
5 Yugoslavia (Slovenia) (1919)
6 USA (1933–7)
7 S Africa/SW Africa (1942)
8 Canada (1929)
9 Great Britain (1910)
10 Southern Rhodesia (1931)

• 5 •

1 The Five Sisters of Kintail
2 Stalin
3 Half-a-crown (5 x 6d)
4 Woolworth's
5 Pam (Betjeman)
6 Mr Meagles (*Little Dorrit*)
7 The Five Members (Pym, Hampden, Hesilrige, Holles, Strode)
8 The Vipers (Aytoun)
9 Three and Seven (Kipling)
10 (Calouste Sarkis) Gulbenkian

• 6 •

1 Peppermint
2 Oxlip
3 Hinny
4 Ugli
5 Liger
6 Clementine
7 Whippet
8 Tudor (Union) Rose
9 Beefalo
10 Josta

• 7 •

1 (Jack) Striker and Dani(elle) Reynolds
2 Tommy and Tuppence (Beresford)
3 Bodie and Doyle
4 Crockett and Tubbs
5 Cagney and Lacey
6 Hunter and McCall
7 Dempsey and Makepeace
8 Hardcastle and McCormick
9 (George) Bulman and Lucy (McGinty)
10 Lone Ranger and Tonto

• 8 •

1 King Ahaseurus
2 Ring-tail
3 The Pope
4 Österreichring
5 The Piggy (-wig)
6 The Ring of the Nibelungs
7 The Doge of Venice
8 Ring o'Roses
9 Meadow-fairies (*Merry Wives of Windsor*)
10 (Richard) Tattersall's

• 9 •

1 Chris Old
2 Old Mother Riley
3 The Old Man of the Sea
4 (The Pleasant Comedie of) Old Fortunatus
5 Old Grog
6 Old Fog
7 Old Hickory
8 That Old Man Eloquent (Milton)
9 Old Mother Hubbard (and her dog)
10 Old Maid

• 10 •

1 Manchester (Mrs Gaskell)
2 Exeter (Thackeray)
3 Rochester (Dickens)
4 Southampton (Meredith)
5 Derby (George Eliot)
6 Clovelly (Dickens and Collins)
7 Puddleton (Hardy)
8 Peebles (Buchan/Douglas)
9 Newcastle-under-Lyme (Bennett)
10 Manchester (Golding)

· 11 ·

1 Apples – Switzerland
2 Cacti – Mexico
3 Molasses – Brazil
4 Dates – Egypt
5 Water-melons – Russia
6 Grape-skins – Portugal
7 Gentians – Switzerland
8 Potatoes – Finland
9 Milk – Russia
10 Plums – Bulgaria

· 12 ·

1 The Flower of Bristowe
2 Bristol University
3 Christmas Steps
4 John Cabot
5 American Consulate
6 Methodist Chapel
7 Chocolate (Joseph Fry)
8 The Llandoger Trow (*Treasure Island*)
9 (Payment) on the nail
10 Bristol

· 13 ·

1 Brownsea Island (Baden-Powell's camps)
2 Steep Holm
3 Walney Island
4 Tresco
5 Isle of Man
6 Lindisfarne (tide tables)
7 Foulness Island
8 Benbecula (BB was Bonnie Prince Charlie in disguise)
9 St Michael's Mount
10 Eilean Donnan

· 14 ·

1 *The School by the Sea* (Angela Brazil)
2 School of Whales
3 *The Schoolmaster* (Haydn)
4 The Fleshly School of Poetry
5 *Clifton School* (locomotive)
6 *The School for Scandal*

7 (Henry Rowe) Schoolcraft
8 *School for Fathers* (Wolf-Ferrari)
9 School of Athens (Raphael)
10 St Custard's School (Searle)

· 15 ·

1 Force majeure
2 William Wilberforce
3 Perforce
4 Brute Force
5 Task Force
6 Force 1 (Beaufort)
7 Royal Air Force Fighter Command
8 Forcemeat Balls
9 Force the Voucher
10 Hardraw Force

· 16 ·

1 Walter
2 Basenji ('The jumping-up-and-down dog')
3 Trappists/Cistercians of the Strict Observance
4 'Come with me to the Casbah'
5 'You dirty rat'
6 'Play it again, Sam'
7 'Elementary, my dear Watson'
8 *Britannia* (HM Yacht)
9 Harpo Marx
10 Hamlet

· 17 ·

1 Canoe
2 Two
3 (I'm a) Gnu
4 Caribou
5 Clerihew
6 Igloo
7 Queue
8 Sioux
9 (You're) Through
10 Pooh (Milne's original 'House at Pooh Corner')

• 18 •

1 Halfpenny
2 Dennis Taylor
3 Nemo
4 Ryder Cup (Curtis Strange and Ken Brown)
5 United Newspapers
6 Halley's Comet
7 Lester Piggott
8 (José Ladislao) Biro
9 Headingley (P C lunch-time guard)
10 Prince William

1986–1987

• 1 •

1 Coca-Cola
2 John Collinson (Bridge)
3 Charles Bradlaugh
4 Tower Bridge
5 St Hugh (Oxford College for women)
6 Tuxedo (G Lorrilard)
7 Home Rule Bill ('Bob's your Uncle' = Salisbury)
8 Avon
9 Alfonso XIII (Spain – posthumous birth)
10 'Bubbles' (Sir W M James/Millais)

• 2 • *Ship Museums*

1 Leningrad
2 Hannibal (Miss)
3 Barcelona
4 Newport (RI)
5 Sydney
6 Toronto
7 Gdynia
8 Marietta (Ohio)
9 Oslo
10 London

• 3 •

1 Amateur Athletic Association
2 Pattie, Maxine, LaVerne
3 Fair Rent, Free Sale, Fixity of Tenure
4 Napoleon, Francis II, Alexander I (France, Russia, Austria – Austerlitz)
5 Latitude, Lead, Look-out
6 Gloucester, Hereford, Worcester
7 Peerless, Pierce-Arrow, Packard
8 Deanna Durbin, Helen Parrish, Nan Grey
9 Reading, (W)riting, (A)rithmetic
10 Ramsbottom and Enoch and Me (Harry Korris)

• 4 •

1 Scapula, clavicle, humerus, ulna, radius, carpals, metacarpals, phalanges (Bones of the upper limb)
2 Ilerda, Pharsalus, Zela, Thapsus, Munda (Caesar's victories in battle)
3 Cambrian, Ordovician, Silurian, Devonian, Carboniferous, Permian, Triassic, Jurassic, Cretaceous (Geological Periods)
4 Augustus, Tiberius, Caligula, Claudius, Nero, Galba, Otho, Vitellius, Vespasian, Titus, Domitian (Roman Emperors)
5 Lacrimal, frontal, trochlear, superior division of oculomotor, naso-ciliary, inferior division of oculomotor, abducens (nerves passing through Superior Orbital Fissure)
6 Norman, Plantagenet, Lancaster, York, Tudor, Stuart, Hanover, Windsor (royal houses)
7 3.14159265358979 (π)
8 Superior, Michigan, Huron, Erie, Ontario (Great Lakes, west to east)
9 Red, orange, yellow, green, blue, indigo, violet (spectrum)
10 Mercury, Venus, Earth, Mars, Jupiter, Saturn, Uranus, Neptune, Pluto (planets)

• 5 •

1 Swindon
2 Tadcaster
3 Stratford
4 Portsmouth
5 Bradford
6 Manchester
7 Devizes
8 Snaith
9 Brighton
10 Burnham-on-Sea

• 6 •

1 Rugby Union
2 Surrey (near Weybridge)
3 One foot on the ground
4 USA (pre-war)
5 12 (Devon County Wanderers XII representing England)
6 All Paris XII (France)
7 (Dick) Fosbury
8 A wink (Tiddly wink)
9 Eton Fives Court
10 Cricket

• 7 •

1 Constipation
2 Haemorrhage
3 Diarrhoea
4 Septic tonsils/sore throat
5 Feverish conditions
6 Pernicious Anaemia
7 Tuberculosis
8 Colouring plasters, varnishes, etc.
9 Impotence
10 Roundworms and threadworms

• 8 •

1 Nietzche
2 (Adam) Smith
3 Wordsworth
4 (W B) Yeats
5 (Oscar) Wilde
6 (Bertrand) Russell
7 Pavlov
8 Tennyson

9 Pope
10 (E A) Poe

• 9 •

1 *Gone with the Wind*
2 *The Time Machine*
3 *David Copperfield*
4 *To Have and Have Not*
5 *Peyton Place*
6 *Roots*
7 *Jaws*
8 *Of Mice and Men*
9 *The Great Gatsby*
10 *Treasure Island*

• 10 •

1 Queen Anne's Lace
2 Quisling
3 Quai d'Orsay
4 Q/Quiller Couch (Chap. 31)
5 Quintain
6 Q-ship
7 Quince
8 Qattara
9 (Ellery) Queen
10 Queens (NY)

• 11 •

1 Fougasse
2 (David) Langdon
3 (Gerard) Hoffnung
4 Giovannetti
5 (Russell) Brockbank
6 Heath Robinson
7 (Norman) Thelwell
8 (Ronald) Searle
9 (Osbert) Lancaster
10 (Roland) Emmett

• 12 •

1 The dish and the spoon
2 Jack (and Jill)
3 Old Man (Goosey Gander)
4 Mary (Contrary)
5 Tom (the Piper's Son)
6 Jack (be nimble)

7 Humpty Dumpty
8 Little Miss Muffet
9 Old Mother Hubbard
10 Solomon Grundy

• 13 •

1 Marks and Spencer
2 Royal Bank of Scotland
3 TSB
4 Littlewoods
5 Diners Club International
6 Barclaycard
7 Debenhams
8 Tesco
9 Lloyds Bank (Access)
10 American Express

• 14 •

1 George
2 Peter
3 Colin
4 Bill
5 Albert
6 Jacob
7 Roger
8 Ernie
9 Jack
10 John

• 15 •

1 49th Parallel (54)
2 AFM (51) – 'Orders'
3 (H J) Heinz (57)
4 Playing Cards (52)
5 Ariovistus (58) – BC
6 Mendelssohn (56) – Opus
7 USA (50)
8 Sir Richard Grenville (53)
9 Praseodymium/Pr (59) – atomic number
10 Peking (55) – days

• 16 •

1 Gold-bricking
2 The Gold Purse of Spain
3 Black Gold

4 The Gold Rush
5 Goldilocks
6 The Gold Bug (Poe – *Dollar* magazine)
7 Goldcrest
8 Fool's Gold
9 Goldbach's Conjecture
10 Gold stick

• 17 •

1 Danzig
2 Athos
3 Vatican
4 Gibraltar
5 San Marino
6 Luxembourg
7 Monaco
8 Andorra
9 Liechtenstein
10 Trieste

• 18 •

1 Billy Smart's Circus
2 Fudge (boxer – 'American Patrol')
3 Betting shops
4 Ferdinand Marcos
5 Princess Anne
6 Hedgehogs (North Ronaldsay)
7 Queen Elizabeth (and Prince Philip) in New Zealand
8 Wicket (1st New Zealand Test)
9 Scillonians
10 Llanfairpwllgwyngyllgogery-chwyrndrobwllllantisiliogogogoch Station (Pringle shop)

1987–1988

• 1 •

1 Kiel Canal
2 Coin-in-the-slot gas meters
3 Appendix (first operation on infected appendix)
4 St John's Ambulance Brigade
5 Motor Race

6 The Deemster (Hall Caine)
7 Sherlock Holmes (at 221B Baker Street)
8 Henry Mayo Bateman
9 Knicker elastic/braided elastic
10 Esperanto (What's that?)

• 2 •

1 Tegestology
2 Storiology
3 Dendrochronology
4 Caliology
5 Exobiology
6 Uranology
7 Argyrothecology
8 Phitology
9 Pseudology
10 Cirplanology

• 3 •

1 Carole Bouquet
2 Ursula Andress
3 Jill St. John
4 Lois Chiles
5 Daniela Bianchi
6 Barbara Bach
7 Mie Hama
8 Barbara Carrera
9 Tanya Roberts
10 Diana Rigg

• 4 •

1 Iran
2 Germany
3 Hong Kong
4 Burma
5 Sierra Leone
6 Surinam
7 Aden
8 Indonesia
9 Netherlands
10 Malaysia

• 5 • *Railways*

1 Burma
2 Finland

3 Paraguay
4 Luxembourg
5 Turkey
6 Poland
7 Brazil
8 Hungary
9 Hong Kong
10 USSR

• 6 •

1 Bombay (Island)
2 Wharves (tidal)
3 Bombay bloomers
4 East India Company
5 Bombay duck
6 Five
7 Bombay oyster
8 Gateway of India
9 Indira Dock (renamed)
10 Bombay

• 7 •

1 *Nicholas Nickleby*
2 *Dombey and Son*
3 *Mr Robert Bolton*
4 *David Copperfield*
5 *Hard Times*
6 *Barnaby Rudge*
7 *The Pickwick Papers*
8 *Great Expectations*
9 *The Old Curiosity Shop*
10 *Sketches by Boz*

• 8 •

1 Centre Point
2 Middle Watch
3 Centre Court
4 Middle Ear
5 Centre of England
6 Middle Passage (slavery)
7 Centre Board
8 Middle Kingdom
9 Centre Forward
10 Middle Mouse (Anglesey)

• 9 •

1 Mary, Queen of Scots
2 Henry III
3 James I of Scotland
4 Edward IV
5 Richard II
6 John II of France
7 Charles I
8 David Bruce of Scotland
9 Edward II
10 David II of Scotland

• 10 •

1 Carmen/*Carmen*
2 Lakmé/*Lakmé*
3 Norma/*Norma*
4 Otello/*Otello*
5 Mignon/*Mignon*
6 Tosca/*Tosca*
7 Siegfried/*Siegfried*
8 Butterfly/*Madame Butterfly*
9 Tancredi/*Tancredi*
10 Serse/*Serse*

• 11 •

1 Kia-ora
2 Adidas
3 Lego (Leg godt)
4 Aspro
5 Pifco
6 Marmite
7 Viyella (in Derbyshire)
8 Esso
9 Spar
10 Volvo

• 12 •

1 Pargeter
2 Lorimer
3 Fletcher/Flower
4 Cooper
5 Bodger
6 Fuller
7 Tedder
8 Lever
9 Palmer
10 Plummer

• 13 •

1 On
2 Oz (Ebsen, original 'Tin Man' contracted Aluminium poisoning)
3 Ob
4 Op
5 Or
6 Oo
7 Ox
8 Og
9 Od (Mrs Browning/von Reichenbach)
10 Oa (Islay)

• 14 •

1 Phaeton
2 Penny-farthing
3 Fiacre
4 Hansom
5 Jeep
6 Juggernaut
7 Surrey
8 Berlin
9 Sulky
10 Black Maria

• 15 •

1 Iron (Michigan)
2 Iron Age
3 *The Iron Heel* (Jack London)
4 Iron sleet (Gray)
5 Iron Crown (of Lombardy – with a nail from the Cross)
6 Iron Gate(s)
7 Iron Mask
8 Iron Lung
9 *Iron Duke* (HMS)
10 Irony

• 16 •

1 *Yorkshire Evening Post*
2 *Times*
3 *Daily Mirror*
4 *Daily Express*
5 *Observer*
6 *News Chronicle (Daily News* and *Daily Chronicle)*

7 *Citizen*
8 *Guardian*
9 *Daily Courant* (or *Oxford Gazette*)
10 *Yorkshire Post*

• 17 •

1 Horseshoe (Blondin, blindfold)
2 Backpack
3 Treenail
4 Wallpaper
5 Shoetree
6 Headstone
7 Paperback
8 Nailhead
9 Packhorse
10 Stonewall (Jackson/Whittier)

• 18 •

1 Scarborough FC
2 Crufts (Afghan)
3 Ted (Blunkett)
4 999 calls
5 Golden Gate Bridge
6 Rosie (Barnes)
7 14 (Sunflowers - 24¾M)
8 Duchess of Windsor (£31M)
9 Greg Norman (Larry H Mize)
10 Church of England Deaconesses

1988–1989

• 1 •

1 Bishop of Wakefield
2 *National Geographic Magazine*
3 K (Kodak)
4 Fridtjof Nansen
5 Suez Canal
6 Rudyard Kipling
7 The first Beauty Contest /Concours de Beauté
8 Benjamin Harrison
9 Jack the Ripper
10 Listowel and Ballybunion Railway (trestle monorail)

• 2 •

1 The Man with the Twisted Lip
2 The Blanched Soldier
3 The Solitary Cyclist
4 The Retired Colourman
5 The Noble Bachelor
6 The Veiled Lodger
7 The Norwood Builder
8 The Missing Three-quarter
9 The Crooked Man
10 The Stockbroker's Clerk

• 3 •

1 Oscar Niemeyer
2 Henry Hobson Richardson
3 Le Corbusier
4 Peder Vilhelm Jensen-Klint
5 Jørn Utzon
6 Eliel Saarinen
7 Sir Owen Williams
8 Frank Lloyd Wright
9 Gustave Eiffel
10 Walter Gropius

• 4 •

1 (Auguste) Comte
2 (Emile) Coué
3 (Emile) Zola
4 (Augustine) Birrell
5 (Claude Henri) Saint-Simon
6 Joe Miller (Joe Millerism)
7 (Thomas) Bowdler
8 (Mrs) Malaprop
9 (Friedrich) Mesmer
10 (Mrs) Grundy

• 5 •

1 Shakespeare
2 Emmeline Pankhurst
3 Charles James Fox
4 King George III
5 Thackeray
6 Thomas Guy
7 Abraham Lincoln
8 Mahatma Gandhi
9 Alcock and Brown
10 Princess Pocahontas

• 6 •

1 Chrysanthemum
2 (White) Moss Rose
3 Marigold
4 Lupin
5 Daisy (Bell)
6 Narcissus
7 Primrose (*Macbeth* II iii)
8 (Scarlet) Pimpernel
9 Bluebell (Girls)
10 Petunia

• 7 •

1 A soldier/marine
2 Female lorry driver
3 The Royal Navy
4 British War Medal and Victory Medal
5 Manual work
6 It doesn't matter (Ça ne fait rien)
7 All clear and air raid warnings sirens
8 Military Policemen
9 Road transport for aircraft
10 Anti-aircraft guns

• 8 •

1 Davenport
2 Tabouret
3 Tallboy
4 Canterbury
5 What-not
6 Chiffonier
7 Cellaret
8 Teapoy
9 Dumb waiter
10 Commode

• 9 •

1 Bass and Flinders
2 Round the World (J C Voss, 1901–04)
3 USS *Skate* (North Pole)
4 Largest object ever stolen
5 the supremacy of Screw over Paddle
6 *Merrimack* and *Monitor* (US)
7 Liberty Ships

8 *President* ('Original Six' US frigates)
9 John Paul Jones (1799)
10 Napoleon (to St Helena on HMS *Northumberland*)

• 10 •

1 Skimbleshanks (T S Eliot)
2 *The Lion* (Manchester–Liverpool Railway)
3 The Motorman
4 The Locomotive
5 Sugar Hill (Haarlem)
6 (Arthur) Honneger
7 Carker (*Dombey and Son*)
8 Commuter
9 Chatanooga Choo Choo
10 The General

• 11 •

1 North Yorks Moors
2 Quantocks
3 Malvern Hills
4 Chilterns
5 Grampians
6 Brecon Beacons
7 Dartmoor
8 Mendips
9 Exmoor
10 Bodmin Moor

• 12 •

1 Wordsworth, William
2 David, Livingstone
3 Hans Christian Andersen
4 Duke of Clarence
5 Constable, John
6 Wolfgang Amadeus, Mozart
7 Cromwell, Oliver
8 Vincent Van Gogh
9 Byron
10 Edward (V)

• 13 •

1 Question mark (quaestio)
2 Mark time

3 St Mark
4 Assay Office Mark
5 Mark Antony
6 Mark Twain
7 Mark Rutherford (pseudonym)
8 Mark Causeway
9 Mark Banco
10 Exclamation mark (lo)

• 14 •

1 Melba
2 (Brillat-) Savarin
3 St Honoré
4 Rossini
5 Mirepoix
6 Pavlova
7 Bath Oliver
8 Praline (Duplessis-Praslin)
9 Pumpernickel
10 Sally Lunn

• 15 •

1 Quarter Guinea
2 Farthing and halfpenny (¼d and
   ½d)
3 Hadrian (117–38 AD)
4 Guernsey
5 Trident for spear (Britannia)
6 1763
7 Nickel brass
8 1/52 shilling
9 Sovereign
10 Nine pence/9d

• 16 •

1 A sucker
2 Violet Elizabeth Bott
3 Felix
4 The Runaway Train
5 Topsy
6 Johnny Walker
7 Giacomo Jocante
8 Little Audrey
9 Henry Crun
10 Adam (shortest poem –
   'microbes')

• 17 •

1 Iboland
2 Acheson (Truman)
3 Beagle
4 Jehu
5 Eye-offending
6 Aysgarth Falls
7 Ephesus
8 Daedalus
9 Gaol (not 'Jail')
10 Seesaw

• 18 •

1 Playschool
2 Walter Gabriel/Chriss Gittins
3 David Bairstow
4 *Young Endeavour*
5 Greg Louganis
6 Barnardo
7 Irving Berlin
8 First (Anglican) woman bishop
   (Massachusetts)
9 Beatrice Elizabeth Mary 8. viii. 88
10 Harry Ramsden

1989–1990

• 1 •

1 *New York Herald* (first overseas
   edition)
2 Dr Herman Hollerith
3 2 guineas
4 First fruit machine
5 Influenza
6 Harry Freeman
7 Moulin Rouge
8 Docker's Tanner
9 (Oklahoma) LAND (Settlement)
10 Double Room WITH BATH

• 2 •

1 Bear's foot
2 Camel's hair
3 *The Horse's Mouth*

4 Whale's bone (NOT whale-bone)
5 Cat's brains
6 Lamb's tail
7 Elephant's eye
8 Hound's tooth
9 Dragon's blood
10 Bee's knees

• 3 •

1 Herman Melville
2 Hermit Crab
3 Hermetic(ally) sealed
4 Hermeneutics
5 The Hermitage
6 Hermitage
7 Herma Ness
8 Hermes
9 Mount Hermon
10 Herm

• 4 •

1 Luton
2 Glasgow
3 Belfast/Aldergrove
4 Manchester
5 Aberdeen
6 Jersey
7 Inverness
8 Heathrow
9 Prestwick
10 Isle of Man/Ronaldsway

• 5 •

1 The Game Chicken
2 *The Game and Play of Chesse*
3 Fair Game
4 Whist (*Bleak House*)
5 The waiting game
6 Cricket (Surrey!)
7 The Great Game
8 Paille Maille (Pall Mall)
9 Monopoly
10 Gossamer

• 6 •

1 Pya (Burma)
2 Seniti (Tonga)
3 Bani (Romania)
4 Satang (Thailand)
5 Mongo or Mung (Mongolia)
6 Tambala (Malawi) or Ngwee (Zambia)
7 Centavo (Nicaragua)
8 Avo (Macao)
9 Chon (Korea)
10 Kobo (Nigeria)

• 7 •

1 Francis and Peter Stirling (2nd Lt)
2 Hopalong Cassidy and California
3 Boston Blackie and the Runt
4 Charlie Chan and No. 1 son (Jimmy)
5 Dagwood Bumstead and Blondie
6 Judge and Mrs Hardy
7 Dr Gillespie and Dr Kildare
8 Ma and Pa Kettle
9 Inspector Hornleigh and Sergeant Bingham
10 Mexican Spitfire and Uncle Matt AND Lord Epping

• 8 •

1 Bern
2 Copenhagen
3 Belgrade
4 Godthaab (Greenland)
5 Luxembourg
6 Sofia
7 Stockholm
8 Reykjavik
9 Brussels
10 Dublin

• 9 •

1 Mascles
2 Contre-ermine
3 Gentleman
4 Passion nails
5 Canting (arms)

6 Shake-fork
7 Proper
8 Leopard
9 Label
10 Difference

• 10 •

1 *One Fat Englishman*
2 *Two on a Tower*
3 *Three Lives*
4 *The Four Winds of Love*
5 *Five Finger Exercise*
6 *Six Characters in Search of an Author*
7 *Seven Men*
8 *Eight o'Clock Tales*
9 *Nine Coaches Waiting*
10 *Ten Days That Shook the World*

• 11 •

1 Lt Gen. Holland M Smith
2 Lt Gen. Joseph W Stillwell
3 Lt Gen. William Joseph Slim
4 Vice Admiral William Frederick Halsey
5 Major Gen. Curtis LeMay
6 Admiral Sir Andrew Browne Cunningham
7 Lt Gen. George Smith Patton (Jr)
8 General Carl Spaatz
9 Field Marshal Sir Henry Maitland Wilson
10 Major Gen. Walter Bedell Smith

• 12 •

1 Zinn(ia)
2 Begon
3 Rudbeck
4 Bignon
5 Raffles
6 Fuchs
7 Garden
8 de Lobel
9 Poinsett
10 Tradescant

• 13 •

1 Namibia/SW Africa
2 Australia/Tasmania
3 Japan
4 New Zealand
5 Samoa
6 Jamaica
7 Colombia
8 Canada/Newfoundland
9 Mauritius
10 Uganda

• 14 •

1 PS *Britannia*
2 RMS *Laconia*
3 RMS *Queen Mary*
4 SS *Ivernia*
5 RMS *Caronia*
6 MV *Britannic*
7 RMS *Aquitania*
8 RMS *Campania*
9 RMS *Carmania*
10 *Queen Mary*

• 15 •

1 Brueghel (Jan and Pieter)
2 Adam (Robert and James)
3 Gershwin (George and Ira)
4 Waugh (Alec and Evelyn)
5 Bellini (Gentile and Giovanni)
6 Amati (Andrea and Nicola)
7 Cooper (Alexander and Samuel)
8 Grimm (Jacob and Wilhelm)
9 Beggarstaff (James and William)
10 Booth (John Wilkes and Edwin)

• 16 •

1 Carroll Gibbons
2 (Charles Woodrow) 'Woody Herman'
3 (George Robert) 'Bob' Crosby
4 Glenn Miller
5 Paul Fenhoulet
6 Heinz Wehner
7 Nat Gonella
8 King Oliver

9 Eric Robinson
10 Stephane Grapelli AND Django Reinhardt

• 17 •

1 Fell (fell, fell and fell again)
2 Bail
3 Trap
4 Fret
5 Tack
6 Game
7 Long
8 Buff
9 Wear
10 Last

• 18 •

1 Hoglet (no previous dictionary def.)
2 Peter Scudamore
3 *Bismarck* found (off Brest)
4 The Portland Vase
5 Neil Fox
6 Steve Cauthen (Kentucky, Epsom, Irish, French)
7 Concorde
8 Globe Theatre (probable site)
9 St Leger
10 Mel Blanc (died, July)

1990–1991

• 1 •

1 London Omnibus Workers
2 Borodin
3 First English newspaper headline (*Star*)
4 Electric Chair (first execution)
5 (Siemen's) Submarine cable
6 First underground railway – City and South London Line
7 *Comic Cuts*
8 Idaho (Gem State with Wyoming – ES)
9 Forth Rail Bridge
10 Queen Wilhelmina

• 2 •

1 Bottom of the deep (Henry IV)
2 Bottomry
3 Mr and Mrs Ramsbottom
4 Bottom
5 Law of a Bottomless Pit (Arbuthnot)
6 Bottoms Up!
7 Six Mile Bottom
8 Foggy Bottom (Washington DC)
9 A bottom of good sense (Johnson)
10 Bell-bottoms

• 3 •

1 Royal Portrush (14th)
2 Hillside
3 Ashridge (9th)
4 Wentworth (West Course)
5 North Wales (16th and 17th)
6 Prince's, Sandwich
7 Royal Porthcawl (12th)
8 Royal Dornoch
9 Carnoustie (10th)
10 St Andrew's

• 4 •

1 Redbreast (Dickens)
2 Redrattle
3 Redwoods
4 Red and raw (*Love's Labour's Lost*)
5 The Red Book of Hergest
6 Redgauntlet
7 Redlaw
8 Redbridge
9 Red Cross
10 Little Red Riding Hood

• 5 •

1 USS *Skate* and *Seadragon* (2.viii.62)
2 David Bushnell's (1776)
3 Merchantman (sub.)
4 Two (Sopwith Schneider) float seaplanes
5 721
6 Italian (human torpedo crews – Alexandria)
7 Lt Cdr Martin Nasmith's (in E11)

8 A, B and C class – RN submarines
9 USSR
10 RN Submarine Service

• 6 •

1 22 (Titanium)
2 45 (Rhodium)
3 72 (Hafnium)
4 61 (Promethium)
5 81 (Thalium)
6 67 (Holmium)
7 53 (Iodine)
8 27 (Cobalt)
9 28 (Nickel)
10 38 (Strontium)

• 7 •

1 William Astor
2 La Tour d'Auvergne
3 Henry David Thoreau
4 Jørgen Jørgensen
5 Nicolas Boileau
6 Robert Campin
7 François de Bonivard
8 Thomas Carlyle
9 Thomas Simpson
10 Jean Dunois

• 8 •

1 Tony Martin
2 Dinah Washington
3 Sophie Tucker
4 Peggy Lee
5 Little Richard
6 Conway Twitty
7 Brook Benton
8 Bobby Darin
9 Nina Simone
10 Chubby Checker

• 9 •

1 St Hubert Hound
2 Eivissenc
3 Dandie Dinmont
4 Papillon/Squirrel Dog
5 Parson Jack Russell Terrier

6 Sealyham
7 Perdigueiro (perdiz)
8 Cairn
9 Schipperke
10 Little Bedlington

• 10 •

1 Little Cowfold (Belloc)
2 Little Lord Fauntleroy
3 Little-endians
4 Little Russian
5 Little Rock (Arkansas)
6 Little Belt (1811, sloop v. frigate)
7 Little Parliament
8 Little Jack Horner
9 Little Britain
10 Little Gentleman in Velvet

• 11 •

1 Rotherham
2 Keighley
3 Whitby
4 Sheffield
5 Kingston-upon-Hull
6 Bradford
7 Selby/Goole
8 Bridlington
9 Middlesbrough
10 Wakefield

• 12 •

1 (John) Sloan
2 (John S) Copley
3 (Winslow) Homer
4 (Grant) Wood
5 (Grandma A M R) Moses
6 (George W) Bellows
7 (Benjamin) West
8 (Ben) Shahn
9 (Linton) Park
10 (Thomas) Eakins

• 13 • *All on 1st April*

1 1973
2 1904
3 1944

4 1955
5 1918
6 1924
7 1908
8 1943
9 1948
10 1974

• 14 • *RNLI*

1 Tobermory
2 Tynemouth
3 Yarmouth, IOW
4 Campbelltown
5 Galway Bay
6 Bridlington
7 Stromness
8 Filey
9 Peterhead
10 Moelfre

• 15 • *Disney characters*

1 Julius (the cat)
2 Oswald, the Lucky Rabbit
3 Goofy
4 Goofy (Italy, Norway, Yugoslavia)
5 The Three Little Pigs
6 Mickey Mouse
7 Donald Duck
8 Crows (*Dumbo*)
9 Peg Leg Pete
10 The Sorcerer (*Fantasia*)

• 16 •

1 Savoy Palace
2 Eltham Palace
3 Greenwich (Old Palace)
4 Nonsuch
5 Edinburgh Castle
6 Brighton Pavilion
7 Osborne House
8 Balmoral (V and A)
9 Sandringham House
10 Queen Mary's Dolls House

• 17 •

1 Pack of cards
2 Trombones
3 MPs
4 The Light Brigade
5 Methuselah
6 'Fourteen Hundred'/Stock Exchange Cry (for a stranger)
7 Mash/MASH
8 *Mallard*
9 *Flying Scotsman*
10 Pennsylvania (Hotel)

• 18 •

1 Sir Richard Hadlee
2 Big Ben
3 14 Wrens (first to crew at sea in RN)
4 *One Man and His Dog* (Katy Cropper with Trim)
5 Faeroe Islands (playing in Sweden v. Austria)
6 E and W (Germany) did 'meet'
7 St Basil's, Moscow
8 Australia's Parliament (Peacock v. Hawke)
9 Gennady Gerasimov
10 12.34.56, 7/9/90

1991–1992

• 1 •

1 Cruft's Great Dog Show
2 First penalty kick (Wanderers v. Accrington)
3 Trans-Siberian Railway
4 German Old Age Pensioners (first)
5 Blackpool Tower foundation stone
6 George Robey (PM of Mirth)
7 Travellers' cheques (first user – American Express)
8 Märklin (Clockwork, 1.75 gauge)
9 Fingerprinting
10 Stamp Distribution SyndiCATE/ SDS (machine sales)

44444

• 2 •

1 Peter I
2 Benedict XV
3 Anastasius II
4 Gregory VII
5 Alexander VI (Borgia)
6 John XXIII
7 Sergius II
8 Joan
9 Gregory XVI
10 Adrian IV

• 3 •

1 The Isle of Man (*Swallowdale*)
2 Gibber (*Missee Lee*)
3 NO GO (*The Picts and the Martyrs*)
4 A kitten (*We Didn't Mean to Go to Sea*)
5 The Roaring Donkey (*The Big Six*)
6 Lt Col T E Jolys (*The Picts and the Martyrs*)
7 Pin Mill (*Secret Water*)
8 An adder (*Swallows and Amazons*)
9 Tom Dudgeon (*Coot Club*)
10 Walker (*Secret Water*)

• 4 •

1 Forenoon (watches)
2 Whitehead (Poet Laureate)
3 Tudor (Royal House)
4 Marie Curie (Nobel Prize, Chemistry)
5 Ash Wednesday (Red Letter Days)
6 *Gone with the Wind* (Pulitzer Prizes – Fiction)
7 Nebuchadnezzar (wine bottles)
8 Pond (Astronomers Royal)
9 Malcolm (Kings of Scotland)
10 Tammuz (Jewish calendar)

• 5 •

1 (Old) Nurburgring (North Loop)
2 Imola
3 Adelaide
4 Spa
5 Daytona
6 Monza
7 Monaco
8 Suzuka (Japan)
9 Hockenheim
10 Brooklands

• 6 •

1 Cribbage
2 Ombre
3 Cinch (also called double pedro/ five high)
4 Piquet
5 Loo
6 Hearts
7 Napoleon
8 Faro
9 Skat
10 Pinochle

• 7 •

1 Apollo
2 Mars
3 Jupiter
4 Hera
5 Venus
6 Artemis
7 Athena
8 Vulcan
9 Juno
10 Io

• 8 •

1 Coot
2 Madge
3 Starling
4 Martlet
5 Redcap
6 Magpie
7 Goose
8 Peregrine
9 Stint
10 Turkey

9.

1 Simon de Montfort (1264)
2 Countess Markiewicz (1918)

3 Benjamin Spiller (1818)
4 Clement Attlee (1937)
5 Betty Harvie-Anderson (1970)
6 Dadabhai Naoroji (1892)
7 Keir Hardie (1892)
8 John Bellamy (1773)
9 Ian Gow (1989)
10 Sir Alan Herbert (1934) –
   possible alternative Mr Williamson
   (1898)

• 10 •

1 McBurney's
2 Munchausen's
3 Sydenham's
4 Fallot's
5 Klinefelter's
6 Bell's
7 Kienböck's
8 Dupuytren's
9 Erb's
10 Meckel's

• 11 •

1 Norma Shearer
2 Mae West (at 5)
3 Clara Bow
4 Lana Turner
5 Marilyn Monroe
6 Kim Novak
7 Greta Garbo
8 Ann Sheridan
9 Linda Darnell
10 Bea Lillie

• 12 •

1 Tank troops
2 Air-mail letters (on blue paper)
3 Greenwich Mean Time
4 Information from Spies
5 The middle of nowhere
6 Blend, Low silhouette, Irregular
   shape, Small, Secluded (escape
   drill)
7 Meal – ready to eat / 'Meal rejected
   by Ethiopians'
8 Helicopter pilot

9 Cutlery
10 Marines – female (broad-'based' –
   Gulf War slang)

• 13 •

1 Lancashire
2 Gloucester
3 Stilton
4 Leicester
5 Caithness
6 Morven
7 Cheddar
8 Cheshire
9 Caerphilly (blown 12′ off vert)
10 Wensleydale

• 14 •

1 Maria and Elizabeth Brontë
   (1814 and 1815)
2 Patrick Brontë
3 Smith Elder and Co. (pub)
4 Elizabeth Branwell (guardian)
5 The Great Glasstown
   Confederation (writings as
   children)
6 Elizabeth Firth and Mary
   Barder
7 Maria Branwell (and met
   Patrick)
8 Wellington (Charlotte's toy
   soldier)
9 Branwell Brontë
10 Charlotte Brontë

• 15 •

1 Surtsey
2 Grand Canyon
3 Dead Sea
4 Mount Etna
5 Matterhorn (Perren – 144 climbs
   out of his intended 150)
6 Ayre's Rock
7 Mount Everest
8 Ignaçu Falls
9 Monument Valley
10 Giant's Causeway

• 16 •

1 Agamemnon (Atlantic cable, used by Queen and President)
2 King Alfred
3 Henry VIII (Trinity House)
4 Queen Victoria
5 Queen Elizabeth II
6 William IV (as Prince William, Duke of Clarence)
7 Catherine the Great
8 Sovereign of the Seas / Sovereign / Royal Sovereign
9 Charles II ('Yacht' – Dutch 'jacht')
10 King Orry

• 17 •

1 Mimi
2 Kaka
3 Co-co
4 Juju
5 Nana
6 Gigi
7 Ha-ha
8 Dada
9 Yoyo
10 Baba

• 18 •

1 Magic Circle
2 Edith Cresson (French Prime Minister: President Mitterand – 'God')
3 *Pravda*
4 Helen Sharman
5 Thunderbirds / Tracy Family (TV return – boys named after astronauts)
6 Jean Simmons (Stella in film)
7 John Daly (US PGA – Nick Price withdrew to be with his wife, thus creating a place for Daly)
8 Longstone / Farne Lighthouse (now automatic)
9 Bob Hope
10 Andrew Scott (Van Gogh)

1992–1993

• 1 •

1 Three-year-old (multiple Classics winner)
2 Ravachol
3 Basketball
4 (first) Colour half-tone
5 Put it in tubes
6 (Marquis of) Queensberry Rules (Sullivan v Corbett)
7 Raised type / Braille
8 North Pier (Norwegian ship damaged pier and sank)
9 Aston Villa
10 7′ – 4′8½″ railway gauge

• 2 •

1 Homburg
2 Stetson
3 Davy Crockett
4 Trilby
5 Dolly Varden
6 Bowler (Hat)
7 Anthony Eden
8 (Johnny) Fedora
9 Tam O'Shanter
10 Busby

• 3 •

1 Lady Day
2 Spy Wednesday
3 Collop Monday
4 Wrenning Day
5 Hock-Day (Monday / Tuesday)
6 Coronation Day
7 Carling / Carle / Care Sunday
8 Mumping Day
9 Man Friday
10 Sheffield Wednesday

• 4 •

1 Fighting among the players
2 On horseback
3 1850 (by Wisden himself)

4 Sir Arthur Conan Doyle
5 E B Alletson (189 for Notts)
6 Rachel Heyhoe-Flint
7 C K Nayudu
8 William ('Fergie') Ferguson (scorer)
9 Playing soccer (for Doncaster Rovers)
10 Middlesex (badge)

• 5 •

1 Castor (beaver)
2 Beetle
3 Hawk
4 Chad
5 Mouse
6 Morse (Walrus)
7 Grouse
8 (Old) Fox
9 Penguin
10 (Teddy) Bear

• 6 •

1 Yorkshire
2 Hertfordshire
3 Derbyshire
4 Warwickshire
5 Dorset
6 Lincolnshire
7 Buckinghamshire
8 Leicestershire
9 Devon
10 Nottinghamshire

• 7 •

1 *Bread*
2 *Watching*
3 *The Upper Hand*
4 *Cheers*
5 *As Time Goes By*
6 *On the Up*
7 *The Cosby Show*
8 *Waiting for God*
9 *One Foot in the Grave*
10 *Bread*

• 8 •

1 Oder-Neisse Line
2 Tram Line
3 Fall Line
4 Siegfried Line
5 Line of the Treaty of Tordesillas / Line of Demarcation (1494)
6 International Date Line
7 Settle–Carlisle Line
8 Thin Red Line
9 Datum Line
10 Bee Line

• 9 •

1 Hoo
2 Wither
3 Watt
4 Wen
5 Witch
6 Howe (1st Earl)
7 Wye
8 Ware
9 Hughes
10 Hulme (Denny 1967)

• 10 •

1 Le Chevalier de Maison Rouge
2 The Man in the Iron Mask
3 Louise de la Vallière
4 Marguerite de Valois
5 Chicot the Jester
6 The Regent's Daughter
7 The Count of Monte-Cristo
8 The Conspirators
9 The Vicomte de Bragalonne
10 The Black Tulip

• 11 •

1 Lemon-week
2 Yellow River
3 Red Button
4 Green Room
5 Black Nell
6 Grey Eminence
7 Orange Grass
8 Blue John

9 Purple Emperor
10 Brown Bomber

• 12 •

1 most southerly point of Wales
2 most easterly point of Scotland
3 most westerly point of Northern Ireland
4 most westerly point of England
5 most westerly point of Scotland / island / GB
6 most westerly point of Wales
7 most southerly point of Northern Ireland
8 most southerly point of Scotland
9 most easterly point of Wales
10 most northerly point of England

• 13 •

1 Robin Hood
2 Aladdin
3 Puss-in-Boots
4 Dick Whittington (and his cat)
5 Peter Pan
6 Jack and the Beanstalk
7 Robinson Crusoe
8 Cinderella
9 Mother Goose
10 Humpty Dumpty

• 14 •

1 Catseye studs
2 Clarence Birdseye
3 *Eyeless in Gaza*
4 Cockeyed
5 Black-eyed Susan
6 Eye of the Baltic
7 Eye
8 Deadeye / Dead-Man's Eye
9 All my eye and Betty Martin
10 Eye of newt

• 15 •

1 Georges Nagelmackers
2 Paris (Gare de l'Est was then Gare de Strasbourg)

3 Orient Express
4 Frankfurt (into the buffet – brake failure)
5 Simplon Tunnel
6 Railway delay (That snowstorm!)
7 Mata-Hari
8 Magda Lupescu
9 The kitchen chef
10 'Murdered' on the Orient Express

• 16 •

1 The Neck-Verse
2 (Black as) Newgate's Knocker
3 William Penn
4 William Joyce ('Lord Haw-Haw')
5 a rat
6 The Distribution of Livery Cloth
7 The Lady of Justice
8 The United Nations Gang (2 Puerto Ricans, 2 West Indians, 2 Irishmen, 2 Englishmen)
9 None
10 Scarlet Band (worn by High Court Judge)

• 17 •

1 'Too Darn Hot'
2 'Anything Goes'
3 'Let's Do It'
4 'Just one of Those Things'
5 'The Lady is a Tramp'
6 'I'm Always True to You, Darling, in My Fashion'
7 'My Heart Belongs to Daddy'
8 'Begin the Beguine'
9 'I've Got You Under My Skin'
10 'Miss Otis Regrets'

• 18 •

1 Zadok (record on Classic FM radio)
2 Gary (Mason – London Crusaders – Rugby League)
3 Vale of Glamorgan (smallest elected majority)
4 Dundee (*Dundee Courier* – 170 years of advertisements)

5 Solo Synchronised Swimming
6 Baroness Thatcher of Kesteven
7 (Astronaut) Sergei Krikalyev
8 *Queen Elizabeth II* (RMS)
9 Bernard Weatherill (then Speaker)
10 Lord's (MCC v Germany)

1993–1994

• 1 •

1 HMS *Havock* and *Hornet*
2 Shredded Wheat
3 Francis Carruthers Gould (first staff cartoonist)
4 Thomas Edison (first film studio – revolved towards light)
5 Manx Electric Railway (D and LCET)
6 Oxford University
7 Peter Rabbit
8 Liverpool Overhead Railway
9 (first hollow cast lead) 7 Model Soldiers (Messrs Britain mnf.)
10 Corinth Canal

• 2 •

1 This Little Pig (No. 3)
2 (Drowning of) Gadarene Swine
3 The Year of the Pig
4 the Pig-fish
5 The Empress of Blandings
6 Napoleon Pig
7 Little Pig Robinson
8 Pannage
9 Pig-wife
10 Landrace

• 3 •

1 1938 (Hurricane)
2 1703 (Great Storm)
3 1902 (Mt Pelée)
4 1888 (Blizzard)
5 1912 (Fog, *Titanic*, 'Unsinkable Molly Brown')
6 1945 (Fog, Air Crash)

7 1939 (Earthquake)
8 1816 (Frost)
9 1833 (Krakatoa)
10 1966 (Flood)

• 4 •

1 The primrose way (Macbeth)
2 Bluebell Line
3 a rose-red city (Petra)
4 The Scarlet Pimpernel
5 Daisy cutter
6 Corporal Violet
7 Tiger Lily
8 The Lavender Hill Mob
9 Stocks and Shares
10 Hyacinth Bucket

• 5 •

1 Salmon
2 Sea Otter fur
3 Cordova
4 Skagway
5 Halibut
6 'Gold'
7 Soapy (con-man)
8 Raven
9 (The purchase of) Alaska ($7,200,000 from Russia)
10 The rest of mainland USA (the Alaskan view)

• 6 •

1 Psyche
2 Thetis
3 Agincourt
4 Amphitrite
5 Renown
6 Vengeance
7 Bellerophon
8 Henry Grâce à Dieu
9 Iphigenia
10 Andromache

• 7 •

1 Lauren Bacall
2 Sophia Loren
3 Joan Crawford

4 Vivien Leigh
5 Rita Hayworth
6 Marlene Dietrich
7 Julie Andrews
8 Jean Harlow
9 Ginger Rogers
10 Brigitte Bardot

• 8 •

1 Foggy Bottom (Washington DC Metro)
2 Madeleine (Paris Metro)
3 Pimlico (London Underground)
4 Saarlandstrasse (Hamburg U-Bahn)
5 Four Lane Ends (Newcastle Metro)
6 Namesty Republicky (Prague Metro)
7 Wall (New York Subway)
8 Charlottenlund (Copenhagen S-tog)
9 Dhoby Ghaut (Singapore MRT)
10 Möckenbrücke (Berlin U-Bahn)

• 9 •

1 Sir J Bazalgette
2 Sir Giles Gilbert Scott
3 Thomas Telford
4 Thomas Rickman
5 Abraham Darby
6 Robert Stevenson
7 Isambard Kingdom Brunel
8 Sir Benjamin Baker and Sir John Fowler
9 Sir Horace Jones (and Sir John Barry)
10 John Rennie

• 10 •

1 Merry-go-round
2 Merry Monarch (Charles II)
3 Merrythought
4 Meg Merrilies
5 *The Merry Wives of Windsor*
6 Merry Dun of Dover
7 Merry Men of May
8 Henry Seton Merriman
9 The Merry Widow
10 The Merrie Citie

• 11 •

1 Harold Larwood
2 Sam Snead
3 Eric Bristow
4 Babe Ruth
5 Stanley Matthews
6 Rod Laver
7 Jean Borotra
8 Tom Morris
9 George Headley
10 Bill Shoemaker (9000+ winners)

• 12 •

1 Satin
2 Angora
3 Damask
4 Nylon
5 Fustian
6 Chenille
7 Poplin
8 Seersucker
9 Nankeen
10 Denim

• 13 •

1 Buck Ruxton
2 Norman Cecil Rutherford
3 Frederick Henry Seddon
4 John Reginald Halliday Christie
5 Neville Heath
6 John Donald Merrett
7 Hawley Harvey Crippen
8 Guenther Fritz Podola
9 Arthur Boyce
10 Jack the Ripper

• 14 •

1 Rudge
2 Ariel
3 BSA
4 Vincent
5 Matchless
6 Royal Enfield
7 Scott
8 Triumph
9 Norton
10 Velocette

• 15 •

1 Stattis Fair
2 Hood Game
3 (Outgoing and incoming) mayors
4 Marbles (individual)
5 The Merry-go-round Mayor
6 Hare Pie Scramble *AND* Bottle Kicking
7 Tuppenny Starvers
8 Bakers and Sweeps
9 Nutters
10 The Whuppity Scourie

• 16 •

1 Running the Gauntlet
2 The Rack
3 Ostracism
4 Garrotte
5 Keel-hauling
6 Peine Forte et Dure
7 Lynching/Hanging *BEFORE* Trial
8 Guillotine/Louisette
9 Strappado
10 Drawn, Hanged, Drawn, Beheaded and Quartered

• 17 •

1 Myrrh
2 Flysch
3 Styx (Milton)
4 Fry
5 Glyph
6 Pygmy
7 Syzygy
8 Fyrd
9 Pnyx
10 Tryst

• 18 •

1 Andy Nicol (Rugby Union – sixth-minute injury)
2 Andorra (independence)
3 Aintree/Grand National (starter, jockey/horse)
4 Buckingham Palace

5 Manchester Academy of Fine Arts (Carly Johnson – aged 4)
6 Holbeck Hall Hotel
7 Roy Race (of the Rovers – started in the *Tiger*)
8 Coronation Anniversary Crown/£5
9 Housebreaking/Burglary
10 President Clinton

1994–1995

• 1 •

1 Chewing gum
2 Thirlmere Dam / Manchester Water Supply
3 Stamps (previously only official cards with printed stamps)
4 Striptease
5 Napoleon Bird (of Stockport – on the piano)
6 Alfred Dreyfus
7 *The Yellow Book*
8 North Borneo
9 Marks and Spencer
10 Nicholas II

• 2 •

1 Tishri (Jewish Calendar)
2 February
3 November
4 August
5 *The Hunt for Red October*
6 (Jane) Avril
7 July
8 May (*Canterbury Tales*)
9 May-Duke (Médoc)
10 Joulukuu (Finnish)

3.

1 Hiawatha's Photographing
2 *A Tour of Russia* (Journal)
3 In acrostics
4 Syzygy
5 Lanrick
6 Wilhem von Schmitz

7 *Crundle Castle*
8 *Through the Looking Glass*
9 A Kill-Ease and Taught-Us
10 I Love Man / Isle of Man

4.

1 Sagittarius
2 Gemini
3 Capricornus
4 Scorpio
5 Pisces
6 Aries (R A M)
7 Taurus
8 Libra
9 Leo
10 Cancer

• 5 •

1 Murrey
2 Umber
3 Jade
4 Maroon
5 Mustard
6 Bay
7 Dun
8 Or
9 Sepia
10 Sorrel

• 6 •

1 Paul Nicholas
2 Vera McKechnie
3 Oliver Postgate
4 Sir Michael Hordern
5 Eric Thompson
6 Ringo Starr / Michael Angelis
7 Kenneth Williams
8 Arthur Lowe
9 John Alderton
10 Christopher Plummer

• 7 •

1 Old Dominion
2 Old Moore's Almanac
3 Old Humphrey
4 Old Dreadnought
5 Old Rowley
6 Old Mortality
7 Old Tom
8 Old Man of the Sea
9 Old Rough and Ready
10 Old Fogs

• 8 •

1 Rudolf, the Prisoner (of Z)
2 Francis Wortley, Dragon (of W)
3 Dr Primrose, the Vicar (of W)
   George-à-Green, the Pinner (of W)
4 Sir Kenneth of Scotland, Knight (of the L)
5 Michael Henchard, the Mayor (of C)
6 Christy Mahon, the Playboy (of the WW)
7 Uncas, the Last (of the M)
8 Lucy, the Bride (of L)
9 Soames Forsyte, the Man (of P)
10 Silas Marner, the Weaver (of R)

• 9 •

1 Viola
2 Pipe
3 Sax
4 Lute
5 Flute
6 Chimes
7 Cornet
8 Hautboy
9 Flageolet
10 Recorder

• 10 •

1 James Crichton
2 Passepartout
3 Mrs Mopp
4 Mrs Hudson
5 Mark Tapley
6 Uncle Tom
7 Cato
8 Simple
9 Mrs Pearce
10 Rochester

• 11 •

1 Odin's father
2 his spear
3 his steed (8-legged)
4 his wolves
5 his ships
6 Odin
7 his black ravens
8 his throne
9 his ring
10 his wife

• 12 •

1 Dead
2 Red
3 Black
4 Pacific
5 Ross
6 Coral
7 Caribbean (Jamaica)
8 Mediterranean
9 Baltic
10 Aral

• 13 •

1 Flea
2 Maggot
3 Ladybird
4 Ant
5 Earwig
6 Daddy Longlegs/Cranefly
7 Centipede
8 Spider
9 Louse
10 Horsefly/Gadfly

• 14 •

1 Strong Ale/Tipsy cake
2 Curl of hair
3 Salt herring
4 Ass's foal
5 Hammer
6 Croaking frogs
7 Drizzle
8 No warning at all

9 A bent playing card (to cheat the cut)
10 Elm

• 15 •

1 Bristol Fighter
2 Albatros D III
3 Sopwith Camel
4 Ilyushin I 1-2 Sturmoviks (36,000)
5 Messerschmitt 109
6 Mustang P-51 (North American Aviation Inc)
7 Rolls Royce Kestrel
8 de Havilland Mosquito
9 Fokker Eindecker
10 Gloster Gladiators

• 16 •

1 Thomas Jefferson
2 Herbert Clark Hoover
3 Theodore Roosevelt
4 James Monroe
5 Dwight David Eisenhower
6 Harry S Truman
7 Ulysses Simpson Grant
8 John Fitzgerald Kennedy
9 Grover Cleveland
10 Andrew Jackson

• 17 •

1 … is a stew spoiled
2 An invalid
3 Napkin folds
4 Nine
5 Breakfast
6 Fading
7 5 ounces
8 Ostrich feathers
9 Sept(ember)
10 30 mins

• 18 •

1 FA touchlines (first woman to qualify)
2 New Zealand

3 The Old Lady of Threadneedle Street/The Bank of England
4 Suzanne Charlton (married tennis pro, Nick Brown)
5 Fred Lindop (RL to RU)
6 Holland
7 North York Moors/Fylingdales
8 Robin Knox-Johnston and Peter Blake (Eat New Zealand Apples = ENZA non-stop round the world yacht Record)
9 Barbie (Mattel outbid Hasbro for J W Spear and Sons)
10 Sheep broke into 'James Herriot's' garden and broke his leg

1995–1996

• 1 •

1 The Northern Union (which LATER became the Rugby Football League)
2 Heinz Baked Beans (in tomato sauce)
3 First woman dental surgeon (Britain)
4 The (un/stopped) hosepipe
5 The gymslip
6 First theatrical knighthood just conferred on Sir Henry Irving
7 First US Open Golf Championship (Rhode Island)
8 The Kiel Canal
9 Sir Henry Wood (The Proms)
10 King C Gillette (inv. safety razor)

• 2 •

1 The Little Mermaid (Copenhagen)
2 Oscar
3 Nelson's Column
4 Liberty (enlightening the world – New York and France)
5 St Michael and the Devil (Coventry)
6 Mount Rushmore (Washington, Jefferson, LINCOLN and T Roosevelt)

7 Peter Pan (Kensington Gardens)
8 Eros (Piccadilly Circus)
9 Life to Death (Frogner Park, Oslo)
10 The Spirit of Ecstasy (Rolls Royce)

• 3 •

1 The Flying Scotsman
2 Coronation Scot
3 Alabam
4 Claude Monet
5 Birmingham
6 Hector Berlioz
7 Charters and Caldicott/Basil Radford and Naunton Wayne
8 The Whip
9 Will Hay (*Oh Mr Porter*)
10 *The Ghost Train* (Arnold Ridley)

• 4 •

1 Marion's Tortoise (152 y. auth)
2 (Academy Award for) Photography
3 Eric Satie (*Vexations* – roughly one minute, but scored for 840 repeats – approximately 4 hours)
4 Shelley's *Epipsychidion*
5 Deryck Guyler (the voice on the radio)
6 Joe Louis (1937–49)
7 'Lord' Sutch
8 *New Hope for Britain* (Labour Party Manifesto 1983 Gerald Kaufman quote)
9 Supercalifragilisticexpialidocious
10 He who laughs last

• 5 •

1 Sir P F Warner
2 A P Freeman
3 F H Tyson
4 F R Spofforth
5 W Lillywhite
6 J W H T Douglas
7 G L Jessop
8 K Mackay
9 G O B Allen
10 H J Tayfield

• 6 •

1 Monday after New Year's Day
2 Wednesday (Mercredi)
3 Thursday (Lutheran Church)
4 Friday (started, finished, found etc.)
5 Sunday/'Stir Up' Sunday
6 Tuesday/Hock Tuesday
7 Spy Wednesday
8 Sir Robin Day
9 Maundy Thursday
10 Doris Day

• 7 •

1 Vitelline
2 Ratline
3 (Radio) Caroline
4 Praline
5 Emmeline (Pankhurst)
6 Moline
7 Vaseline
8 Cymbeline
9 Carline
10 Line

• 8 •

1 Pollyanna
2 Polly Oliver
3 Polly-wolly-doodle
4 Polly Peachum
5 Polly Peck (Asil Nadir)
6 Polly (Apollinaris water)
7 Polly Flinders
8 Mr Polly
9 Polly (P J) Hervey
10 Polly Scobell (mother of Barbara Cartland)

• 9 •

1 Germany (Deutsch)
2 Reconstructed doll (from parts of others)
3 Effanbee (US doll makers)
4 (Margarete) Steiff (her first toy was an elephant used until 1903/4 as a trademark on ear button)

5 G Drayton (watermelon smile)
6 Automata
7 Kewpie doll
8 Doll's house
9 Teddy bears
10 Teddy's tummy

• 10 •

1 Curtiss JN-4 (Great War trainer)
2 Ford Trimotor
3 DH 100 Vampire
4 Mosquitos
5 Douglas C47/Dakota (as Vietnam gunship)
6 The Gladiators of Malta
7 The Thrust Measuring Rig/TMR
8 Dornier's Do 17
9 Fairey Swordfish
10 Junker's Ju 52/3m

• 11 •

1 The Devil's Missionary
2 The Devil's Own
3 The Devil (on two sticks)
4 The Devil and St Dunstan ('Gone to the Devil')
5 The Devil's Dyke
6 Devil's Bridge
7 The Devil's Arrows
8 The Devil's Bird
9 The Devil's Throat
10 The Devil's Bones

• 12 •

1 Swanee Whistle
2 Turkish (Crescent)
3 Kit (pochette)
4 Tromba Marina (nun's fiddle)
5 Serpent
6 Xylophone
7 Hurdy-gurdy
8 Jew's Harp
9 Banjulele
10 Clarinet

· 13 ·

1 Snoopy's sisters
2 Rerun
3 Puppy Farm (Snoopy etc)
4 Barber
5 Spike, Marbles, (Ugly) Olaf, Andy and Rover
6 Woodstock, Conrad, Bill, Oliver and Harriet
7 *L'il Folks*
8 Linus van Pelt
9 Pigpen
10 The little girl with red hair

· 14 ·

1 '0' gauge (Hornby)
2 Meccano
3 Queen Mary
4 Meccano (Liverpool)
5 Stirling Moss (Dinky)
6 Never produced though in the catalogue
7 (Butthen) Mazak (Dinky casting alloy)
8 Sold for £12,100 (Dinky – 1994 Christie's)
9 India (Dinky-Calcutta)
10 Frank Hornby

· 15 ·

1 J F Kennedy
2 R H Dana
3 George Sand
4 Scheherazade
5 Wimbledon (Head Groundsman)
6 It started to rain/the flood
7 Dunmow
8 Hoover Dam (Nevada/Arizona border – time zone)
9 The Year of Confusion (BC 46)
10 Ray Milland/Dan Birnam (the character)

· 16 ·

1 Waverley Station (after the draining)
2 (Greyfriars) Bobby

3 A bowshot
4 Mons Meg
5 Deacon (William) Brodie (Dr J and Mr H)
6 James de Witt
7 Esses/ss – (Sanctuary line of Holyrood Abbey)
8 The Heart of Midlothian
9 Castle Esplanade (part ceded by Charles I)
10 Edinburgh (Camera Obscura)

· 17 ·

1 Randolph Scott
2 Tex Ritter
3 Hank Williams
4 Roy Rogers
5 Tom Mix
6 The Lone Ranger/Clayton Moore (also Lee Powell or Robert Livingston)
7 Gene Autry
8 John Wayne
9 William Boyd/Hopalong Cassidy
10 Gary Cooper

· 18 ·

1 Lester Piggott
2 Became the longest-lived person on record
3 WO ('The Scotswoman')
4 Concorde prototype (Sothebys)
5 Jesse James
6 Lady Penelope (P sold earlier, now 'hosts' a British chat show)
7 Dr Barnardo (150th anniversary)
8 Buckingham Palace (Volkswagen)
9 Rochester (Bishop)
10 the end of amateurism by the Rugby Football Union

1996–1997

• 1 •

1 Utah
2 Louis Rehn
3 Chop-suey
4 *The Daily Mail* ('The Busy Man's Daily Journal')
5 Phil May
6 Britain's first Poodle Parlour
7 Walter Arnold (first speeding fine – 8 mph in 2 mph area)
8 First Olympic Gold Medal (Hop, step and jump)
9 George Burns
10 The first screen kiss

• 2 •

1 Linz (Mozart *Symphony No. 36*)
2 Mauthausen (concentration camp)
3 Durnstein (Blondel)
4 Badgastein (Radon – hot springs)
5 Bad Ischl
6 Braunau am Inn (Adolf Hitler)
7 Wiener Neustadt (Maximillian's remains)
8 Vienna/Wien (wheel)
9 St Wolfgang (*White Horse Inn*)
10 Mayerling (with Crown Prince Rudolf)

• 3 •

1 Coppersmith Barbet
2 Arrowsmith
3 The Village Blacksmith
4 Granny Smith (apple)
5 Demetrius the Silversmith
6 Oliver Goldsmith (*The Good-Natured Man*)
7 George and Weedon Goldsmith
8 A Locksmith (Key is L's daughter)
9 Psmith
10 Ladysmith

• 4 •

1 Waterloo
2 Dettingen
3 Stamford Bridge (1066)
4 Flodden (Scott – *Marmion*)
5 Blenheim (Southey)
6 Naseby (Macaulay)
7 Bosworth (Shakespeare)
8 Agincourt (Shakespeare)
9 Minden
10 Jutland (Ships sunk)

• 5 •

1 Oxford (Dryden)
2 Birmingham (Chesterton – *The Rolling English Road*)
3 Boston (Ingelow – *High Tide on the Coast of Lincolnshire*)
4 Bristol (Macaulay – *The Armada*)
5 London (Shelley – *Peter Bell the Third*)
6 Cambridge (Brooke – *The Old Vicarage, Grantchester*)
7 Shrewsbury (Shakespeare – *Henry IV Part 1*)
8 Cheltenham (Betjeman)
9 Gloucester (Doctor Foster)
10 St Ives (a man with seven wives)

• 6 •

1 The Old Bachelor (Congreve)
2 Old Man of Coniston
3 Old Peculiar (Theakston's)
4 Old Nod the Shepherd
5 Old King Cole
6 Old Deuteronomy (T S Eliot)
7 Old Forge (USA)
8 An Old Person of Cromer (Lear)
9 Old Vic
10 Sir John Oldcastle (Lollard)

• 7 •

1 The Belfry of Sacre Coeur
2 The Louvre
3 Père-Lachaise Cemetery
4 Montfaucon
5 Avenue Foch (was Ave de l'Imperatrice)

6 Church of St Séverin burial ground
7 Place de la Concorde
8 Arc de Triomphe (Rude's sculpture)
9 Notre Dame (Quasimodo)
10 Les Tuilleries

• 8 •

1 Rudyard Kipling – Porcupine
2 Matthew Arnold – Horse
3 Marriott Edgar – Lion
4 Longfellow – Squirrel
5 Henry Williamson – Stoat
6 John Buchan – Elephant
7 R L Stevenson – Donkey
8 George Orwell – Pig
9 Jean de Brunhoff – Monkey
10 Ernest Thompson Seton – Wolf

• 9 •

1 Brasenose College (Brasenhuis)
2 All Souls College
3 Queen's College (Philippa of Hainault – also his wife)
4 Magdalen College
5 Trinity College (above gate)
6 St John's College
7 Merton College
8 Christ Church
9 Exeter College
10 Keble College (Holman Hunt)

• 10 •

1 Madame Breda (*The Three Hostages*)
2 Frederick Barbon (*Castle Gay*)
3 Rev. John Laputa (*Prester John*)
4 Sir Archibald Roylance (*John Macnab*)
5 Mr Caw (*Huntingtower*)
6 Jannie Grobelaar (*Mr Standfast*)
7 General von Oesterzee (*Greenmantle*)
8 Richard Hannay (*The Thirty-Nine Steps*)
9 Miss Barlock (*The Island of Sheep*)
10 Count Paul Jovian (*The House of the Four Winds*)

• 11 •

1 Alexander Pope – *The Rape of the Lock*
2 Oliver Goldsmith – *The Deserted Village*
3 Thomas Gray – *Elegy Written in a Country Churchyard*
4 Michael Flanders – *The Hippopotamus Song*
5 Lewis Carroll – *The Hunting of The Snark*
6 Lord Byron – *Don Juan (Canto Seven)*
7 William McGonagall – *The Tay Bridge Disaster*
8 John Betjeman – *Hunter Trials*
9 Noel Coward – *Mrs Worthington*
10 Lord Tennyson – *The Brook*

• 12 •

1 Teesdale Sandwort
2 The Langdales
3 Lauderdale
4 Walter Mondale (Carter/Reagan)
5 Mulled ale
6 Wensleydale
7 Colindale (London Underground, Northern Line)
8 Ravenglass and Eskdale Railway (reduced gauge)
9 Gordale
10 Deepdale (Preston)

• 13 •

1 Missouri
2 South Dakota
3 Wisconsin
4 Minnesota
5 Colorado
6 Georgia
7 Washington
8 Kansas
9 Oregon
10 Nevada

• 14 •

1 Cockatoo
2 Cuckoo
3 Baloo
4 Ballyhoo
5 Peterloo
6 Portaloo
7 Nanki-Poo
8 Voodoo
9 Belcoo
10 Old Man Kangaroo

• 15 •

1 The Murray Arms, Gatehouse of Fleet
2 The Englischer Hof, Meiringen (Conan Doyle – *The Adventure of the Final Problem*)
3 The Green Tree, Portaway (John Buchan – *Castle Gay*)
4 The Golden Lily, Amiens (Alexandre Dumas – *The Three Musketeers*)
5 The Golden Sheep, Moy (R L Stevenson – *An Inland Voyage*)
6 The Victoria, Cranbourne
7 The Peacock, Islington (Thomas Hughes – *Tom Brown's Schooldays*)
8 The Bell, Edmonton (William Cowper – *The Diverting History of John Gilpin*)
9 The Angel Inn, Plymouth (C S Forester – *A Ship of the Line*)
10 The Fisherman's Rest, Dover (Baroness Orczy – *The Scarlet Pimpernel*)

• 16 •

1 Certificate and choice of sweet (as a reward for coping with a gigantic meal)
2 490 portions
3 'Goodbye, Mr Chips'
4 Glasgow
5 Pounds of haddock and potatoes and bottles of sauce on the annual shopping list

6 1½d (21 years on the same site in Guiseley – original price)
7 2p (Diamond Jubilee of Guiseley opening by The White Cross Hotel)
8 Harry Corbett ('Sooty')
9 Hong Kong
10 Leeds University School of Medicine (for Scientific Research)

• 17 •

1 See you later, alligator
2 Good-bye
3 Pip-pip
4 Ta-ta (Tatar)
5 Ciao (Chow x 2)
6 T T F N
7 Sayonara
8 Arrivederci
9 Farewell (Jack Judge – *Tipperary*)
10 Vale (Guernsey)

• 18 •

1 Gary Kasparov (v. computer)
2 *The Magnificent Seven* (it was!)
3 Red (reintroduction of red telephone boxes and 15 Red Kites from Spain to the Midlands)
4 Buckingham Palace (Nelson Mandela)
5 Two species of pipistrelle in Britain (45 and 55 kHz)
6 Globe Theatre
7 Carrier Pigeon
8 Dorothy Lamour
9 Gurning
10 Morse (Colin Dexter)

1997–1998

• 1 •

1 Galtee More won the Derby
2 H G Wells (*The Invisible Man*)
3 first to drive from Land's End to John O' Groats
4 fatal stabbing of the actor William Terris
5 Johannes Brahms
6 Riesenrad, the giant Ferris wheel in the Prater, Vienna
7 Tate Gallery opened (on site of former Millbank Prison)
8 Snaefell Mines
9 Women's Institute
10 Malaria parasite

• 2 •

1 Nine points of the law
2 Laverlaw
3 Broad Law (Southern Scotland)
4 my law-giver
5 John Law
6 Denis Law
7 The Law of the Jungle (Kipling)
8 Bonar Law
9 Manx Law
10 Salic Law

• 3 •

1 Chandigarh (*Storm in Chandigarh* – Nayantara Sahgal)
2 Krishnapur (*The Siege of Krishnapur* (J G Farrell)
3 Delhi (Song – 'I wonder what happened to him' – Noel Coward)
4 Malgudi (*The Man-eater of Malgudi* – R K Narayan)
5 Seringapatam (*The Moonstone* – Wilkie Collins)
6 Chandrapore (*A Passage to India* – E M Forster)
7 Meridki (*Plain Tales from the Hills* – Rudyard Kipling)
8 Pankot (*The Raj Quartet* – Paul Scott)
9 Powalgarh (*The Man-eaters of Kumaon* – Jim Corbett)
10 Bhowani Junction (*Bhowani Junction* – John Masters)

• 4 •

1 Mr Prout (*Stalky & Co* – Rudyard Kipling)
2 Mr Brocklehurst (*Jane Eyre* – Charlotte Brontë)
3 Andrew Crocker-Harris (*The Browning Version* – Terence Rattigan)
4 Mr Wardlaw (*Prester John* – John Buchan)
5 Walter Rose (*Eric, or Little by Little* – F W Farrar)
6 Wackford Squeers (*Nicholas Nickleby* – Charles Dickens)
7 Dr Augustus Fagan (*Decline and Fall* – Evelyn Waugh)
8 Mr Samuel Quelch (*Billy Bunter Stories* – Frank Richards)
9 Dr Thorneycroft Huxtable (*The Adventure of the Priory School* – Conan Doyle)
10 Holofernes (*Love's Labour's Lost* – William Shakespeare)

• 5 •

1 Salerno (Italy)
2 Inchon (Korea)
3 South of France viz., St Tropez, Frejus, St Raphael, Ste Maxime area
4 Makin, Tarawa, Abemama (Gilbert Islands)
5 Okinawa (Japan)
6 Dieppe (France)
7 Suez (Egypt)
8 Anzio (Italy)
9 San Carlos (Falkland Islands)
10 Grenada (West Indies)

• 6 •

1 Reinhard Heidrich
2 Chris Hani
3 King Alexander of Yugoslavia
4 President Paul Doumer of France
5 Rasputin
6 Tom Mboya
7 President John F Kennedy
8 Leon Trotsky
9 Mahatma Gandhi
10 Itzhak Rabin

• 7 •

1 M – James Bond stories
2 K – Kellogg's Special K cereal
3 A – frame
4 T – bone steak
5 Z – 10th December 1941
6 E – *Yeomen of the Guard* (Gilbert and Sullivan)
7 R – in the month
8 Y – chromosome
9 X – files
10 C – navigation flag

• 8 •

1 Jack-in-the-box
2 Jack by the Hedge (Garlic Mustard – wild flower)
3 Jack Cade
4 Jack the Ripper (kipper – rhyming slang)
5 Jack Horner
6 Jack Ketch (execution of Monmouth – 1685)
7 Jack Point (*Yeomen of the Guard*)
8 Jack Hobbs (197 centuries – Patsy Hendren had 170)
9 Jack Dempsey
10 Jack Juggler (sixteenth-century comedy based on Plautus's *Amphitruo*)

• 9 •

1 Clouded Yellow (butterfly)
2 Yellow Fever Virus

3 Yellow-Dog Dingo (Rudyard Kipling – *Just So Stories*)
4 Yellow-bellies
5 Yellowhammer or Yellow Bunting
6 Yellow Pine
7 Yellow Submarine (original Beatles' single)
8 Yellow River
9 Yellow Sea
10 Yellowhead Pass

• 10 •

1 Small Copper
2 Comma
3 Grizzled Skipper
4 Queen of Spain Fritillary
5 Scotch Argus
6 Purple Emperor
7 Red Admiral
8 Brimstone
9 Camberwell Beauty
10 Grayling

• 11 •

1 Mansell (Hereford and Worcester)
2 Askham (North Yorkshire)
3 Nymet (Devonshire)
4 Woodham (Essex)
5 Yealand (Lancashire)
6 Wellesbourne (Warwickshire)
7 Mellon (Wester Ross)
8 Acton (Salop)
9 Charlton (Somerset)
10 Sibford (Oxfordshire)

• 12 •

1 Addinsell
2 Alfven
3 Paul McCartney
4 Telemann
5 Lumbye
6 Walton
7 Shostakovich
8 Bernstein
9 C P E Bach
10 Mozart

• 13 •

1 English girls (*Utopia Limited*)
2 the Judicial humorist (*The Mikado*)
3 Reginald Bunthorne (*Patience*)
4 Rudolph (*The Grand Duke*)
5 Mad Margaret (*Ruddigore*)
6 Major General Stanley (*The Pirates of Penzance*)
7 Princess Ida
8 Captain Corcoran (*HMS Pinafore*)
9 Dr Daly (*The Sorcerer*)
10 Life (*The Gondoliers*)

• 14 •

1 George Canning
2 William Gladstone
3 Lloyd George
4 Henry Addington
5 Benjamin Disraeli
6 Harold Macmillan
7 William Pitt, Earl of Chatham
8 Ramsay MacDonald
9 Spencer Perceval
10 Stanley Baldwin

• 15 •

1 The Treaty of Nanking
2 Wan Chai (Hong Kong Metro)
3 horses
4 Kitty Fane (W Somerset Maugham – *The Painted Veil*)
5 The Foreign Correspondents' Club (John le Carré – *The Honourable Schoolboy*)
6 Tsing Ma Bridge
7 The Star Ferry
8 a gong (Noel Coward – *Mad Dogs and Englishmen*)
9 Governor Chris Patten (dogs)
10 *South China Morning Post*

• 16 •

1 Liège (railway station)
2 Spa (Pouhan Pierre-le-Grand)
3 Ostend
4 Mons (Meg)

5 Brussels (R L Stevenson – *An Inland Voyage*)
6 Antwerp (Christopher Plantin)
7 Oudenaarde (1708)
8 Lokeren (Robert Browning – *How they brought the good news from Ghent to Aix*)
9 Orval
10 Baarle Hertog

• 17 •

1 Langness (*Clifton*)
2 Slieau Whallian (*Braddan Vicarage*)
3 The Cerebellum (*Dartmoor*)
4 Foxgloves (*Lynton Verses*)
5 Union Mills (*Chalse A Killey*)
6 Douglas (*Tommy Big-eyes*)
7 Oxford College (*Mary Quayle*)
8 King Knut (*Clevedon Verses*)
9 Rangoon (*Betsy Lee*)
10 Skillicorn (*Spes Altera*)

• 18 •

1 Life Peerage for M C Cowdrey
2 Comet Hale-Bopp
3 BA aircraft (tail decoration)
4 under the proposed new runway at Manchester Airport
5 Laurie Lee
6 a helicopter
7 Lord Moynihan
8 bronze of Raoul Wallenberg unveiled in Great Cumberland Place
9 Globe Theatre
10 Mike Tyson

1998–1999

• 1 •

1 Havana (US warship)
2 Captain Joshua Slocum
3 Emperor Franz-Josef of Austria (assassination in Geneva of Empress)
4 Oscar Wilde (*The Ballad of Reading Gaol*)
5 Fashoda
6 Aubrey Beardsley (death from TB in Menton)
7 Radium
8 Peking (New Territories – Hong Kong)
9 *Fighting Ships*
10 death of Gladstone

• 2 •

1 Macavity (T S Eliot)
2 Steve McQueen
3 The Macallan (Malt Whisky)
4 Barbara McClintock
5 McBurney (Surgery)
6 Dickson McCunn (John Buchan – *The House of the Four Winds*)
7 Flora MacDonald
8 Ed McBain
9 Hairy Maclary (Lynley Dodd)
10 MacArthur

• 3 •

1 Drambuie
2 Cuarenta y Tres (43)
3 Grand Marnier
4 Chartreuse
5 Van der Hum
6 Advocaat
7 Sambuca
8 Galliano
9 Benedictine
10 Cointreau

• 4 •

1 Klaus Barbie
2 Josef Mengele
3 the SS
4 Otto Skorzeny
5 Adolf Eichmann
6 Heinrich Himmler
7 Joseph Goebbels
8 Walter Schellenberg
9 Rudolf Hess
10 Alois Brunner

• 5 •

1 Beachy Head
2 Burnham on Sea
3 South Stack
4 Turnberry
5 Bell Rock
6 Longstone
7 Happisburgh
8 Chickens Rock
9 Eddystone
10 Godrevy Point

• 6 •

1 Francisco Franco – Spain
2 Antonio Salazar – Portugal
3 Hastings Banda – Malawi
4 Idi Amin – Uganda
5 Nicolae Ceausescu – Romania
6 Anastasio Somoza – Nicaragua
7 Porfirio Diaz – Mexico
8 Benito Mussolini – Italy
9 Saddam Hussein – Iraq
10 Pol Pot – Cambodia

• 7 •

1 Nun (wine)
2 Mum (Betjeman – *Christmas*)
3 Gog (*Ezekiel* 38)
4 Laval
5 Minim
6 Glenelg
7 Eve (Ted Hughes)
8 Ewe (Shakespeare – *Othello*)
9 Abba
10 Anna (Old Indian currency)

· 8 ·

1 Green Howards
2 Green Chartreuse
3 Greenstick fracture
4 J R Green (*Short History of the English People*)
5 Green bottles
6 Greenpeace
7 Greenheart
8 Greenhouse
9 Green Bay
10 Green Woodpecker

· 9 ·

1 *The Honorary Consul*
2 *Monsignor Quixote*
3 *Our Man in Havana*
4 *The Power and the Glory*
5 *The Quiet American*
6 *Stamboul Train*
7 *Dr Fischer of Geneva or The Bomb Party*
8 *A Burnt-Out Case*
9 *The Heart of the Matter*
10 *The Comedians*

· 10 ·

1 King Kong
2 Giant Hogweed
3 Goliath
4 wasps (Jonathan Swift – *Gulliver's Travels*)
5 Cormoran
6 Giant Sequoia
7 Atlas
8 The Cerne Giant
9 Giant Despair
10 Ymir

· 11 ·

1 Modern American Usage
2 Opera
3 Railway guide
4 Manx Dictionary
5 Pharmacopoeia
6 Miracles
7 Film and video guide
8 Music
9 Quotations
10 Cricket

· 12 ·

1 Spanier
2 Russell
3 Billy Strayhorn
4 Julius Adderley
5 Jefferson
6 Joe Nanton
7 Emile Lacoume
8 Charlie Parker
9 Louis Armstrong
10 Manone

· 13 ·

1 Zurich (football team)
2 Arosa (John Buchan – *Mr Standfast*)
3 Baden
4 Matterhorn
5 Lucerne (St Leger)
6 Rosenlaui (Conan Doyle – *The Adventure of the Final Problem*)
7 Basle (offering the papacy to Amadeus VII, who took the title Pope Felix V)
8 Château Chillon
9 Burglen (William Tell)
10 Geneva (railway station)

· 14 ·

1 Mayfly
2 Dragonfly (D G Rosseti – *The House of Life*)
3 Butterfly
4 Flea (Jonathan Swift – *On Poetry*)
5 Cicada (Christopher Morley – *End of August*)
6 Ladybird
7 Bluebottle (*The Goon Show*)
8 Bees (Shakespeare – *The Tempest*)
9 Beetle (Volkswagen)
10 Ant (Norfolk river)

• 15 •

1 *Bellipotent* (Herman Melville – *Billy Budd, Sailor*)
2 *Ribiera* (Captain Marryat – *Mr Midshipman Easy*)
3 *Waterwitch* (T E Brown – *Tommy Big-eyes*)
4 *Euphrosyne* (Virginia Woolf – *The Voyage Out*)
5 *Covenant* (R L Stevenson – *Kidnapped*)
6 *Patna* (Joseph Conrad – *Lord Jim*)
7 *Dulcibella* (Erskine Childers – *The Riddle of the Sands*)
8 *Tankadere* (Jules Verne – *Around the World in Eighty Days*)
9 *Goblin* (Arthur Ransome – *We Didn't Mean to Go to Sea*)
10 *Pinafore* (W S Gilbert – *HMS Pinafore*)

• 16 •

1 Pocahontas
2 Sitting Bull
3 Red Jacket
4 Sequoya
5 Samoset
6 Uncas
7 Rain-in-the-Face
8 Geronimo
9 Pontiac
10 Spotted Tail

• 17 •

1 Thomas Hardy – Drummer Hodge
2 Charles Dibdin – Tom Bowling
3 Walt Whitman – Abraham Lincoln
4 John Milton – Lycidas
5 Dylan Thomas – Ann Jones
6 Percy French – George Grossmith
7 John Dryden – Mr Oldham
8 Abraham Cowley – Mr William Harvey
9 Hilaire Belloc – Jim
10 W H Auden – W B Yeats

• 18 •

1 Little Mermaid (Copenhagen statue)
2 Mark Taylor (declared when equalling Bradman's record 334)
3 Drug-running (7 soldiers of 39th Regiment, Royal Artillery)
4 Honda (Isle of Man TT Races)
5 *Beano* (feature in 60th Birthday number)
6 Infinitive (*New Oxford Dictionary*)
7 John Prescott (driving Honda prototype)
8 Burial of remains of Tsar Nicholas II and family
9 The cane (Amendment of School Standards Framework Bill)
10 Arsenal (Premiership and FA Cup double)

1999–2000

• 1 •

1 Robert Wilhelm Bunsen's
2 Johann Strauss the Younger's
3 Trent Bridge, Nottingham (first Test Match on this ground)
4 First Hague Peace Conference
5 Elgar (*Enigma Variations*)
6 John Rylands (Manchester)
7 Queensland
8 *Belgica*
9 Aspirin
10 Thornycroft (Oliver Cromwell)

• 2 •

1 16th – Mary I
2 14th – Richard II
3 19th – William IV
4 18th – George II
5 12th – Richard I
6 20th – Edward VII
7 15th – Richard III
8 17th – Charles I
9 13th – John
10 11th – Canute

• 3 •

1 Renoir, Pierre
2 Nightingale, Florence
3 Samuel Pepys
4 Rembrandt (van) Rijn
5 Johann Sebastian Bach
6 Fridtjof Nansen
7 Joseph Goebbels
8 Emily Brontë
9 Franz Liszt
10 Kipling, Rudyard

• 4 •

1 1483 (King Richards' accessions)
2 Compo (*Last of the Summer Wine*)
3 Stalky (Rudyard Kipling – *Stalky and Co*)
4 Walcott (West Indies cricketers – the three Ws)
5 Balthazar (nativity)
6 Norrland (divisions of Sweden)
7 Kesteven (Lincolnshire)
8 Stapes (ear ossicles)
9 J (Jerome K Jerome – *Three Men in a Boat*)
10 Arvad (Phoenician triple federation of city states – Tripoli)

• 5 •

1 dik-dik
2 dum dum
3 ro-ro
4 baba
5 beriberi
6 Sing Sing
7 couscous
8 tuk-tuk
9 yo-yo
10 dodo

• 6 •

1 Jack Ruby
2 Onyx
3 Garnet
4 Bombay Sapphire (gin)
5 Opal (*Twelfth Night* Act 2 Scene 4)
6 Diamond Sculls
7 Pearl Harbour
8 Moonstone (Wilkie Collins)
9 HMS *Amethyst*
10 Topaz

• 7 •

1 *Robinson Crusoe* (Daniel Defoe)
2 *Jane Eyre* (Charlotte Brontë)
3 *Out of Africa* (Karen Blixen)
4 *Secret Water* (Arthur Ransome)
5 *Jude the Obscure* (Thomas Hardy)
6 *Animal Farm* (George Orwell)
7 *The Prisoner of Zenda* (Anthony Hope)
8 *Allan Quartermain* (Rider Haggard)
9 *Clea* (Lawrence Durrell)
10 *A Tale of Two Cities* (Charles Dickens)

• 8 •

1 Rudyard Kipling – Peacock
2 Richard Adams – Black-headed Gull
3 John Buchan – Goshawk
4 Longfellow – Plover
5 Edward Lear – Pelican
6 Beatrix Potter – Owl
7 Paul Annixter – Seagull
8 Ernest Thompson Seton – Partridge
9 George Orwell – Raven
10 Henry Williamson – Treecreeper

• 9 •

1 Ginger and Pickles
2 Timmy Tiptoes
3 Pig Robinson
4 Peter Rabbit
5 Mr Jeremy Fisher
6 Pigling Bland
7 Mrs Tiggy-Winkle
8 Jemima Puddle-Duck
9 Squirrel Nutkin
10 Mrs Tittlemouse

ANSWERS

• 10 •

1 George II
2 George Cross
3 Georgetown (Guyana)
4 George Street (Edinburgh)
5 *Royal George*
6 Georgie Porgie
7 George Washington
8 George Formby
9 George Eliot
10 George Du Maurier

• 11 •

1 Grey Mare's Tail
2 Little Grey Rabbit
3 his grey mare
4 Earl Grey tea
5 grey squirrel
6 Greyfriars (Edinburgh)
7 greyhound (*Henry IV Part I*, 1. 3)
8 Lady Jane Grey
9 grey matter
10 Earl of Mar's Grey-Breeks

• 12 •

1 Aachen
2 Dresden (porcelain)
3 Mainz
4 Berlin (Christopher Isherwood – *Goodbye to Berlin*)
5 Hamelin (Robert Browning – *The Pied Piper of Hamelin*)
6 Cologne (Graham Greene – *Stamboul Train*)
7 Nuremberg (Longfellow – *Nuremberg*, re Dürer)
8 Karlsruhe (Jerome K Jerome – *Three Men on the Bummel*)
9 Heidelberg
10 Hamburg

• 13 •

1 Wauchope (Hugh MacDiarmid)
2 Dove (Charles Cotton – *Poems on Several Occasions*)

3 Shannon (Edmund Spenser – *The Faerie Queene*)
4 Medway
5 Evenlode (Hilaire Belloc)
6 Irwell (Marriott Edgar – *Three Ha'pence a Foot*)
7 Trent (John Milton – *At a Vacation Exercise*)
8 Thames (Matthew Arnold – *The Scholar Gipsy*)
9 Tees (Lord Macaulay – *A Jacobite's Epitaph*)
10 Severn (Lord Tennyson – *In Memoriam*)

• 14 •

1 Laughing Water (Longfellow – *The Song of Hiawatha*)
2 Laughing stock
3 Laughing Jackass (Kookaburra)
4 Laughing Hyena
5 *The Laughing Cavalier* (Frans Hals – The Wallace Collection)
6 Laughing Fish Point (Lake Superior)
7 *Laughing Gravy* (1931 film)
8 Laughing queen (Leigh Hunt – *The Nile*, referring to Cleopatra)
9 a laughing Devil (Byron – *The Corsair*)
10 Laughing Gas

• 15 •

1 Peter Abelard
2 Adolf Hitler
3 Horatio Nelson
4 John Profumo
5 Dante
6 Prince Charles Edward Stuart (Bonnie Prince Charlie)
7 Edward Kennedy
8 Napoleon Bonaparte
9 Benito Mussolini
10 Samson

• 16 •

1 Shrewsbury
2 Glasgow
3 Liverpool
4 Hexham
5 Dumfries
6 Beverley
7 Penrith
8 London
9 Cambridge
10 Norwich

• 17 •

1 Roland
2 Ovid
3 Mohammed
4 St Swithin's
5 Boadicea's/Boudicca's
6 Alfred's
7 Charles I, II and II (of the Franks)
8 Hengest
9 Vesuvius
10 Wenceslas

• 18 •

1 Anil Kumble, Jim Laker (all ten wickets in a Test Match innings)
2 Tanzania (Julius Nyerere)
3 Lord Menuhin (memorial service in Westminster Abbey)
4 Sir Vivian Fuchs (polar explorer)
5 Greatest period of totality in eclipse of the sun
6 *Mars* (spacecraft)
7 Manchester United defeating Bayern Munich in final of European Champions' League
8 The discovery of George Leigh Mallory's body on Mount Everest
9 London Eye Ferris wheel
10 Morecambe (statue of Eric)

2000–2001

• 1 •

1 King Umberto I of Italy
2 Frank Baum (*The Wonderful Wizard of Oz*)
3 Zeppelin (airship)
4 Casey Jones
5 John Ruskin
6 Crystal Palace (MCC v London County – Doyle's only wicket in first class cricket)
7 Oscar Wilde
8 Max Planck's (*Quantum Theory*)
9 first fully operational submarine (USS *Holland*)
10 Central Line opened

• 2 •

1 Oranges and lemons
2 Orange Tip butterfly
3 Orange-pekoe tea
4 Orangeburg (South Carolina – February 1968)
5 *The Five Orange Pips*
6 *The Love of the Three Oranges* (Gozzi – Prokofiev)
7 Agent Orange
8 Orange Order
9 Orange River
10 *A Clockwork Orange*

• 3 •

1 James the Red Engine
2 Jesse James
3 Clive James
4 St James (The Greater)
5 James Joyce (*Ulysses*)
6 James James Morrison Morrison Weatherby George Dupree (A A Milne)
7 James Bay (Canada)
8 Henry James
9 King James II
10 P D James

• 4 •

1 *Flying Scotsman*
2 Pullman
3 The Long Man of Wilmington
4 the common man
5 beggarman
6 Kentish Man
7 *Manxman*
8 Flashman
9 dragoman
10 Chinaman

• 5 •

1 Hot Lips Page
2 Fats Waller
3 Cootie Williams
4 Sonny Rollins
5 Jelly Roll Morton
6 Stuff Smith
7 Miff Mole
8 Duke Ellington
9 Bix Beiderbecke
10 Dizzy Gillespie

• 6 •

1 Nicosia (Cyprus)
2 Ottawa (Canada)
3 Sofia (Bulgaria)
4 Amman (Jordan)
5 Wellington (New Zealand)
6 Monrovia (Liberia)
7 Oslo (Norway)
8 Jakarta (Indonesia)
9 Tallinn (Estonia)
10 Ulan Bator (Mongolia)

• 7 •

1 Lacrosse
2 Contract Bridge
3 Shinty
4 Bowls
5 Croquet
6 Rowing
7 Table Tennis
8 Curling
9 Road Walking
10 Eton Fives

• 8 •

1 *Here's Harry*
2 *Only Fools and Horses*
3 *Up the Elephant and Round the Castle*
4 *Hancock's Half Hour*
5 *Sykes*
6 *My Wife Next Door*
7 *George and Mildred*
8 *The Larkins*
9 *Bread*
10 *Upstairs, Downstairs*

• 9 •

1 bullseye
2 goldeneye (diving duck)
3 fisheye
4 a joyless eye (Shelley – *To the Moon*)
5 London Eye (architects of Ferris wheel)
6 lazy eye
7 Dick Deadeye (Gilbert – *HMS Pinafore*)
8 pink-eye
9 black eye
10 Ireland's Eye

• 10 •

1 *La Sonnambula* (Bellini)
2 *La Cenerentola* (Rossini)
3 *La Prophète* (Meyerbeer)
4 *The Gipsy Baron / Der Zigeunerbaron* (Johann Strauss)
5 *Martha* (Flotow)
6 *The Magistrate / Der Corregidor* (Wolf)
7 *La Favorita* (Donizetti)
8 *La Traviata* (Verdi)
9 *Madame Butterfly* (Puccini)
10 *The Bartered Bride* (Smetana)

• 11 •

1 silly billy
2 hocus-pocus
3 lazy daisy
4 brain drain
5 fuddy-duddy
6 jet set

7 mumbo-jumbo
8 willy-nilly
9 Delhi Belly
10 hurdy-gurdy

• 12 •

1 Belarius (*Cymbeline*)
2 Lucentio (*The Taming of the Shrew*)
3 Viola (*Twelfth Night*)
4 Portia (*The Merchant of Venice*)
5 Duke Vicentio (*Measure for Measure*)
6 Sir John Falstaff (*The Merry Wives of Windsor*)
7 Rosalind (*As You Like It*)
8 Julia (*Two Gentlemen of Verona*)
9 Helen (*All's Well That Ends Well*)
10 Kent (*King Lear*)

• 13 •

1 Newfoundland (off Cape Race)
2 Halifax, Nova Scotia
3 Lebanon (off Tripoli)
4 Nantucket Sound
5 St Lawrence River
6 Tobago
7 River Mersey
8 River Thames (London)
9 Philippines (Tablas Strait)
10 Gibraltar

• 14 •

1 Alvis
2 Humber
3 Armstrong Siddeley
4 AC
5 Rover
6 Packard
7 Hispano Suiza
8 Bugatti
9 Farman
10 Graf und Stift

• 15 •

1 Crete
2 Naxos
3 Lesbos
4 Corfu
5 Skyros
6 Samos
7 Rhodes
8 Patmos
9 Kos
10 Ithaca

• 16 •

1 Black Cobra (Rudyard Kipling)
2 Whiteadder
3 A Python (Hilaire Belloc)
4 A Rattlesnake (Lewis Carroll)
5 An Asp
6 The Serpent's
7 Anaconda
8 Snake Pass
9 Blackadder (Rowan Atkinson)
10 Grass Snake

• 17 •

1 Andrew Jackson
2 William Harrison
3 Andrew Johnson / Bill Clinton
4 Thomas Jefferson
5 Theodore Roosevelt
6 John Adams
7 Lyndon B Johnson
8 James A Garfield
9 Woodrow Wilson
10 Franklin D Roosevelt

• 18 •

1 Garry Kasparov (failed to win any games in World Chess Championship defeat)
2 HM Queen Elizabeth II (request for no garlic during State Visit to Italy)
3 Elizabeth Taylor and Julie Andrews received DBE at same ceremony
4 Shane Warne in *Wisden's* Five Cricketers of the Century
5 *Who Wants to be a Millionaire* (wrong answer forfeited £218,000)
6 David Beckham (statue)

7 David Hempelman-Adams (balloon flight over the North Pole)
8 Alec Stewart – Queen Elizabeth, the Queen Mother
9 Hansie Cronje (Piet Cronje was defeated Boer general)
10 The third secret of Fatima (Portugal – 1917)

2001–2002

• 1 •

1 President McKinley
2 Tottenham Hotspur (beat Sheffield United in Cup Final)
3 President Theodore Roosevelt (entertained Booker Washington)
4 London's first electric tram
5 Uganda Railway linking Mombasa and Lake Victoria (Patterson – *The Man-eaters of Tsavo*)
6 Birmingham (Lloyd-George)
7 Frederick Bechstein (Wigmore Street)
8 Edmund Barton (PM of Commonwealth of Australia)
9 King C Gillette
10 Maurice Maeterlinck (*The Life of the Bee*)

• 2 •

1 *The Master of Ballantrae*
2 *Kidnapped*
3 *The Body Snatchers*
4 *The Black Arrow*
5 *Catriona*
6 *Travels with a Donkey in the Cévennes*
7 *An Inland Voyage*
8 *Treasure Island*
9 *The Strange Case of Dr Jekyll and Mr Hyde*
10 *Weir of Hermiston*

• 3 •

1 Stendhal – Shetland
2 The Oval – to halve
3 Lara – Aral
4 Keys – Skye
5 Ascot – Tosca
6 Gonville – live long
7 Caracas – cascara
8 TT races – scatter
9 buckle – Lübeck
10 coasters – Socrates

• 4 •

1 Mo (Norway)
2 St Pawl (Malta)
3 Esch (Luxembourg)
4 Marche (Belgium)
5 Sanlucar (Spain)
6 Rothenburg (Germany)
7 Brive (France)
8 Bassano (Italy)
9 La Chaux (Switzerland)
10 Bergen (Holland)

• 5 •

1 Bubonic Plague (1665)
2 Foot and Mouth Disease (first case – 1839)
3 Typhoid / Enteric Fever (first outbreak – 1839)
4 Anthrax (long-standing contamination ex-World War II)
5 Malaria (last English stronghold)
6 Yellow Fever (1865)
7 Typhus (gaol fever 1522)
8 Cholera (Broad Street – Dr John Snow 1849)
9 Smallpox (1952)
10 Poliomyelitis (1834 first case of Infantile Paralysis)

• 6 •

1 W H Bragg
2 Frederick Banting
3 Barbara McClintock
4 Frederick Sanger

5 Nevill Mott (followed Chadwick at Caius)
6 Gerhard Domagk
7 Werner Forssman
8 Marie Curie
9 Ivan Pavlov
10 Niko Tinbergen

• 7 •

1 perch
2 pike
3 skate
4 dab
5 sole
6 bass
7 gudgeon
8 miller's thumb
9 grayling
10 char

• 8 •

1 Buckingham (George Villiers, Duke of)
2 Rockingham (Charles Watson-Wentworth, Marquis of)
3 Walsingham (Sir Francis)
4 Nottingham
5 Chillingham cattle
6 Gingham
7 Sandringham House
8 Gressingham Ducks
9 Marjorie Allingham
10 John Bellingham

• 9 •

1 *The Blue Boy* (Gainsborough)
2 Bluebonnet
3 Bluecoats (Christ's Hospital)
4 Blue Carbuncle (Conan Doyle)
5 Blue John
6 *The Blue Lamp*
7 Bluebell Line
8 Prussian Blue
9 Blue Peter
10 Blue Mosque (Istanbul)

• 10 •

1 pig
2 chicken
3 dog
4 cow
5 horse
6 turkey
7 sheep
8 goose
9 goat
10 duck

• 11 •

1 Hidalgo
2 Sherry Spinner
3 Sandeman (*Armada Cream*)
4 a bun and glass of sherry (*The Gondoliers* – W S Gilbert)
5 *Tio Pepe*
6 Emilio Lustau
7 wine districts (*pagos*) around Jerez
8 Pedro Domecq
9 Williams and Humbert's (*A Winter's Tale*)
10 Pedro Ximenes (grape variety)

• 12 •

1 Victoria Plum
2 Victoria Cross
3 Victoria Beckham (*Learning to Fly*)
4 Victoria Falls Bridge (1907)
5 *Victoria Louise*
6 Victoria Press
7 Queen Victoria (St Paul's – 1872)
8 Victoria Day
9 *Princess Victoria*
10 Victoria de los Angeles

• 13 •

1 Wulf Schmidt
2 Oleg Penkovsky
3 Juan Pujol Garcia
4 Elyesa Bazna
5 William G Sebold
6 Dusko Popov
7 Michael Goleniewski

8 Jonny Jebsen
9 Ursula Kuczynski
10 Arthur Owens

• 14 •

1 *Ecclesiastes*
2 *I Samuel (Saul)*
3 *Exodus (The 'Adulterous Bible', 1631)*
4 *Jonah (Jonah and the Grampus)*
5 *Zephaniah*
6 *II Kings (the Destruction of Sennacherib)*
7 *Leviticus*
8 *Isaiah* (Chapter 37)
9 *Esther* (Chapter 8 verse 9)
10 *Malachi*

• 15 •

1 Florence
2 Pisa (*Ponte al Mare, Pisa* – Shelley)
3 Syracusa (Archimedes)
4 Amalfi (*Flight the Fourth* – Longfellow)
5 Palermo (Sicilian Vespers, 1282)
6 Bari (St Nicholas)
7 Turin (Martini and Rossi vermouth)
8 Padua (*The Taming of the Shrew* – Shakespeare)
9 Mantua (*Rigoletto*)
10 Salerno (US Fifth Army, 9th September 1943)

• 16 •

1 Castor and Pollux
2 Ross and Norris McWhirter
3 Antipholus of Ephesus and Antipholus of Syracuse (*The Comedy of Errors*, Shakespeare)
4 Neville and Helena Landless (*The Mystery of Edwin Drood* – Charles Dickens)
5 Manuel and Esteban (*The Bridge of San Luis Rey* – Thornton Wilder)
6 Heracles and Iphicles
7 Philip and Dolly Clandon (*You Never Can Tell* – G B Shaw)

8 Daisy and Demi-John (*Good Wives* et al – Louisa M Alcott)
9 Romulus and Remus
10 Ronald and Reginald Kray

• 17 •

1 *Amistad* (1839)
2 *Batavia* (1629)
3 *E A Bryan* (Port Chicago 1944)
4 Invergordon (1931)
5 *Caine* (Herman Wouk)
6 USS *Somers*
7 *Alexander*
8 HMS *Bounty*
9 HMS *Hermione*
10 *Potemkin*

• 18 •

1 new car licence numbers
2 Mir space station
3 Des O'Connor (autobiography – *Bananas Can't Fly*)
4 River Tyne (Millennium Bridge – The Eyelid)
5 Glenalmond
6 brain (BSE research)
7 Ian Woosnam's
8 St Catharine's College, Cambridge
9 Hull Crown Court (Trial of Leeds United footballers)
10 Prince Charles (slapped with flower in Riga)

2002–2003

• 1 •

1 collapse of campanile of St Mark's, Venice
2 King Alfonso XIII of Spain
3 *Just So Stories* (Rudyard Kipling)
4 collapse of stand at Ibrox Park, Glasgow
5 Cecil Rhodes (Scholarships to Oxford)
6 Thornycroft's (Boudicca)

7 creation of London's first crematorium

8 Holloway Prison

9 A J Balfour succeeded his uncle, Lord Salisbury

10 Sunderland (transfer from Sheffield United)

• 2 •

1 Pamplona (Hemingway)

2 Madrid (restaurant)

3 Valladolid (Laurie Lee – *As I Walked Out One Midsummer Morning*)

4 Córdoba

5 Alcalá de Henares

6 Seville (*Don Giovanni*)

7 Cádiz (Drake)

8 Aranjuez (Rodrigo)

9 Corunna / La Coruña (Woolf – *The Burial of Sir John Moore*)

10 Toledo (el Greco)

• 3 •

1 Robert Jenkins

2 Samson

3 Tycho Brahe

4 Squirrel Nutkin

5 Douglas Bader

6 John the Baptist

7 Long John Silver (R L Stevenson – *Treasure Island*)

8 James Scott, Duke of Monmouth

9 King Christian IV of Denmark

10 Horatio Nelson

• 4 •

1 Dirck (Browning – *How they brought the good news from Ghent to Aix*)

2 Herminius (Macaulay – *The Battle of Lake Regillus*)

3 Dick Turpin

4 Hopalong Cassidy

5 Heimdall

6 Nigel Loring (Conan Doyle – *The White Company*)

7 Sir Andrew Aguecheek (Shakespeare – *Twelfth Night*)

8 Cosmo Gaffikin (Siegfried Sassoon – *Memoirs of a Fox-hunting Man*)

9 Don Quixote

10 Mary O'Hara

• 5 •

1 poor little rich girl

2 mad about the boy

3 Mrs Worthington's daughter ('Mrs Worthington')

4 a bit ('I Wonder What Happened to Him')

5 the bar on the Piccola Marina

6 Tunbridge Wells ('There Are Bad Times Just Around the Corner')

7 Fiddledidee ('I've Been to a Marvellous Party')

8 all night ('Let's Do It')

9 on the road to Samarkand ('I Like America')

10 London Pride

• 6 •

1 Forty Foot Drain (Cambridgeshire)

2 Fournocks (Co. Meath)

3 Two Bridges (Devonshire)

4 Ruyton-XI-Towns (Shropshire)

5 The Twelve Pins (Co. Galway: Percy French – *To the West*)

6 Five-Mile-Town (Co. Tyrone: W R Rodgers – *The Character of Ireland*)

7 Ninewells (Dundee)

8 Seven Stones Reef (Scilly Islands)

9 The Three Sisters (Glencoe, Argyllshire)

10 Nine Mile Bar (Kirkcudbrightshire)

• 7 •

1 Parker (published *Advertisements*)

2 Hubert Walter (Richard I)

3 Dunstan (coronation of King Edgar)

4 Sheldon (Sheldonian Theatre, Oxford)

5 Arundel

6 Sudbury (Wat Tyler)

7 Davidson

8 Stigand

9 Pole (Mary I)
10 Theodore

• 8 •

1 Rembrandt
2 Peter Paul Rubens
3 Paul Cézanne
4 Vincent van Gogh
5 Frans Hals
6 Carel Fabritius
7 Paul Gauguin
8 Albrecht Dürer
9 Goya
10 el Greco (*Count Orgaz*)

• 9 •

1 Edam
2 Yarg
3 Wensleydale
4 Roquefort
5 Fontina
6 Banon
7 Cheshire (Ye Olde Cheshire Cheese)
8 Stilton
9 Reblochon
10 Jarlsberg

• 10 •

1 Edward IV
2 Louis XIV of France
3 William IV
4 Henry VIII
5 Louis XV of France
6 George II
7 Frederick IV of Denmark
8 George IV
9 Charles II
10 Edward III

• 11 •

1 zygoma
2 hamate
3 patella
4 clavicle
5 fibula
6 ethmoid

7 hyoid
8 lunate
9 pisiform
10 incus

• 12 •

1 Claire Bloom (*Leaving a Doll's House*, 1996)
2 Terry-Thomas (*Filling the Gap*, 1959)
3 Alec Guinness's (*My Name Escapes Me – Memoirs of a Retiring Actor*, 1996)
4 Errol Flynn's (*My Wicked Wicked Ways*, 1959)
5 Christopher Lee (*Tall, Dark and Gruesome*, 1977)
6 Michael Wilding (*Apple Sauce –* posthumously, 1982)
7 Bob Hope (*I Owe Russia $2000*, 1976)
8 Anthony Quinn (*One Man Tango*, 1995)
9 Peter O'Toole (*Loitering With Intent*, 1993)
10 Omar Sharif (*The Eternal Male*, 1977)

• 13 •

1 Turnberry (13th)
2 Twinkleberry (Beatrix Potter – *The Tale of Squirrel Nutkin*)
3 Hillberry (Isle of Man TT course)
4 Huckleberry Finn (Mark Twain)
5 Chuck Berry
6 Cranberry Tart (Edward Lear – *The Jumblies*)
7 Burberry
8 Mulberry (World War II)
9 Dogberry (Shakespeare – *Much Ado About Nothing*)
10 Strawberry (Beatles' song)

• 14 •

1 scirocco
2 harmattan
3 shamal
4 gregale

5 mistral
6 khamsin
7 pampero
8 levanter
9 chinook
10 Fremantle doctor

• 15 •

1 Berne
2 Brussels (Manneken Pis)
3 Helsinki
4 Linz
5 Rome (Trevi Fountain)
6 Madrid (Fuente de Cibeles)
7 Copenhagen (Gefion Fountain – creation of Zealand)
8 Alton Towers (Pagoda Fountain)
9 Nuremberg
10 Gothenburg

• 16 •

1 3.10 (western film)
2 one (nursery rhyme)
3 10.27 (John Buchan – *The Thirty-Nine Steps*)
4 12 noon (Noel Coward – *Mad Dogs and Englishmen*)
5 ten to three (Rupert Brook – *Grantchester*)
6 a quarter past one (Agatha Christie – *Murder on the Orient Express*)
7 11 am (11th November 1918 Armistice)
8 8.40 am
9 8.45 (Jules Verne – *Around the World in Eighty Days*)
10 8 pm

• 17 •

1 Christ's College, Cambridge
2 Jesus College
3 Robinson College
4 Queens' College
5 Pembroke College (Wren)
6 Magdalene College (Pepys)
7 Trinity College (Byron by Thorvaldsen)

8 Sidney Sussex College
9 Gonville and Caius College (gates)
10 St John's College (Wordsworth)

• 18 •

1 Kenneth Wolstenholme
2 Dotty, Princess Royal's English Bull Terrier
3 Lady Thatcher's (statue in Guildhall Library)
4 successful nesting of Bee-eaters
5 Lonnie Donegan
6 Graham Henry – Wales
7 La Linea (Southern Spain)
8 Metropolitan Museum of Art, New York (Lombardo's fifteenth-century statue)
9 Lord Howe
10 elevation to city

2003–2004

• 1 •

1 Mrs Emmeline Pankhurst
2 20 mph
3 Apolinario Mabini (Philippino politician)
4 E D Morel's (*The West African Mail*)
5 Lord Macaulay's
6 W and G Foyle's
7 Major General Sir Hector Macdonald
8 Paul Gauguin
9 Tour de France
10 Pope Pius X

• 2 •

1 Patrick Steptoe (test tube babies)
2 Gregory Pincus (the birth pill)
3 Christiaan Barnard
4 Humphry Davy
5 Louis Braille
6 Luc Montagnier (HIV)
7 Antonio Egaz Moniz (pre-frontal leucotomy)

8 René Laënnec
9 Selman Waksman (Streptomycin)
10 Gregor Mendel

• 3 •

1 Vincent van Gogh
2 Maurice Utrillo
3 John Constable (Salisbury)
4 Camille Pissaro (Dieppe)
5 Jean-Baptiste Camille Corot (Mantes-la-Jolie)
6 Claude Monet (Rouen)
7 Canaletto (Westminster Abbey)
8 Pieter Jansz. Saenredam
9 Carl Larsson
10 Marcel Duchamp

• 4 •

1 King Oliver
2 Scott Joplin
3 Duke Ellington
4 Hoagy Carmichael
5 P Babarin
6 Spencer Williams
7 Count Basie
8 Kid Ory
9 Jelly Roll Morton
10 W C Handy

• 5 •

1 sweetbreads
2 Bombay duck
3 lemon cheese
4 Scotch woodcock
5 Welsh rabbit
6 mince pies
7 toad in the hole
8 Cullen skink
9 hot dog
10 devils on horseback

• 6 •

1 pi
2 kappa
3 mu
4 Omega (watch)
5 gamma gobulin

6 alpha rhythm
7 lambda
8 beta (drug development)
9 Delta (south-west Holland)
10 iota

• 7 •

1 Arnhem
2 Rotterdam (Erasmusbrug 1996)
3 The Hague (suburb Scheveningen)
4 Amsterdam (Van der Valk)
5 Delft (assassination of William the Silent)
6 Eindhoven (Philips)
7 Utrecht (1713)
8 'sHertogenbosch (Hieronymus Bosch)
9 Leeuwarden (long-distance skating race)
10 Flushing / Vlissingen (Arthur Ransome – *We Didn't Mean to Go to Sea*)

• 8 •

1 Crazy Horse (Ogala Sioux chief)
2 8 horsepower
3 Dala / Dalarna horse (Swedish souvenir)
4 Horseshoe Farm, Finchley
5 Horse's Neck
6 The Wooden Horse
7 Whitehorse (Yukon Territory, Canada)
8 the horseleach (*Proverbs* 30. 15)
9 Horsehead
10 a Stalking Horse (challenged Margaret Thatcher's leadership of the Conservative party in 1989)

• 9 •

1 Barcelona
2 Bordeaux
3 Seville
4 Venice
5 Como
6 Lisbon
7 Marseille

8 Gent
9 Angers
10 Porto

• 10 •

1 Yew (Nevern, Pembrokeshire –
   weeps a thick blood-like sap)
2 Douglas Fir (Dunkeld – highest tree
   in Britain)
3 Birch
4 Willows
5 Glastonbury Thorn / Hawthorn
   (Arimathea legend)
6 The Walnut Tree (Inn at Aldington)
7 Oak (Charles II)
8 Monkey Puzzle / Chile Pine
9 Lime tree (Kent CCC, Canterbury)
10 Chestnut tree (Longfellow – *The
   Village Blacksmith*)

• 11 •

1 Black Sea
2 Black Prince
3 Penny black
4 black spot (R L Stevenson – *Treasure
   Island*)
5 Mr Blackboy (Dickens – *David
   Copperfield*)
6 Black Paquito (Shaw – *Captain
   Brassbound's Conversion*)
7 Black Hastings (war horse of Sir
   Geoffrey Peveril – Scott – *Peveril of
   the Peak*)
8 blackhead
9 Black Annis
10 Black Mamba

• 12 •

1 *The Lord of the Rings* (Tolkien)
2 *The Old Bachelor* (William Congreve)
3 *The Master of Ballantrae* (R L
   Stevenson)
4 *The Deemster* (Hall Caine)
5 *The Man with the Golden Gun* (Ian
   Fleming)
6 *The Faithful Ally* (Eric Linklater)
7 *The Black Dwarf* (Sir Walter Scott)

8 *The Spy* (James Fennimore Cooper)
9 *The Spy Who Came in from the Cold*
   (John le Carré)
10 *The Red Pony* (John Steinbeck)

• 13 •

1 Matthew
2 Andrew
3 James (the Great) (Coquille St
   Jacques)
4 Bartholomew
5 Peter
6 Judas Iscariot
7 John
8 Jude
9 Thomas
10 Matthias

• 14 •

1 Rook (*frugilegus*)
2 Dunnock / Hedge Sparrow
   (*Prunella*)
3 Cattle Egret (*Bubulcus*)
4 Puffin (*Fratercula*)
5 Moorhen (*Gallinula chloropus*)
6 Wigeon (*penelope*)
7 Little Grebe (*Tachybaptus*)
8 Eider (*Somateria mollissima*)
9 Nightjar (*Caprimulgus*)
10 Great Grey Shrike (*Excubitor*)

• 15 •

1 Jane (Rapturous Maidens – *Patience*
   – W S Gilbert)
2 women (relating to Kent – *Pickwick
   Papers* – Charles Dickens)
3 Cagliari (Provinces of Sardinia)
4 Götterdämmerung (*The Ring Cycle*
   – Wagner)
5 Oona O'Neill (Charlie Chaplin's
   wives)
6 Peter Schidlof (The Amadeus
   Quartet)
7 The Dry Salvages *(The Four Quartets*
   – T S Eliot)
8 Fitzurse (murderers of Thomas
   a'Becket)

9 Mount Olive (*The Alexandria Quartet* – Lawrence Durrell)

10 roast beef (little pigs)

• 16 •

1 Powerscourt (Co. Wicklow)
2 Cauldron Snout (River Tees)
3 Mynach Falls (Devil's Bridge, Dyfyd)
4 Plodda Falls (Glen Affric, Inverness-shire)
5 Pistyll Rhaeadr (Powys)
6 Glenmaye (Manx fairytale)
7 Lodore Falls (Cumbria – Southey – *Rhymes for the Nursery*)
8 Falls of Clyde (New Lanark – painting in Scottish National Gallery)
9 Aira Force (Cumbria – Wordsworth – *The Somnambulist*)
10 Grey Mare's Tail (Dumfries and Galloway)

• 17 •

1 founder of IKEA
2 Svante Arrhenius
3 Jakob Johan Anckarström (King Gustav III's assassin)
4 Dag Hammarskjöld
5 Alfred Nobel
6 Ingemar Johansson (World Heavyweight Boxing Champion)
7 King Karl X Gustav
8 Queen Kristina
9 Selma Lagerlöf
10 Carl von Linné / Linnaeus

• 18 •

1 Sir Ranulph Fiennes
2 David Beckham (boot kicked by Ferguson)
3 flight across English Channel without power
4 Andrew Hall (four Test innings for South Africa)
5 Silvio Berlusconi
6 Robert Coleman Atkins

7 Aaron Barschak (gatecrashing Prince William's 21st birthday party)
8 Bob Hope (own one-liner)
9 Peterborough (changed to London Spy – *Daily Telegraph*)
10 Referendum on European Monetary Union

2004–2005

• 1 •

1 Rockall (wreck of *Norge*)
2 Oseberg ship
3 Charles Rennie Mackintosh (The Willow Tea Rooms in Sauchiehall Street, Glasgow)
4 Sisavang Vong of Laos
5 Anton Chekhov
6 *Madame Butterfly*
7 Royal Horticultural Society
8 St Louis (3rd Olympic Games)
9 Fire on paddle steamer *General Slocum* in New York harbour
10 launching of Tr.S.S. *Manxman*

• 2 •

1 Francis Davey (Daphne du Maurier – *Jamaica Inn*)
2 The Vicar of Bray
3 Rev. Sam Weech (*The Titfield Thunderbolt*)
4 William Collins (Jane Austen – *Pride and Prejudice*)
5 Mr Chadband (Charles Dickens – *Bleak House*)
6 Mr Roundhay (Conan Doyle – *The Adventure of the Devil's Foot*)
7 Mr Brocklehurst (Charlotte Brontë – *Jane Eyre*)
8 Dr Daly (W S Gilbert – *The Sorcerer*)
9 Rev. John Laputa (John Buchan – *Prester John*)
10 Rev. Josiah Crawley (Anthony Trollope – *Framley Parsonage*)

• 3 •

1 Walker Art Gallery (George Stubbs)
2 the Boswells (Carla Lane – *Bread*)
3 Sir John and Cecil Moores
4 Wellington/Waterloo Monument (Melville Monument)
5 Carl Bernard Bartels (sculptor of the Liver Birds)
6 Mersey Rail Tunnel (1886)
7 Nathaniel Hawthorne (1856–57)
8 Adelphi Hotel
9 Church of Our Lady and St Nicholas (1810)
10 Custom House (Jules Verne – *Around the World in Eighty Days*)

• 4 •

1 Mary Wilson
2 Dr Hawley Harvey Crippen
3 Dr Edward Pritchard
4 Dr Neill Cream
5 Frederick Gordon Radford
6 Lady Frances Howard, Countess of Essex
7 Dr Henry George Lamson
8 Graham Young
9 John Armstrong
10 Major Herbert Armstrong

• 5 •

1 Deal Pier (1873)
2 Cromer Pier (1993)
3 Bangor Pier (1914)
4 Southend-on-Sea Pier (1908)
5 Britannia Pier, Great Yarmouth (1859)
6 Penarth Pier (1947)
7 Yarmouth (Isle of Wight) Pier (1876)
8 North Pier, Blackpool (1897)
9 Saltburn Pier (1924)
10 Skegness Pier (1919)

• 6 •

1 Vasa Loppet (Swedish long-distance ski race)
2 Glacier Express
3 Offa's Dyke Path
4 Pennine Way
5 Leighton Buzzard Light Railway
6 Wuppertal Schwebabahn (monorail)
7 E20
8 Hadrian's Wall
9 Channel Tunnel
10 Barcelona Metro

• 7 •

1 James I to Anne of Denmark
2 William I to Matilda of Flanders (Eu)
3 Henry VI to Margaret of Anjou (Titchfield Abbey)
4 Edward IV to Elizabeth Grey née Woodville (Grafton Regis)
5 Henry VIII to Jane Seymour
6 Edward I to Eleanor of Castille (Las Huelgas)
7 Richard I to Berengaria of Navarre (Limassol)
8 Charles II to Catherine of Braganza (Portsmouth)
9 William IV to Adelaide of Saxe-Meiningen
10 Edward III to Philippa of Hainault

• 8 •

1 William Tell
2 King William IV
3 Williamsburg (Virginia)
4 Williamanmary (Sellar & Yeatman – *1066 And All That*)
5 *Sir William Hardy* (*Rainbow Warrior*)
6 Prince William Sound (*Exxon Valdes*, 1989)
7 Father William (Lewis Carroll – *Alice's Adventures in Wonderland*)
8 *William the Lawless* (Richmal Crompton)
9 King William II
10 Sweet William

ANSWERS

• 9 •

1 Yes Tor (Devon)
2 Ben Lomond (trad. Scottish song – *Loch Lomond*)
3 Snowdon (John Betjeman – *A Bay in Anglesey*)
4 Bredon Hill (A E Housman – *A Shropshire Lad*)
5 Brandon Mountain (Co. Kerry – St Brendan)
6 Plynlimon (Lewis Glen Cothi in George Borrow – *Wild Wales*)
7 Leith Hill (Surrey)
8 Black Combe (William Wordsworth – *View from the top of Black Combe*)
9 Ben Bulben (W B Yeats – *Under Ben Bulben*)
10 Malvern (Lord Macaulay – *The Armada*)

• 10 •

1 Leonard Bernstein
2 Sir Jacob Epstein
3 Helena Rubinstein
4 Frankenstein
5 Wallenstein
6 Albert Einstein
7 Sergei Eisenstein (*The Battleship Potemkin*, 1925)
8 Karl Bechstein
9 Sir John Rothenstein
10 Field Marshal Fritz von Manstein (Operation to relieve Stalingrad)

• 11 •

1 White's Club, 69 St James's Street (1733 Hogarth)
2 Temple of Artemis at Ephesus (356 BC – birth of Alexander the Great)
3 Rome (64 AD – Nero)
4 Reichstag, Berlin (1933)
5 Matilda (Hilaire Belloc)
6 Harrods (1883)
7 Ålesund, Norway (1904)
8 Argyll Concert Rooms, London (1830)

9 Great Fire of London (1666)
10 Chicago (1871)

• 12 •

1 Jonathan Edwards (triple jump world record, Gothenburg, 1995)
2 Cambridge University VIII (Boat Race record time, 1998)
3 Jim Laker (England v. Australia, Old Trafford, 1956)
4 Greg Norman (record four round score, Open Championship, Sandwich, 1993)
5 Arsenal (unbeaten Premiership record, 2003/2004)
6 Jack Hobbs (career batting record)
7 Björn Borg (v. John McEnroe, Wimbledon Final, 1980)
8 Paula Radcliffe (marathon world record, London, 2003)
9 Roger Bannister (four minute mile, Oxford, 1954)
10 John McGuinness (outright mountain circuit lap record, Formula 1 TT, Isle of Man, 2004)

• 13 •

1 Wight (French name)
2 Irish Sea
3 Hebrides (Overture)
4 Trafalgar
5 German Bight (Heligoland until 1956)
6 Dogger
7 Bailey
8 Fisher (Bud. cartoonist)
9 Lundy
10 FitzRoy (Capt. Robert Fitzroy, first director of Met. Office)

• 14 •

1 Brown Hairstreak butterfly
2 Brown Clee (Shropshire)
3 Father Brown (G K Chesterton)
4 brown sauce
5 Thomas Brown ('I do not love thee Dr Fell')

6 Brown's Hotel (London)
7 John Brown (militant abolitionist – 1859)
8 *Walnut Brown* (Sherry - Williams and Humbert)
9 *Brown on Resolution* (C S Forester)
10 Brownshirts (SA)

• 15 •

1 The Peach State
2 On Blueberry Hill
3 gooseberry
4 International Date Line (Kiribati, 1994/5)
5 Pears soap
6 Canaan Sodindo Banana (Zimbabwe, 1980–7)
7 Harry Lime (Graham Greene – *The Third Man*)
8 cherry-picker
9 Mark Lemon (founder and first editor of *Punch*)
10 Plum Warner (MCC in Australia, 1932/33)

• 16 •

1 Duntisbourne (Gloucestershire)
2 Hemingford (Huntingdonshire)
3 Manningford (Wiltshire)
4 Lillingstone (Buckinghamshire)
5 Ashford (Shropshire)
6 Kibworth (Leicestershire)
7 Carew (Pembrokeshire)
8 Cropwell (Nottinghamshire)
9 Pillerton (Warwickshire)
10 Itchen (Hampshire)

• 17 •

1 foxtrot
2 Edward Fox
3 The Red Fox (R L Stevenson – *Kidnapped*)
4 the quick brown fox
5 *The Fox and the Goat*
6 The Foxglove (William Withering)
7 George Fox (Society of Friends)
8 *The Springfield Fox*

9 Uffa Fox (Flying Fifteen yacht)
10 Fox Glacier (South Island, New Zealand)

• 18 •

1 Kelly Holmes (Olympic gold medals at 800 and 1500 metres)
2 Crystal Palace (Hollioake relay world record for CHASE)
3 Calayan Rail (previously unknown bird in Philippines)
4 King William's College General Knowledge Paper (motto)
5 Mike Ruddock (six Joneses in Welsh Rugby XV)
6 Geoffrey Rees-Jones's (former Headmaster – King William's College)
7 Princess Alice
8 Eurostat Yearbook (map on cover omitted Wales)
9 Charley (hurricanes/Florida)
10 Fred Dibnah (steam tractor at his funeral)

2005–2006

• 1 •

1 Aldwych Theatre
2 *The Scarlet Pimpernel* (Baroness Orczy)
3 Prince Carl of Denmark elected King Haakon VII of Norway (Wilhelm had been elected King George I of Greece)
4 Henri Rousseau's (*Le Lion Affamé* at the exhibition of Les Fauves)
5 Robert Koch's (Nobel Prize)
6 Automobile Association
7 Potemkin Mutiny
8 *De Profundis* (Oscar Wilde – posthumously)
9 Charing Cross Station (Avenue Theatre)
10 *The Merry Widow* (Lehar)

• 2 •

1 Carolina and Paolino's (Cimarosa –
   The Secret Marriage)
2 The Owl and the Pussy-Cat
   (Edward Lear – *The Owl and the
   Pussy-Cat*)
3 Lohengrin and Elsa's (Wagner
   – *Lohengrin*)
4 *The Marriage of Figaro* (Nancy
   Storace and Francesco Benucci at
   the Burgtheater, Vienna, 1ˢᵗ May
   1786)
5 Gino Carella and Lilia Herriton's
   (E M Forster – *Where Angels Fear to
   Tread*)
6 Jude Fawley and Arabella Donn's
   (Thomas Hardy – *Jude the Obscure*)
7 David Copperfield and Agnes
   Wickfield's (Dickens – *David
   Copperfield*)
8 Mr Rochester and Jane Eyre's
   (Charlotte Brontë – *Jane Eyre*)
9 Ko-Ko (W S Gilbert – *The Mikado*)
10 Minnehaha and Hiawatha's
   (Longfellow – *The Song of Hiawatha*)

• 3 •

1 T E Brown (*Bella Gorry – The
   Pazon's Story*)
2 John Betjeman (*The Exile*)
3 Henry Cadman (*Harry Druidale,
   Fisherman from Manxland to
   England*)
4 Wilkie Collins (*Armadale*)
5 Sir Walter Scott (*Peveril of The Peak*)
6 F W Farrar (*Eric, or Little by Little*)
7 Hall Caine (*The Manxman*)
8 David Baddiel (*The Secret Purposes*)
9 John Ray (*The Ornithology of Francis
   Willughby*)
10 William Wordsworth (*At Bala-sala,
   Isle of Man*)

• 4 •

1 *I Maccabees*, Handel (*Judas
   Maccabaeus*)
2 *Ruth*, Berkeley (*Ruth*)

3 *Daniel*, Walton (*Belshazzar's Feast*)
4 *Job*, Parry (*Job*)
5 *Judith*, Vivaldi (*Juditha triumphans*)
6 *Song of Songs*, Boyce (*Solomon*)
7 *Genesis*, Massenet (*Eve*)
8 *Lamentations*, Tallis (*Lamentations of
   Jeremiah*)
9 *Exodus*, Schoenberg (*Moses and
   Aaron*)
10 *Jonah*, Carissimi (*Jonas*)

• 5 •

1 St Mark's Fly (*Bibio marci*)
2 St George's Mushroom
3 St Cuthbert's Duck (Eider)
4 St Anthony's Fire (Erysipelas)
5 St Vitus's Dance (Sydenham's
   Chorea)
6 St John's Wort (Tynwald Day)
7 St Elmo's (or St Helen's) Fire
8 St Baldred's Boat and St Baldred's
   Cradle (East Lothian)
9 Coquille St Jacques
10 St Olaf's Candlestick (One-flowered
   Wintergreen)

• 6 •

1 synecdoche
2 tmesis
3 oxymoron
4 anaphora
5 paralipsis
6 hendiadys
7 chiasmus
8 alliteration
9 aposiopesis
10 litotes

• 7 •

1 *The Snowman*
2 *The Swineherd*
3 *The Steadfast Tin Soldier*
4 *The Shepherdess and the
   Chimneysweep*
5 *The Ugly Duckling*
6 *The Little Mermaid*
7 *The Little Match Girl*

8 *The Tinderbox*
9 *The Princess and the Pea*
10 *The Bronze Pig*

• 8 •

1 Fort Worth (Texas)
2 Chatsworth
3 Woolworth's (second store)
4 Molesworth (Willans and Searle)
5 Bosworth (King Richard III)
6 Tamworth (pigs)
7 Winkworth (Arboretum, Surrey)
8 William Wordsworth (Tintern Abbey)
9 Kenilworth (King Edward II)
10 Maria Edgeworth (Thady Quirk in *Castle Rackrent*)

• 9 •

1 Barrique
2 Louis Roederer's *Cristal*
3 Aube
4 Taittinger
5 thick-bodied bottle
6 Clicquot *Rosé*
7 Henri Abele
8 Pommery
9 Mercier
10 Balthazar

• 10 •

1 Vichy (Carottes à la Vichy)
2 Chantilly
3 Caen (Tripe à la mode de Caen)
4 Riom (Grenouilles à la mode de Riom)
5 Pithiviers (Gâteau de Pithiviers)
6 Crécy (Potage Crécy)
7 Nantua
8 Nice (Salade Niçoise)
9 Monaco/Monte Carlo (Oignons à la Monégasque)
10 Pézenas (Petits pâtés de Pézenas)

• 11 •

1 Celestine V
2 Paul VI (at Manila, 1970 Benjamin Mendoza y Amor Flores)
3 Benedict IX
4 Pius XI (collapse of roof of Vatican library. *cf.*, John XXI's death at Viterbo)
5 Formosus
6 Clement VI (*Lettres sans Titre, XIX*)
7 Leo X
8 Urban IV (Great Comet, 1264)
9 John XII
10 Calistus III (Sano di Pietro – Pinacoteca, Siena)

• 12 •

1 *The Guns of Navarone*
2 *Death Train*
3 *Fear is the Key*
4 *When Eight Bells Toll*
5 *Ice Station Zebra*
6 *The Golden Rendezvous*
7 *Bear Island*
8 *Puppet on a Chain*
9 *Caravan to Vaccarès*
10 *HMS Ulysses*

• 13 •

1 doe and dough
2 tun (54 gallons) and ton (a century)
3 ilium and ileum
4 purl (knitting) and pearl
5 Toad and towed (Kenneth Grahame – *The Wind in the Willows*)
6 links and Lynx (constellation)
7 bore and boar
8 drupe and droop
9 queue and cue
10 martin and marten

• 14 •

1 trouble (DOT – devoid of trouble)
2 Odd (a nickname for OEC with duplex steering)

3 Francis-Barnett (who had this motto in the 1920s, when their frames were made of bolted up straight tubes)

4 OK Supreme Lighthouse model (Pharos of Alexandria, built by Ptolemy II)

5 Velocette (while *1926–27–29 TT WINNERS* was on their tanks, Harold Willis, their development engineer, called this *1066 and all that*)

6 Big Port AJS (port is passed to the left)

7 Brough Superior (built by George Brough, whose father had built the Brough)

8 Norton Spares Used (1930s nickname for the NSU. Walter Moore, the designer, had left Norton and joined NSU, hence the similarity of the two makes)

9 Banana (the Wooler was nicknamed *The Flying Banana* by Graham Walker because of its yellow tank extending beyond the steering head. It finished 34th)

10 Royal Enfield Bullet (company slogan – *Made like a gun*)

• 15 •

1 Totteridge and Whetstone (treatise on algebra by Robert Recorde *The Whetstone of Witte*)

2 Whitechapel

3 Roding Valley (*roding* is territorial flight of woodcock)

4 Temple (badges of Inner and Middle Temple)

5 Maida Vale (Battle of Maida 1806)

6 Fairlop (great oak blown down in 1820)

7 Vauxhall

8 Arno's Grove

9 Marble Arch

10 Angel (English gold coin from 1465)

• 16 •

1 Red Arsenic

2 Red Fox (R L Stevenson – *Kidnapped*)

3 Red Biddy (with red wine)

4 Redstart

5 The Red Barn (1827)

6 Lilias Redgauntlet (Sir Walter Scott – *Redgauntlet*)

7 The Red Queen (Lewis Carroll – *Through the Looking Glass*)

8 *Red Cotton Night-cap Country* (Robert Browning)

9 Redruff (Ernest Thompson Seton – *Wild Animals I Have Known*)

10 Little Red Riding Hood

• 17 •

1 Ferguson and Muirhead (*The Adventure of the Sussex Vampire*)

2 Jabez Wilson (*The Red-headed League*)

3 Sam Brewer (*The Adventure of Shoscombe Old Place*)

4 Dr Percy Trevelyan (*The Adventure of the Resident Patient*)

5 Westhouse and Marbank (*A Case of Identity*)

6 Sherlock Holmes (*The Adventure of the Musgrave Ritual*)

7 Graham and McFarlane (*The Adventure of the Norwood Builder*)

8 Dr Hill Barton (*The Adventure of the Illustrious Client*)

9 Stimson and Co. (*The Disappearance of Lady Frances Carfax*)

10 Mrs Oakshott (*The Adventure of the Blue Carbuncle*)

• 18 •

1 Southend-on-Sea pier

2 Twelve Apostles (limestone pillars, Victoria, Australia)

3 Dresden (reconsecration of Frauenkirche)

4 Lime tree at St Lawrence Ground, Canterbury, blown down

5 Epidermolysis bullosa (crossing of Humber by Graham Boanas)
6 Ecuador (Alfredo Palacio)
7 Galapagos Giant Tortoise (Aged 175)
8 Epsom (Motivator won the Derby from A Walk in the Park)
9 Horatio Nelson's ('Kiss me Hardy')
10 Sir John Mills (title of his autobiography)

2006–2007

• 1 •

1 King Christian IX of Denmark (Europe's 'Grandfather')
2 Japanese battleship *Satsuma* (rivalling Britain's *Dreadnought* launched earlier in 1906)
3 Theodore Roosevelt (Nobel Peace Prize – Russo-Japanese War)
4 John Betjeman (see *By the Ninth Green, St Enodoc*)
5 Coca-Cola (caffeine replaced cocaine)
6 Balloon *United States* (winner of first international balloon race)
7 suffragette (*Daily Mail*)
8 *Sirio* (Italian liner)
9 Alfred Dreyfus
10 Northern Rugby Football Union (Rugby League)

• 2 •

1 Nicely-Nicely Jones (Damon Runyon – *Guys and Dolls*)
2 Bustopher Jones (The Cat About Town. T S Eliot – *Old Possum's Book of Practical Cats*)
3 Tom Jones (Henry Fielding)
4 Catherine Zeta Jones (wife of Michael Douglas and daughter-in-law of Kirk Douglas)
5 Edward Burne-Jones (*The Briar Rose* painting cycle, depicting the Sleeping Beauty legend at Buscot Park, Oxon)
6 Brian Jones (founder of The Rolling Stones. Proverbially 'gather no moss' – Sisyphus rolled a stone eternally up hill, but when nearly at the top it always rolled down again)
7 Inigo Jones (Covent Garden and the Banqueting Hall at Whitehall, in front of which King Charles I was beheaded)
8 Athelney Jones (Sir A Conan Doyle – *The Sign of Four*)
9 Bridget Jones (Helen Fielding)
10 Edward German (originally Edward German Jones, wrote a light opera – *Tom Jones*)

• 3 •

1 Copernicus (presented with his *Revolutionibus Orbium Coelestium* – 1543)
2 Galileo (his *Sidereus Nuncius* contradicted long-established Aristotelian cosmology and Catholic teaching)
3 Römer (measurement of the speed of light by measuring times of eclipse of Jupiter's moons – 1676)
4 Halley (died 1742, predicted return of comet in 1758)
5 Olbers (his 1826 *Paradox* was resolved by Hubble's 1920s discovery of the expansion of the universe)
6 Adams and Le Verrier (predicted the position of Neptune – confirmed in 1846)
7 Venus (transits – *planets* = Greek *wanderer*)
8 1930 (Gustav Holst – his wartime seven-part *The Planets* suite made incomplete by discovery of Pluto)
9 Penzias and Wilson ('noise' generated shortly after the big bang about 13 billion years ago)

10 Gravitational lensing (detection of more than 100 exo-planets, orbiting distant stars – last ten years)

• 4 •

1 Waterloo and City Line
2 The Rock Island Line
3 Plimsoll Line
4 Clapton Line (green line on gums)
5 Caroline (of Ansbach, consort of King George II)
6 Bibby Line (Manx Flag)
7 Maginot Line
8 Mason-Dixon Line
9 bowline
10 Hindenburg Line

• 5 •

1 Wells Cathedral
2 St Paul's Cathedral ('RESURGAM' inscribed above the door of the south transept)
3 Peterborough Cathedral (Catherine of Aragon)
4 Ely Cathedral
5 Oxford Cathedral (Thomas Hardy – *Jude the Obscure*)
6 Chichester Cathedral (stained glass window designed by Marc Chagall)
7 Worcester Cathedral (King John's tomb. Ref. A A Milne – *Now We Are Six*)
8 Lincoln Cathedral (Imp in Angel Choir)
9 Durham Cathedral (St Cuthbert's ducks)
10 Exeter Cathedral (John Betjeman)

• 6 •

1 Armagh (W R Rodgers – *Europa and the Bull*)
2 Dundalk (Patrick Kavanagh – *The Great Hunger*)
3 Lifford
4 Finnea (John Betjeman – *An Impoverished Irish Peer*)

5 Cavan (Percy French – *Song of William Inspector of Drains*)
6 Wicklow (Seamus Heaney – *Exposure*, from *Singing School*)
7 Galway (Louis MacNeice)
8 Derry (Charlotte Elizabeth Tonna)
9 Coleraine (Thackeray – *Peg of Limavady*)
10 Kilkenny

• 7 •

1 James I (Samuel Taylor Coleridge – *Notebook*)
2 childishness (Shakespeare – *As You Like It*)
3 Trinity College Boat Club, Cambridge (First and Third)
4 *Fourth Protocol* (Frederick Forsyth)
5 Edward V (Robert Stillington, Bishop of Bath and Wells questioned validity of Edward IV's marriage to Elizabeth Woodville)
6 *Inn of the Sixth Happiness* (film)
7 7th cranial nerve (facial)
8 8th hole at Royal Troon (The Postage Stamp)
9 Mozart's 9th Piano Concerto (*Jeunehomme* – written for Victoire Jenamy)
10 10th President of the USA, John Tyler (Tyler Too)

• 8 •

1 Orinoco (Womble)
2 Octodecimo
3 Oloroso
4 Orsino (Shakespeare – *Twelfth Night*)
5 Orgoglio (Spenser – *The Faerie Queene*)
6 *Otago*
7 Orvieto
8 Oviedo
9 Orbetello
10 Okolo (Gabriel Okara – *The Voice*)

• 9 •

1 Tallow Road station (John Betjeman – *A Lament for Moira McCavendish)*
2 Belgrade (Cecil Roberts – *Victoria Four Thirty)*
3 Gare de l'Est (Maurice Dekobra – *The Madonna of the Sleeping Cars/La Madone des Sleepings)*
4 Pathoda (John Masters – *Bhowani Junction)*
5 Leeds (John Buchan – *The Thirty-Nine Steps)*
6 Liège (Graham Greene – *Stamboul Train)*
7 Emden (Erskine Childers – *The Riddle of the Sands)*
8 Bombay (Jules Verne – *Around the World in Eighty Days)*
9 Carlisle (T S Eliot – *Skimbleshanks: the Railway Cat)*
10 Carlsruhe (Jerome K Jerome – *Three Men on the Bummel)*

• 10 •

1 *Buddleia* (Adam Buddle, Rector of North Fambridge)
2 *Lobelia* (Matthias de Lobel)
3 *Begonia* (Michel Bégon)
4 *Wisteria* (Caspar Wistar)
5 *Camellia* (George Josef Kamel)
6 *Forsythia* (William Forsyth, George III's gardener)
7 *Dahlia* (Anders Dahl, named by Prof. Antonio José Cavanilles)
8 *Rudbeckia* (Olof Rudbeck)
9 *Bougainvillea* (Louis Antoine de Bougainville)
10 *Zinnia* (Johann Gottfried Zinn)

• 11 •

1 Sicilius's Ghost (W H Shakespeare – *Cymbeline)*
2 Marley's Ghost (Charles Dickens – *A Christmas Carol)*
3 The Monkey's Paw (W W Jacobs)
4 Rolls Royce Silver Ghost

5 The statue of the Commendatore (W A Mozart – *Don Giovanni)*
6 The Ghost of Molly Malone (Irish folk-song)
7 Sir Roderic Murgatroyd (W S Gilbert – *Ruddigore)*
8 Brisbane (F Marion Crawford – *The Upper Berth)*
9 Tom Pearce's grey mare (*Widecombe Fair* – Dartmoor folk-song)
10 Ann Boleyn's Ghost (Bob Weston & Bert Lee – *With Her Head Tucked Underneath Her Arm)*

• 12 •

1 a Cardinal's hat (Richard Harris Barham – *The Jackdaw of Rheims)*
2 a lum hat (David Rorie – *The Lum Hat Wantin' The Croon)*
3 Albert's cap (Marriott Edgar – *Albert and the Lion)*
4 men's Sunday hats (Robert Browning – *The Pied Piper of Hamelin)*
5 a mantilla (John Buchan – *Greenmantle)*
6 a straw hat (Robert Louis Stevenson – *Travels with a Donkey in the Cévennes)*
7 red knitted caps (Arthur Ransome – *Swallows and Amazons)*
8 The Beryl Coronet (Sir A Conan Doyle)
9 a solar topee (Noel Coward – *Mad Dogs and Englishmen)*
10 Baggy Green Caps (Simon Briggs)

• 13 •

1 Quicksilver (Mercury)
2 Silverspot (Ernest Thompson Seton)
3 Silverstone (Old English)
4 Silverfish
5 silver claws and a silver eye (Walter de la Mare – *Silver)*
6 Lord Silverbridge (Anthony Trollope – *The Duke's Children)*

7 a little silver trout (W B Yeats –
   Song of Wandering Aengus)
8 Silver Wedding of King George
   VI and Queen Elizabeth (postage
   stamp)
9 a Silver Churn (W S Gilbert
   – *Patience*)
10 The Silver Tassie (Sean O'Casey)

• 14 •

1 Peter the Great
2 Edward Lear (*The Old Man With a
   Beard*)
3 Sweyn Forkbeard (son of Harald
   Bluetooth)
4 Goatsbeard (a. k. a.
   Jack-go-to-bed-at-noon)
5 The Ancient Mariner (S T
   Coleridge)
6 Robinson Crusoe (Daniel Defoe)
7 shaved off one half of their beards
   (*II Samuel* 10, 1-4)
8 The Bearded Wonder (Brian
   Johnston – Bill Frindall)
9 Svengali (George du Maurier
   – *Trilby*)
10 she plucked Gloucester's Beard
   (W H Shakespeare – *King Lear* III,
   I, 35)

• 15 •

1 Edgar (*King Lear*, III, iv, 123)
2 Bassanio (*The Merchant of Venice*, II,
   ii, 129–30)
3 Helen (*All's Well That Ends Well*, IV.
   v, 16)
4 Sir John Falstaff (*Henry IV Part 1*.
   II, v, 538–9)
5 Prospero (*The Tempest*, I, ii, 466)
6 Pistol (*Henry V*, v, I, 9)
7 Bottom (*A Midsummer Night's
   Dream*, IV, ii, 38)
8 Touchstone (*As You Like It*, I. ii. 60)
9 Clown (*The Winter's Tale*, IV, iii, 44)
10 Christopher Sly (*The Taming of the
   Shrew*, Ind. ii. 7)

• 16 •

1 Kia (Cerato)
2 Toyota (Corolla)
3 Fiat (Panda)
4 Suzuki (Liana)
5 Volkswagen (Phaeton)
6 Skoda (Octavia – Shakespeare –
   Antony and Cleopatra)
7 Hyundai (Getz)
8 Renault (Kangoo)
9 Daihatsu (Charade)
10 Honda (Civic)

• 17 •

1 Wolfe Macfarlane (R L Stevenson –
   The Body-Snatcher)
2 Dr Stephen Maturin (Patrick
   O'Brian – *Post Captain*)
3 Dr Edouardo Plarr (Graham Greene
   – *The Honorary Consul*)
4 Dr Aziz (E M Forster – *A Passage to
   India*)
5 Sir Patrick Cullen (George Bernard
   Shaw – *The Doctor's Dilemma*)
6 Doc Daneeka (Joseph Heller
   – *Catch-22*)
7 The Doctor of Physic in *The
   Canterbury Tales* (Geoffrey Chaucer)
8 Dr John H Watson (Sir A Conan
   Doyle – *A Study in Scarlet*)
9 Dr Caius (W H Shakespeare – *The
   Merry Wives of Windsor*)
10 Dr Hannibal Lecter (Thomas Harris
   – *The Silence of the Lambs*)

• 18 •

1 Tiger Woods (caddie dropped nine
   iron into lake beside seventh green
   in Ryder Cup; Woods went on to
   win his match with Robert Karlsson
   3 & 2)
2 P W Botha (autobiography – *Voice in
   the Wilderness*)
3 Pluto (demoted to Dwarf Planet
   by the International Astronomical
   Union, as orbit overlaps that of
   Neptune)

4 The Gambia (presidential election)
5 Darrel Hair's
6 Desert Orchid (death)
7 Pam Ayres
8 Buckingham Palace
9 Grantchester (Rupert Brooke statue by Paul Day)
10 Paul McCartney's ('When I'm Sixty-Four' – 1967)

2007–2008

• 1 •

1 Oklahoma (United States)
2 Irish 'Crown Jewels' (Regalia of the Order of St Patrick – Dublin Castle)
3 Persil (released by Henkel)
4 Baden-Powell (four patrols in first experimental scout camp on Brownsea Island)
5 Rudyard Kipling (Nobel Prize for Literature – 'You're a better man than I am Gunga Din')
6 *Playboy of the Western World* (J M Synge – first performance at the Abbey Theatre, Dublin)
7 Horace Rayner (shot William Whiteley, claiming that he was Whiteley's illegitimate son)
8 *Thomas W Lawson*
9 Colin Blythe (bowling for Kent v. Northamptonshire at Northampton)
10 International Auto-Cycle Tourist Trophy on the Isle of Man

• 2 •

1 St Dominic's (Talbot Baines Reed – *The Fifth Form at St Dominic's*)
2 Lowood (Charlotte Brontë – *Jane Eyre*)
3 Beardsley College (Vladimir Nabokov – *Lolita*)
4 Dotheboys Hall (Charles Dickens – *Nicholas Nickleby*)

5 Fernhurst (Alec Waugh – *The Loom of Youth*)
6 Marcia Blaine School for Girls (Muriel Spark – *The Prime of Miss Jean Brodie*)
7 St Custard's (Geoffrey Willans – *Down with Skool*)
8 Roslyn School (F W Farrar – *Eric, or Little by Little*)
9 Hogwarts School (J K Rowling – *Harry Potter and the Philosopher's Stone*)
10 Greyfriars School (Frank Richards – *Billy of Greyfriars School*)

• 3 •

1 William Henry Ireland (wrote *Vortigern*, but claimed it was a lost Shakespeare play)
2 Eric Hebborn (Conrad Oberhuber identified similarities in style of alleged painting by Savelli Sperando and Francesco del Cossa)
3 The Zinoviev Letter
4 Konrad Kujau (Hitler Diaries – 1983)
5 Han van Meegeren (charged with collaboration, undertook to paint *Jesus with the Doctors* under police supervision, but was then charged with forgery)
6 Alceo Dossena
7 George Psalmanazar (in his fictitious *Description of Formosa*)
8 Piltdown Man (lower jaw of orang-utan and teeth of chimpanzee, as well as a mediaeval human skull)
9 Tom Keating (forgeries of Shoreham by Samuel Palmer)
10 Lothar Malskat (turkey in the 'repainting' of frescos)

• 4 •

1 Rorke's Drift (eleven VCs)
2 Graham's Town (Rudyard Kipling – *The Elephant's Child, Just So Stories*)
3 Chaka (John Buchan – *Prester John*)
4 Basil d'Oliveira

5 Sol Plaatje (translation of *The Comedy of Errors* into Setswana)

6 The Bushman (Laurens van der Post – *The Lost World of the Kalahari*)

7 Cecil Rhodes ('So little done, so much to do')

8 Hendrik Verwoerd (assassinated by Dimitri Tsafendas)

9 *Drommedaris* (settlement of the Cape by Jan van Riebeeck in 1652)

10 Machadodorp (Paul Kruger)

• 5 •

1 Land's End (Cornish name)

2 Stretford End (Jim Laker's 19 wickets against Australia 1956)

3 *Endgame* (Samuel Beckett)

4 Turnip Townshend

5 *The End of the Affair* – Graham Greene

6 Manhood End (Rudyard Kipling – *Eddi's Service*)

7 Mile End (Daniel Defoe – *The History and Remarkable Life of the Truly Honourable Colonel Jack*)

8 Howard's End (E M Forster)

9 Southend (originally south end of Prittlewell)

10 Great End (Cumbria)

• 6 •

1 Metropolitan Nikodim (originally Boris Rotov – Vatican 1978)

2 Vyacheslav Molotov (Cocktail)

3 Anton Chekhov (*Uncle Vanya* and *Three Sisters*)

4 Piotr Tchaikovsky (Nadeja von Meck)

5 Tsar Ivan IV - the Terrible (seven wives)

6 Grigory Orlov's (Catherine the Great)

7 Alexander Pushkin

8 Dmitri Mendelayev (Mendelevium – Md)

9 Yuri Gagarin

10 Ivan Pavlov (conditioned reflex)

• 7 •

1 Lenski (*Eugin Onegin*)

2 Hamlet and Laertes (*Hamlet*)

3 Lt. Col. Fawcett (1843)

4 William Pitt the Younger (1798)

5 Prof. Moriarty (Conan Doyle – *The Adventure of the Final Problem*)

6 Liszt's (Princess Belgiojoso – piano duel with Sigismonde Thalberg)

7 Sohrab (Matthew Arnold – *Sohrab and Rustum*)

8 Lord Mohun's (1712)

9 Earl of Shrewsbury (by George Villiers, 2nd Duke of Buckingham 1668)

10 Goliath (*I Samuel 17*)

• 8 •

1 John Gow, a.k.a. Smith

2 Captain Hook (J M Barrie – *Peter Pan*)

3 Captain Sharkey (Conan Doyle)

4 Caroline North (Radio Station)

5 Anne Bonney

6 Billie Bones (R L Stevenson – *Treasure Island*)

7 Frederic (W S Gilbert – *The Pirates of Penzance*)

8 François l'Olonnais (ref. Alexander Exquemelin – *The Buccaneers of America*)

9 Peter Blood (Rafael Sabatini – *Captain Blood*)

10 Conrad (Byron – *The Corsair*)

• 9 •

1 a little farm at the bottom of Arkansaw (Mark Twain – *Huckleberry Finn*)

2 The Manor Farm (George Orwell – *Animal Farm*)

3 Talbothays Dairy Farm (Thomas Hardy – *Tess of the D'Urbervilles*)

4 Salt Lake Farm (Dylan Thomas – *Under Milk Wood*)

5 Caen Farm (Henry Williamson – *Tarka the Otter*)

6 Philip's Farm (Tennyson – *The Brook*)

7 Cold Comfort Farm (Stella Gibbons)

8 Västra Vemmenhög (Selma Lagerlöf – *The Wonderful Adventures of Nils*)

9 Blaweary (John Buchan – *Castle Gay*)

10 Renshent (T E Brown – *Tommy Big-Eyes*)

• 10 •

1 Winchester Light Automatic Rifle

2 Grantchester (Rupert Brooke – *The Old Vicarage, Grantchester*)

3 Mr Rochester (Charlotte Brontë – *Jane Eyre*)

4 Melchester United (*Roy of the Rovers*)

5 G K Chesterton (Father Brown stories)

6 Sir Francis Chichester's (Circumnavigations of *Gipsy Moth IV* and *Golden Hind*)

7 Silchester

8 Chesterfield

9 Barchester (Anthony Trollope – *Barchester Towers*)

10 Colchester United Football Club

• 11 •

1 Hole in the heart (Ventricular Septal Defect)

2 *The Heart of the Matter* (Graham Greene)

3 *Kind Hearts and Coronets*

4 Purple Heart (drug)

5 *Heart of Darkness* (Joseph Conrad)

6 Heartsease (*Viola tricolor*, a.k.a. Love-in-idleness; see Shakespeare – *A Midsummer Night's Dream* II, i.)

7 Sick Heart River (John Buchan – *Sick Heart River*)

8 *Heartbeat*

9 Queen of Hearts (Lewis Carroll – *Alice in Wonderland*)

10 Heart of Midlothian

• 12 •

1 'Dear Lord and Father of mankind'

2 'I vow to thee, my country, all earthly things above'

3 'O Jesus, I have promised'

4 'When I survey the wondrous cross'

5 'Come down, O Love divine'

6 'Guide me, O thou great Redeemer'

7 'Glorious things of thee are spoken'

8 'The day thou gavest, Lord, is ended'

9 'Let us with a gladsome mind'

10 'In the bleak mid-winter'

• 13 •

1 Sergeant Pepper (The Beatles)

2 Lieutenant Godet (Baroness Orczy – *Sir Percy Hits Back*)

3 Colonel Bramble (André Maurier – *The Silence of Colonel Bramble*)

4 Sergeant Major Williams's (*It Ain't Half Hot, Mum*)

5 Major Jonquier (C S Forester – *The Gun*)

6 Captain Havermeyer (Joseph Heller – *Catch 22*)

7 Major General Stanley (W S Gilbert – *The Pirates of Penzance*)

8 Corporal Himmelstoss (Erich Maria Remarque – *All Quiet on the Western Front*)

9 Private Mulvaney (Rudyard Kipling – *Plain Tales from the Hills*)

10 Brigadier Gerard (Sir A Conan Doyle)

• 14 •

1 Dean Martin (Dino Paul Crocetti)

2 St Martin of Tours

3 martingale

4 freemartin

5 Martinique (Mont Pelée, eruption on Ascension Day 1902)

6 Martinware

7 Sand Martin (Bee-eater and Kingfisher also nest in holes)

8 Julian Pemartin (inspired by
l'Opera in his building at Jerez de la
Frontera)
9 Martindale (*The Complete Drug
Reference*, first published 1883, now
in its 35th edition)
10 Martin Chuzzlewit (Charles
Dickens)

• 15 •

1 Peter Duck
2 George Owdon and Ralph Strakey
(*The Big Six*)
3 *Margoletta* (*Coot Club*)
4 Mastadon (*Secret Water*)
5 *Wild Cat* (*Missee Lee*)
6 Great Northern Diver (*Great
Northern*)
7 the summit of Kanchenjunga
(*Swallowdale*)
8 Mumps (*Winter Holiday*)
9 Mariehamn (*We Didn't Mean to go to
Sea*)
10 Timothy (*Pigeon Post*)

• 16 •

1 Coimbra
2 Leiden (Hortus Botanicus)
3 Tartu (Estonia)
4 Salamanca
5 Bristol (Wills and Fry)
6 Turku
7 Cambridge (Christ's College)
8 Padua
9 Göttingen
10 Dublin (Trinity College)

• 17 •

1 Paddington (Michael Bond)
2 Little Venice (Paddington)
3 Bart Simpson
4 Whitechapel
5 Victoria Embankment (Cleopatra's
Needle)
6 Connaught Hotel (Coburg until
1917)

7 Jack Straw's Castle (Hampstead)
8 Waterloo (railway station – Marshal
Blücher's arrival at battle)
9 Hyde Park Corner (horse in
Wellington Monument)
10 Lambeth (W Somerset Maugham –
Liza of Lambeth)

• 18 •

1 Jelly beans (appeared on the pitch
at Trent Bridge while Zaheer Khan
was batting)
2 Royal Philharmonic Orchestra
(played in a rubbish tip with
instruments made of rubbish)
3 Baroness Thatcher (speaking of her
statue in the Members Lobby at
Westminster)
4 Kingston, Jamaica (Death of Bob
Woolmer)
5 Alan Coren (The Sage of
Cricklewood and author of *The
Cricklewood Diet*)
6 Ian Botham's knighthood ('Beefy'
recalling the regal naming of sirloin)
7 Trinity College Great Court,
Cambridge (Sam Dobin beat time of
David Cecil, Baron Burghley)
8 Prince Harry (of his mother at 10th
Anniversary Memorial Service)
9 Kevin Rudd (elected Prime Minister
of Australia)
10 Oleg Gordievsky (honour for former
Soviet spy)

2008–2009

• 1 •

1 Henry Ford
2 W G Grace (his last first-class
match – Gentlemen of England v.
Surrey)
3 *The Chocolate Soldier* (Oscar Straus
operetta, after *Arms and the Man*)

4 Elizabeth Garrett Anderson (First woman doctor and now first Mayor – Aldeburgh)
5 Vladivostok (New York to Paris road race)
6 King Edward VII's (Cullinan Diamond – Crown Jewels)
7 Sir Henry Campbell-Bannerman
8 *The Wind in the Willows* (Kenneth Grahame – Toad)
9 Winston Churchill
10 Assassination of his father King Carlos I and Crown Prince Luiz in Lisbon

• 2 •

1 Lawrence Durrell – *Clea*
2 Dashiell Hammett – *The Maltese Falcon*
3 Charles Dickens – *Great Expectations*
4 John Steinbeck – *The Red Pony*
5 Thomas Gray – *Elegy Written in a Country Churchyard*
6 Jane Austen – *Pride and Prejudice*
7 Oscar Wilde – *The Picture of Dorian Gray*
8 Gabriel García Márquez – *One Hundred Years of Solitude*
9 E M Forster – *Where Angels Fear to Tread*
10 Lewis Carroll – *Through the Looking Glass*

• 3 •

1 Samuel Morse (first telegram to his partner Alfred Vail 'What hath God wrought?')
2 Flora Poste to Mrs Smiling (Stella Gibbons – *Cold Comfort Farm*)
3 Captain Kendall (of the *Montrose*, reporting Crippen as passenger)
4 The stationmaster at Voi (Tsavo, Kenya, World War I)
5 Davies's (to Carruthers re Rippingille stove, Erskine Childers – *The Riddle of the Sands*)

6 '*Unpack*' (Alfred Emanuel Smith – 1932)
7 Mercer (Conan Doyle – *The Adventure of the Creeping Man*)
8 '*Better drowned than duffers if not duffers wont drown*' (Arthur Ransome – *Swallows and Amazons*)
9 Leithen (John Buchan – *The Power-House*)
10 Murder of General Gordon (Queen Victoria to Gladstone)

• 4 •

1 Fair Isle (Old Scandinavian *faar* (sheep) + *ey* (island)
2 Staffa (Mendelssohn – *The Hebrides Overture – Fingal's Cave*)
3 Egilsay (blow to the head by Haakon's cook Lifolf)
4 Isle of May (King David I to the Benedictines of Reading)
5 Lismore (St Moluag's questionable victory over St Mulhac in a boat race)
6 Eriskay (Charles Edward Stuart, the Young Pretender, aboard *Du Teillay*)
7 North Ronaldsay
8 Gruinard Island (Anthrax)
9 Ailsa Craig (Robert Burns – *Duncan Gray*)
10 Bass Rock (R L Stevenson – *Catriona*)

• 5 •

1 Quisling
2 Jussi Björling (*Pearl Fishers'* duet)
3 Ugly Duckling
4 gosling
5 Terschelling
6 Hans Memling
7 angling
8 fingerling
9 Grayling
10 Riesling

• 6 •

1 Charles VI of France
2 Pope Alexander VI
3 Haakon VI of Norway
4 Frederick VI of Denmark (Louise Augusta, daughter of Friedrich Struensee)
5 Rama VI (Vajivarudh, King of Siam)
6 George VI of Great Britain (Albert, Prince Consort and Princess Alice, Grand Duchess of Hesse)
7 James VI of Scotland (Margaret Tudor)
8 Mehmet VI, Sultan of the Ottoman Empire (Turkey)
9 Constantine VI, Byzantine Emperor
10 Henry VI of England (Shakespeare plays)

• 7 •

1 Esperanto (Ludovic Lazarus Zamenhof)
2 Romanian
3 Basque
4 Finnish (it is not even Indo-European)
5 Albanian
6 Wendish, also known as Sorbian or Lusatian (spoken in certain districts of Eastern Germany)
7 Romansch (also known as Ladin and as Rheto-Romanisch)
8 Catalan (the construction using the present of the verb to go, so that it looks like 'I am going to')
9 Bulgarian
10 Slovene

• 8 •

1 Abalone
2 Cockle shells
3 Shrimps (potted)
4 *The Amorous Prawn* (renamed *The Playgirl and the War Minister*)

5 Norway Lobster and Dublin Bay Prawn
6 Mussel (Loretto School at Musselburgh)
7 Oysters (Sam Weller in *Pickwick Papers*)
8 Crabs' (Dylan Thomas – *Under Milk Wood*)
9 Periwinkle (flowers in vegetable kingdom)
10 The Lobster (Lewis Carroll – *Alice in Wonderland*)

• 9 •

1 *Bellini*. Rome and Palermo or Siracusa (*La Sonnambula*)
2 *Johannes Kepler*. Wiesbaden and Prague
3 *Casanova*. Venice and Ljubljana
4 *Hans Christian Andersen*. Copenhagen and Munich (*The Constant Tin Soldier*)
5 *Jean Monnet*. Brussels and Basel
6 *Sibelius*. St Petersburg and Helsinki (*King Christian II*)
7 *Bartók Béla*. Budapest and Vienna (*Bluebeard's Castle*)
8 *Francisco de Goya*. Paris and Madrid (*Maja*)
9 *Pegasus*. Amsterdam and Zurich
10 *Salvador Dali*. Barcelona and Milan (*La Persistencia de la Memoria*)

• 10 •

1 Tiber (Lord Macaulay – *Horatius, The Lays of Ancient Rome*)
2 Thames (Robert Bridges – *There is a Hill Beside the Silver Thames*)
3 Weser (Robert Browning – *The Pied Piper of Hamelin*)
4 Nile (Jules Verne – *Five Weeks in a Balloon*)
5 Danube (John Buchan – *Greenmantle*)
6 Jordan (*Joshua 3. 13-17*)

7 Oise (Robert Louis Stevenson – *An Inland Voyage*)

8 Ohio (Mark Twain – *The Adventures of Huckleberry Finn*)

9 Amazon (Rudyard Kipling – *The Beginning of the Armadillos, Just So Stories*)

10 Oxus (Matthew Arnold – *Sohrab and Rustum*)

• 11 •

1 Rose Stanley (Muriel Spark – *The Prime of Miss Jean Brodie*)

2 Accrington Stanley FC (evolved from Stanley Villa FC in 1893)

3 Stanley Mortensen in Stanley Matthews's Match (Only 20th Century Cup Final hat-trick – Blackpool 4 Bolton Wanderers 3 1953)

4 Stanley Baldwin ('…my lips are not yet unsealed…' – 10th December 1935)

5 Port Stanley

6 Major-General Stanley (Vegetable, animal and mineral – W S Gilbert – *The Pirates of Penzance*)

7 Stanley Holloway (*Old Sam*)

8 James Stanley, 7th Earl of Derby, Lord of Mann

9 Stanley Webber (Harold Pinter – *The Birthday Party*)

10 Henry Morton Stanley ('Dr Livingstone I presume?')

• 12 •

1 The Blue Dragon (*Martin Chuzzlewit*)

2 The Sol's Arms (*Bleak House*)

3 The Six Jolly Fellowship Porters (*Our Mutual Friend*)

4 The Pegasus's Arms (*Hard Times*)

5 The Goat and Boots (*Sketches by Boz*)

6 The Magpie and Stump (*Pickwick Papers*)

7 The Three Cripples (*Oliver Twist*)

8 The Saracen's Head (*Nicholas Nickleby*)

9 The Three Jolly Bargemen (*Great Expectations*)

10 The Maypole Inn (*Barnaby Rudge*)

• 13 •

1 James Buchanan

2 William Henry Harrison

3 James Maddison

4 Dwight D Eisenhower ('I like Ike')

5 William McKinley

6 Calvin Coolidge

7 George Washington

8 Theodore Roosevelt (Bull Moose)

9 James Monroe (Monrovia)

10 John Adams and Thomas Jefferson

• 14 •

1 New Zealand (*ling* in Wellington)

2 Samoa (*pi* in Apia)

3 Japan (*OK* in Tokyo)

4 Romania (*char* in Bucharest)

5 Canada (*Taw* in Ottawa)

6 Belgium (*russe* in Brussels)

7 Hungary (*ape* in Budapest)

8 Pakistan (*lama* in Islamabad)

9 Botswana (*boron* in Gaborone)

10 Philippines (*nil* in Manila)

• 15 •

1 Moll Yellowhammer (Thomas Middleton – *A Chaste Maid in Cheapside*)

2 Clarice Starling (Thomas Harris – *The Silence of the Lambs*)

3 Fanny Robin (Thomas Hardy – *Far From the Madding Crowd*)

4 Bernard Nightingale (Tom Stoppard – *Arcadia*)

5 Sir Mulberry Hawk (Charles Dickens – *Nicholas Nickleby*)

6 James Raven (Graham Greene – *A Gun for Sale*)

7 James Shearwater (Aldous Huxley – *Antic Hay*)

8 Edwina Crane (Paul Scott – *The Towers of Silence*)
9 Atticus Finch (Harper Lee – *To Kill a Mockingbird*)
10 Sergeant Kite (George Farquhar – *The Recruiting Officer*)

• 16 •

1 Houghton Ruby
2 Sherry Spinner
3 Thunder and Lightning
4 Dunkeld
5 Mallard and Claret
6 Yellow Sally
7 Tup's Indispensable
8 Alexandra
9 Soldier Palmer
10 Stoat's Tail

• 17 •

1 Digne (Victor Hugo – *Les Misérables*)
2 Bethune (Alexandre Dumas – *The Three Musketeers*)
3 Rouen (Gustave Flaubert – *Madame Bovary*)
4 Bayonne (Ernest Hemingway – *The Sun Also Rises*)
5 Alençon (Patrick O'Brian – *The Surgeon's Mate*)
6 Gap (Frederick Forsyth – *The Day of the Jackal*)
7 Montpellier (Conan Doyle – *The Adventure of the Empty House*)
8 Rheims (Thomas Barham – *The Jackdaw of Rheims*)
9 Harfleur (Shakespeare – *King Henry V*)
10 Amiens (John Buchan – *Mr Standfast*)

• 18 •

1 Sir Edmund Hillary KG
2 Melton Mowbray Pork Pie
3 Rebecca Romero (Rowing 2004, Cycling 2008)

4 Lily Savage/Paul O'Grady (*At My Mother's Knee… and Other Low Joints*)
5 Sir Ian Botham (Leukaemia Walks)
6 Ripon Cathedral
7 Liverpool
8 *Sirius Star* (Capture by Somali Pirates)
9 Marion Jones
10 Lucian Freud's

2009–2010

• 1 •

1 Smoking (Premiere of Wolf-Ferrari's *Il Segretto di Susanna*)
2 First Kibbutz (at Degania Aleph)
3 Angelo Raffaele Lerro
4 Lapwings (First birds ringed in Britain)
5 Peary, North Pole
6 Rimsky-Korsakov's (*The Golden Cockerel*)
7 Selma Lagerlöf (Nobel Prize for Literature)
8 São Tomé and Principe (objection to ill-treatment of workers in the cocoa plantations)
9 Hubert Latham's (failed cross-channel flight, five days before Bleriot's successful attempt)
10 pH (invented by Sören Sörensen, Director of the Carlsberg Laboratory)

• 2 •

1 John Belcher (gifts from Sydney Stanley a.k.a *The Spider*)
2 Sir John Trevor
3 Neil Hamilton
4 Richard Rigby
5 Sir Thomas Osborne, Earl of Danby
6 Henry Fox
7 Thomas Mardy-Jones

8 David Blunkett
9 Francis Bacon
10 David Lloyd-George

• 3 •

1 Cologne/Köln (*Stamboul Train* – Graham Greene)
2 Dresden (*Three Men on the Bummel* – Jerome K Jerome)
3 Frankfurt-am-Main (*Meister Floh* – E T A Hoffmann)
4 Berlin (*Mr Norris Changes Trains* – Christopher Isherwood)
5 Mainz (*Mathis der Maler* – Paul Hindemith)
6 Lübeck (*Buddenbrooks* – Thomas Mann)
7 Wittenberg (*Michael Kohlhaas* – Heinrich von Kleist)
8 Hamburg (*Smiley's People* – John Le Carré)
9 Flensburg (*The Riddle of the Sands* – Erskine Childers)
10 Hamelin/Hameln (*The Pied Piper of Hamelin* – Robert Browning)

• 4 •

1 Roger Federer (v. Rafael Nadal in 2008)
2 Dorothea Lambert Chambers v. Dora Boothby (1913)
3 Manolo Santana (v. Dennis Ralston in 1966)
4 Margaret Court v. Billie Jean King (1970)
5 René Lacoste (1925, 1928)
6 Anthony Wilding v. H. Roper Barrett (1911 Barrett retired at 2 sets all)
7 Baron Gottfried von Cramm
8 Frank Shields withdrew, giving his opponent (Sidney Wood) a walk-over (1931)
9 Bob Falkenberg (v. John Bromwich in 1948)
10 William Renshaw (1882, 1883 and 1889)

• 5 •

1 Hameln (Albert Pierrepoint, executioner – December 1945)
2 William Calcraft (Michael Barrett, in front of Newgate Prison, 1868)
3 Admiral Byng's (Shot on board the *Monarque* in 1757 for failure to engage the French off Minorca)
4 Ko-Ko (*The Mikado* – W S Gilbert)
5 Margaret, Countess of Salisbury (Tower Green 1541)
6 William Duell (1740)
7 Catherine Hayes (Tyburn 1726)
8 Charles Wooldridge (subject of Oscar Wilde's *Ballad of Reading Jail*)
9 Boiling alive (Richard Rose at Smithfield 1532)
10 John Lee (James Berry, executioner – 1885)

• 6 •

1 Sweetbreads
2 Samuel Whitbread
3 Breadalbane
4 Bread of Heaven
5 Pitta bread
6 Breadfruit plants (Capt. Bligh on *Bounty* at Otaheite)
7 Bread basket of Europe
8 The greatest thing since sliced bread
9 Bread sauce
10 Naan bread

• 7 •

1 Van Der Valk (Amsterdam detective – TV signature tune: *Eye Level*)
2 Vancouver Island
3 Murgatroyd Van Rust (Ogden Nash – *Nevertheless*)
4 Rip van Winkle (Washington Irving)
5 Hugo Van der Goes (*The Portinari Altarpiece*)
6 Pieter Van der Faes (Sir Peter Lely – Oliver Cromwell)
7 Sir John Vanbrugh

8 Jeroen van Aeken/Jerome van Aken (Hieronymus Bosch)

9 Jean Van de Velde (Open Golf, Carnoustie, 1999)

10 Hendrik Willem Van Loon (*Van Loon's Lives*)

• 8 •

1 Bongo (African antelope)
2 Mango
3 Ringo Starr (replaced Pete Best)
4 Congo red
5 Santo Domingo (temporarily Ciudad Trujillo)
6 Django Reinhardt (two fingers became joined as a result of fire)
7 Yellow Dog Dingo (Rudyard Kipling – *Just So Stories*)
8 Chicken Marengo
9 Drongo
10 Tango (originated in Buenos Aires)

• 9 •

1 Horsham (W J King's *Mallard Ale*)
2 Blandford St Mary (Badger's *Pickled Partridge Ale*)
3 Alva (Harviestoun Brewery's *Ptarmigan*)
4 Market Weston, Diss (Old Chimneys Brewery's *Hairy Canary*)
5 Old Allangrange, Munlochy (Black Isle Brewery's *Goldeneye Pale Ale*)
6 Wiveliscombe (Cotleigh Brewery's *Nutcracker*)
7 Great Oakley, Corby (Great Oakley's *Wagtail*)
8 Malvern (Malvern Hills Brewery's *Swedish Nightingale Real Ale*)
9 Earl Soham, Woodbridge (Earl Soham Brewery's *Gannet Mild*)
10 Exminster (Exeter Brewery's *Avocet Ale*)

• 10 •

1 Alexander the coppersmith (*II Timothy 4.14*)
2 King Alexander III of Scotland (annexed the Isle of Man)
3 Cecil Frances Alexander (*All things bright and beautiful*)
4 Alexander Fleming (*Penicillium*)
5 Alexander Samsonov (Russian Army commander at Battle of Tannenburg)
6 Tsar Alexander I of Russia (Feodor Kuznich)
7 King Alexander I of Jugoslavia
8 Alexander Pope ('a long disease' - *An Epistle to Dr Arbuthnot*)
9 Alexander Bell (telephone)
10 Alexander Beetle (*Now We Are Six* – A A Milne)

• 11 •

1 101st (*The Clock Symphony* – Haydn)
2 5th (Cranial Nerve – Trigeminal)
3 38th (Parallel – Korean War)
4 15th (July – St Swithin's Day)
5 10th (Pope Pius)
6 137th (Psalm)
7 4th (King William's College)
8 6th (*Diary of a Sixth Form Mouse* – *The Fifth Form at St Dominic's* – Talbot Baines Reed)
9 11th (Armistice Day)
10 3rd (*The Third Man* – Graham Greene)

• 12 •

1 Margaret of Anjou, Queen of Henry VI
2 Catherine of France, Queen of Henry V (her preserved corpse)
3 Emma of Normandy, Queen of Ethelred II, the Unready, and Canute
4 Eleanor of Castile, Queen of Edward I
5 Eleanor of Provence, Queen of Henry III

6 Caroline of Brunswick, Queen of
    George IV
7 Queen Mary I (Sawston Hall)
8 Caroline of Ansbach, Queen of
    George II
9 Mary of Teck, Queen of George V
10 Queen Anne (with Sarah Churchill,
    Lady Marlborough)

• 13 •

1 St Albans
2 Lincoln
3 Norwich (pelican)
4 Chichester (nesting peregrine
    falcons)
5 Salisbury (spire became highest
    after the spire of the central tower at
    Lincoln was blown down)
6 Ely (Bishop Alcock, founder of Jesus
    College)
7 Gloucester
8 Rochester (Bishop Walter de
    Merton)
9 Chester
10 St Paul's, London (Duke of
    Wellington)

• 14 •

1 Kingsholm, rugby football
    (Gloucester RFC)
2 Lord's, cricket (Lords and Ladies
    a.k.a. Cuckoo Pint)
3 Boleyn Ground, football (West
    Ham United *a.k.a.* Upton Park)
4 Billown, motor-cycle racing (Isle
    of Man: Compo Simmonite – Bill
    Owen)
5 Devonshire Park, lawn tennis
    (Eastbourne, Sussex)
6 Altcar, hare-coursing
7 The Belfry, golf
8 The Roodee, horse-racing (Chester)
9 The Crucible, snooker ('A pipkin or
    crucible': *Patience* – W S Gilbert)
10 Cowdray Park, polo

• 15 •

1 Macula
2 Vistula (Most Poniatowskiego,
    Warsaw)
3 Dracula
4 St Peter ad Vincula (Tower of
    London)
5 Tarantula
6 Scrofula
7 Fistula
8 Furcula (Wishbone)
9 Fratercula (Puffin)
10 Benbecula

• 16 • *National versions of Monopoly*

1 B-dul Kogalniceanu (Bucharest,
    Romania)
2 Børsgade (Copenhagen, Denmark)
3 Collyer Quay (Singapore)
4 Palisády (Bratislava, Slovakia)
5 Hamngatan (Stockholm, Sweden)
6 Avenue (de) Matignon (Paris,
    France)
7 Calle Fontanella (Barcelona,
    Spain)
8 Narva maantee (Tallin, Estonia)
9 Abbey Street (Dublin, Ireland)
10 Annankatu (Helsinki, Finland)

• 17 •

1 Chateaubriand (Steak – Vicomte de)
2 Dunce (John Duns Scotus)
3 Melba (Toast/Peach – Nellie
    Melba)
4 Mercator (Projection)
5 Soubise (Sauce – Prince de Soubise)
6 Sten (Gun)
7 Sandwich (4th Earl of Sandwich)
8 Rastafarian (Selassie's title Ras
    Tafari)
9 Caesar (Salad)
10 Bacitracin (antibiotic)

• 18 •

1 Hazel Blears
2 David Haye's (defeat of Nikolai Valuev to become WBA Heavyweight Champion)
3 Carol Ann Duffy (Poet Laureate)
4 Fake blood capsule (Heineken Cup Quarter Final)
5 Michael Martin (on resigning as Speaker)
6 *Ellan Vannin* (Mersey 1909 IOM Post Office issue)
7 Runaway balloon hoax (cf. Ian McEwan – *Enduring Love*)
8 Giles Brandreth (*Something Sensational to Read in the Train: the Diary of a Lifetime*)
9 Keith Floyd
10 Manx language (no longer regarded as extinct)

2010–2011

• 1 •

1 Boutros Ghali
2 E M Forster (published *Howard's End*)
3 Kissing - French Railways
4 *Pluviôse* (submarine) and *Pas de Calais* (cross-channel ferry)
5 Hawley Harvey Crippen (5 grains of Hyoscine Hydrobromide from Lewis & Burrow's)
6 Count Lev Tolstoy
7 Prince Nicholas, Montrenegro
8 Sir Henry Irving's
9 Halley's Comet and Mark Twain (20th and 21st April – Twain had 'come in' 2 weeks after the comet's 1835 appearance)
10 *The Firebird/L'Oiseau de Feu* (Stravinsky's ballet)

• 2 •

1 Dexter Gordon (disc – *Dexter Blows Hot and Cool*)
2 Catherine Gordon (mother of Lord Byron)
3 Hezekiah Leroy Gordon
4 Gordon Bennett
5 General Charles (Chinese) Gordon
6 Gordon Highlanders
7 Gordon's Gin (trademark)
8 Gordon Richards (won 1000 Guineas, Oaks and St Leger on Sun Chariot in 1942)
9 Flash Gordon
10 Duff Gordon (sherry)

• 3 •

1 8th at Gleneagles (Whaup's Nest)
2 4th at St Andrews (Ginger Beer – Fentiman's logo)
3 7th at Royal Troon (Tel-el-Kebir – Battle in Egypt)
4 7th at Castletown (Race Course – site of earlier Derby races)
5 5th at Royal Liverpool, Hoylake (Telegraph)
6 15th at Royal Dornoch (Stulaig – island north of Lochboisdale)
7 12th at Manor House (Doolittle – Hugh Lofting creation)
8 12th at Forest of Arden (Coots Island)
9 15th at Royal Portrush (Purgatory)
10 18th at Prestwick (Clock)

• 4 •

1 Victor Borge
2 Karl Nielsen's (featured on Danish 100 kroner note)
3 Michael Laudrup (Lazio, Juventus, Barcelona, Real Madrid, Vissel Kobe and Ajax)
4 King Valdemar Atterdag
5 Knud Rasmussen
6 King Hardicanute

7 Thomas Dinesen (VC – brother of Karen Blixen)

8 H C Andersen's (*The Little Mermaid* – sculpture)

9 Tycho Brahe (Tycho's (exploding) Star – Cassiopeia)

10 King Christian VII (by Struensee)

• 5 •

1 Llandovery
2 Christ's Hospital
3 King William's
4 Charterhouse
5 Dulwich (Shackleton's whaler *James Caird*)
6 St Paul's (153 boys/fishes)
7 Fettes
8 Rugby (Elsee or Boomer Bell)
9 Eton (Canaletto)
10 Highgate

• 6 •

1 Utopia (*A Modern Utopia*)
2 Utah (the Beehive State)
3 Utsire (North and South in shipping forecast)
4 Jørn Utzon (Kuwaut National Assembly and Sydney Opera House)
5 Uther Pendragon
6 Maurice Utrillo
7 Utility (Shakespeare – *King Henry V*, 5. 2. 53–4)
8 Utrecht (Adrian VI, the only Dutch Pope)
9 Utile
10 Alison Uttley

• 7 •

1 Dominic Cork (Test Match debut v. West Indies)
2 Clare College, Cambridge
3 Virginia Mayo
4 Dr Kildare
5 Rinty Monaghan
6 Inspector Wexford (*Simisola*)
7 Tipperary

8 James Galway (CD – *The Celtic Minstrel*)
9 Louth (highest spire of any parish church)
10 Limerick

• 8 •

1 Jonah (2, *10*)
2 Malachi (3, *2*)
3 Amos (7, *14*)
4 Joel (1, *4*)
5 Hosea's (1, *2–8*)
6 Haggai's and Zechariah's (1, *1*)
7 Daniel (7, *5*)
8 Jeremiah's (28, *10–13*)
9 Isaiah (11, *7* and 65, *25*)
10 Ezekiel (37, *1–2*)

• 9 •

1 Filbert (nut)
2 Lambert Simnel
3 St Cuthbert's Duck (aka. Eider)
4 Gimbert (Soham – bomb train explosion, June 1944)
5 Humbert Humbert (Vladimir Nabokov – *Lolita*)
6 Gustave Flaubert (*Madame Bovary*)
7 Mrs Maria Benjamin Fitzherbert (Caroline of Brunswick and Frances Villiers)
8 Dogbert (Scott Adams 1997)
9 Franz Schubert (*Tragic* and *Unfinished* Symphonies)
10 Osbert Lancaster

• 10 •

1 Chelsea Quealey
2 Mutt Carey
3 Turk Murphy
4 Bunk Johnson
5 Huddie Ledbetter – 'Lead Belly'
6 Fate Marable
7 Fats Waller (or Fats Sardi)
8 Miff Mole
9 Pinetop Smith or Pinetop Perkins
10 Woody Herman

• 11 •

1 Z (old English)
2 D-Day
3 X (classification for 'adult' films)
4 a white C (Comma butterfly)
5 Vitamin A
6 O (Giotto's O – Pope Benedict XI)
7 The L-Shaped Room
8 W (tungsten)
9 F (W S Gilbert - *Yeoman of the Guard*)
10 Q-Fever

• 12 •

1 Spotted Dog (*The Thirteen Gun Salute*)
2 Smallpox (*The Nutmeg of Consolation*)
3 Blue ointment (*The Hundred Days*)
4 Peter Haywood (*Desolation Island*)
5 Captain Ole Bugge (*Master and Commander*)
6 The Grapes (*The Surgeon's Mate*)
7 Stockholm (*The Letter of Marque*)
8 The foretopgallant studdingsail booms (*The Wine-Dark Sea*)
9 Eaten by a shark (*Treason's Harbour*)
10 West (*Clarissa Oakes*)

• 13 •

1 Aurunculeia (John Buchan – *The House of the Four Winds*)
2 Bandoola (J H Williams – *Elephant Bill*)
3 The Danish Order of the Elephant (Ridder af Elefantorderen)
4 Hawa'i (mounted by Akbar – Agra 1561)
5 Radha Pyari's (Kala Nag in Kipling's *Toomai of the Elephants*)
6 Surus (Hannibal's favourite elephant)
7 Abu l'Abbas (given to Charlemagne by Harun al Rashid)
8 Suleiman (King João III to the future Maximilian II)

9 Hanno / Annone (King Manuel I to Leo X)
10 Babar and Celeste (Jean de Brunhoff)

• 14 •

1 Barton Swing Aqueduct (Bridgewater Canal)
2 Almond Aqueduct (Union Canal)
3 Stanley Ferry Aqueduct (Aire & Calder Navigation)
4 Marple Aqueduct (Peak Forest Canal)
5 Chirk Aqueduct (John Sell Cotman painting)
6 Longdon on Tern Aqueduct (Shrewsbury Canal)
7 Dundas Aqueduct (Kennet and Avon Canal)
8 Lune Aqueduct (Lancaster Canal)
9 Pontcysyllte Aqueduct (Llangollen Canal)
10 Stretton Aqueduct (Shropshire Union Canal)

• 15 •

1 Bungalow (Snaefell Mountain Railway crossing)
2 Stonebreakers' Hut
3 Governors' Bridge
4 Parliament Square (Statues in Westminster's Parliament Square)
5 Alpine Cottage
6 Keppel Gate
7 Laurel Bank
8 Ginger Hall
9 Brandywell
10 Quarterbridge (over River Glass)

• 16 •

1 Bologna (*Il Matrimonio Segreto* – Cimarosa)
2 Bergamo (*Harlequin* or *The Windows* – Busoni)
3 Messina (*Béatrice et Bénédict* – Berlioz)

4 Cremona (*La Finta Semplice*
   – Mozart)
5 Verona (*Romeo and Juliet* – Gounod)
6 Syracuse (*Tancredi* – Rossini)
7 Montalto (*Pagliacci* – Leoncavallo)
8 Terracina (*Fra Diavola* – Auber)
9 Mantua (*Rigoletto* – Verdi)
10 Rome (*The Rape of Lucretia* – Britten)

• 17 •

1 Shakespeare – *Coriolanus*
2 John Buchan – *The Thirty-Nine Steps*
3 Thomas Hardy – *Tess of the
   d'Urbervilles*
4 Nicholas Monsarrat – *Richer Than
   All His Tribe*
5 Hall Caine – *The Manxman*
6 C S Forester – *Flying Colours*
7 R L Stevenson – *The Beach at Falesá*
8 John Masters – *Bhowani Junction*
9 Max Beerbohm – *Zuleika Dobson*
10 Joseph Conrad – *The Rescue*

• 18 •

1 Aylesbury (unveiling of statue of
   Ronnie Barker by his wife)
2 Kiel (Major Tony Hibbert)
3 Didi Nearne (World War II spy,
   died 2nd September)
4 Seventh Marquess of Townshend
   (longest known holder of a
   peerage)
5 Edward Elgar (image on £20 note)
6 Hip joint (replacement
   commemorating Sir John Charmley
   on 60p stamp)
7 Wittenberg (plastic statuettes of
   Martin Luther)
8 Nick Griffin (excluded from
   Buckingham Palace Garden Party)
9 J P R Williams (attempted to
   influence the breathaliser)
10 Wimbledon (6ft 9in John Isner's
   marathon match with Nicolas
   Mahut)

And finally
a bespoke General Knowledge Paper

Win £1000-worth of books!

This extra set of particularly fiendish questions has been compiled especially for this book by Pat Cullen, and just to tantalise quiz aficionados, the answers are not given here …

Answers will be published online at www.liverpooluniversitypress.co.uk and on Twitter (https://twitter.com/LivUniPress) on 30 June 2012 and will also be available on request from the publisher from that date onwards.

To enter a competition for a prize
of £1000-worth of Liverpool University Press books,
send in a full set of answers by 15 June 2012 to:
LUP World's Most Difficult Quiz
Liverpool University Press
4 Cambridge St
Liverpool
L69 7ZU
or email entries to lup@liv.ac.uk with the subject line
'World's Most Difficult Quiz'.
Entries should include full contact details
(name, address, phone number and email address).

All the correct sets of answers will be placed into a prize draw and a winner picked out on 30 June 2012. The lucky (and erudite) victor will be given £1000-worth of Liverpool University Press books of their choice.

A Bespoke Quiz

· 1 · *In 1811:*

1   which city fell to Auchmuty?

2   what was published by a lady?

3   who hypothesised on molecular equality?

4   who targeted the frames of stockingers and knitters?

5   where did the Danes fail to recapture an English garrison in the Kattegat?

6   what written ordinance had been prompted by an abnormality in haemoglobin metabolism?

7   where did the parish priest from Dolores face the firing squad?

8   which two countries declared their independence?

9   where was The Prophet defeated?

10   who succeeded Joshua Smith?

· 2 · *Comment:*

1   a prop?

2   it is and it isn't?

3   it can't be helped?

4   the whole purpose?

5   love at first sight? (for example)

6   sensing that this has happened before?

7   unlimited authority?

8   the eternal triangle?

9   leading nowhere?

10   set in stone?

• 3 •

1   whence the skipper?

2   whence GW 2275 when its rider was fatally injured?

3   where did Tess say 'Why am I on the wrong side of this door!'

4   where did the great-grandson of Boleslav I, the Cruel, Duke of Bohemia, die?

5   where do monuments commemorate the golden jubilees of grandfather and grand-daughter?

6   where did the action of the wicked stepmother lead to the succession of a seemingly unprepared monarch?

7   where did a secret passage provide access from No. 6 to the court in the Oak Room?

8   which church is dedicated to the sometime wife of the King of Northumbria?

9   where did Louisa fall when jumping with the Captain?

10   where did Jesse Carter develop his business?

• 4 • *Who, prior to execution:*

1   quoted from the 51ˢᵗ Psalm?

2   screamed 'Purim Fest 1946'?

3   stated 'I am the martyr of the People'?

4   when brought the whisky he had requested said 'I think I'll make it a double'?

5   announced 'In death as in life, I defy the Jews who caused this last war, and I defy the power of darkness which they represent'?

6   shook hands with each member of the firing squad and said 'Take a step or two forward lads. It will be easier that way'?

7   studying the axe, said 'This is strong Medicine, but it is a Physician for all diseases and miseries'?

8   said 'Show my head to the people, it is worth showing'?

9   quoted from Horace and then Ovid?

10   quoted from the 71ˢᵗ Psalm?

• 5 • *Who or what:*

1   manages without ice?

2   was Suzuki's mistress?

3   suggests an ante-mortem vigil?

4   is urged to go elsewhere in search of its dinner?

5   provides meat in the summer and collects for the harvest?

6   clad in brown and grey, played at battlecock and shuttledore?

7   was a temporary resident at 1600 Pennsylvania Avenue?

8   is, literally, a religious prophet?

9   is played under ground?

10   had episcopal origins?

• 6 •

1   who sailed eastward from Campobello?

2   whose two ghastly heads swing on the gibbet at Nidarholm?

3   what was striving unceasingly to release the ruthless iron nail?

4   what has a taste more divine, more dulcet, delicious, and dreamy?

5   whose side was gored by cruel rocks, like the horns of an angry bull?

6   where do fountains wrought with richest sculpture stand in the common mart?

7   where are ashes heaped in drifts over vineyard and field and town?

8   where did the melancholy chimes ring strange unearthly changes?

9   who rode silently with muffled oar to the Charlestown shore?

10   who carried away the Dean of Jaen and sold him to Algiers?

• 7 • *What eponym is applied to:*

1 a break at the base of the 5th metatarsal?

2 an uncomplicated break at the front of the ala?

3 a broken wrist resulting from a fall onto the back of the hand?

4 a break involving the inner projection of the lower part of the thigh bone?

5 a break in the upper part of one of the forearm bones with dislocation of the head of its neighbour?

6 a break at the upper end of the outer leg bone with separation from its neighbour, which suffers a break at its lower end?

7 a break above the elbow with displacement backwards of the two intact long bones?

8 a break producing a deformity suggestive of an item of cutlery?

9 a break above the elbow with entrapment of the radial nerve?

10 breaks in the ring of the first cervical vertebra?

• 8 • *Give rank and name (but not in this instance number):*

1 who boarded the *City of Athens* with his friend Martyn?

2 who wrote reports on Ericson, Bennett, Lockhart and Ferraby?

3 who searched for Jack at the Blue Posts, George and Fountain Inns?

4 who claimed to have 'important information' about a planned elopement?

5 to whom was the Princess of Stolp introduced by the Countess Canerine at the Peterhof?

6 who received VIP treatment on his repatriation from the Kola Inlet via Moscow, Teheran, Cairo and Gib?

7 who described the wreck of the treasure ship *Corinne*, lying on the Juister Riff?

8 who plumped for the Handsome Sailor on the gangway of the *Rights*?

9 who broke the political officer's neck in the locked wardroom?

10 who conducted a marriage ceremony aboard HMS *Oedipus*?

• 9 •

1 who did for Harry and Jack with his plan of attack?

2 who suggested in a love poem that his mistress had halitosis?

3 who, in mourning, had no further use for either the sun or the moon?

4 who turned back expecting to catch a bird and disturbed a family of unweaned mice?

5 which bibulous Celt described his youthful self as being, in effect, callow, carefree and locally well-known?

6 in which nonsense poem were different body parts of an eponymous creature credited with the powers of occlusion and apprehension?

7 which timid would-be lover was worried about the ladies noticing that he was getting thin on top?

8 who described fungal abundance among the redundant bathroom furniture?

9 who was mightily taken with a little untidiness in a lady's dress?

10 which lake poet might have found retail therapy debilitating?

• 10 • *Connected by the same waterway:*

1 where is the spätburgunder pre-eminent?

2 where was the Archbishop devoured by rodents?

3 what owes its stellar design to Adriaan Anthoniszoon?

4 where did a heroic rover scout save the bridge from demolition?

5 where are a red ox, a white eagle and a black horn vividly depicted?

6 where, as depicted elsewhere by Memling, was there a massacre of itinerant virgins?

7 where does a cherub suck a finger withdrawn from a bees' nest?

8 where did Clara's beloved husband attempt to drown himself?

9 what did Goethe describe as the source of the Ocean?

10 where did Ludendorff fail to hold up the 9th?

• 11 • *Whose second wife:*

1   was accused of witchcraft?

2   succeeded his mother-in-law in the roll?

3   delivered her stepson in chains to the conquerors?

4   had her jewellery confiscated by his cousin following his deposition?

5   provided him with a premature daughter, following an attempt on his life on Easter Day?

6   produced for him a rightful heir, notwithstanding suggestions of a warming pan delivery?

7   adopted the name of her predecessor and later married one of his successors?

8   uniquely (in that era) succeeded him as Queen Regnant?

9   was likened to a Swabian butcher's best friend?

10   eventually became Abbess of Whitby?

• 12 • *Who:*

1   died in the same incident as Islero?

2   bridged the Rio Manzanares with nine arches?

3   was invited to dinner, Saturday evening at seven, with Robespierre?

4   died on the same date as the Bard of Avon, although in fact ten days earlier?

5   like the Danish Court physician, cuckolded an inadequate Monarch to his political advantage?

6   was the first European to view the Mar del Sur, but later lost his head at the instigation of his father-in-law?

7   was fatally injured in a fall while painting the Mystic Marriage of St Catherine?

8   created the themes used by a blind man in his fantasy for a gentleman?

9   famously depicted the result of an infamous Condor attack?

10   depicted both filicide and cannibalism?

· 13 ·

1   what stolen jewel never reached Van Seddar?

2   what was stolen by Hamilton, Matheson, Stuart and Vernon?

3   who stole 216 new gunmetal shackles from a Norfolk boatyard?

4   whose theft of a spoon with the insignia FV was blamed on the farmer's maidservant?

5   who stole a hammer, but was later murdered by its owner, masquerading as the thief's fiancée?

6   who was caught trying to steal a jewelled snuffbox from the former lover of Catherine II at Covent Garden?

7   who stole Lady Fairfax's watch en route to the Guild Church of St Martin-within-Ludgate?

8   who stole Rachel's birthday present while in a laudanum-induced trance?

9   who received plenary absolution following the theft of a ring?

10 who stole St Edward's Crown from the Tower of London?

· 14 · *Where*:

1   were the Seljuks routed by the Mongols?

2   is the bejewelled weapon, coveted by Harper?

3   was Laurie's passport confiscated by the Syrian Consul?

4   were the hexabrachial giants killed and left in a pile on the beach?

5   was the priestess's light extinguished, resulting in the drowning of her lover?

6   did the thief take Stumm's staff map and escape through the window and over the roof?

7   did the Queen, dressed as Aphrodite, entertain a Roman visitor on her barge?

8   did Doctor Plato and his brother die at the hands of the Emperor?

9   did victory prompt the statement 'Veni, vidi, vici'?

10 were Priscilla and her husband left behind?

• 15 • *Which distillation:*

1   wins at 100 to 1?

2   started as House of Commons?

3   like its origin, is so hard to leave?

4   is charcoal-mellowed drop by drop?

5   includes, specifically, the Macallan and Highland Park in its blend?

6   boasts water from our own spring, our own malted barley and a full barrowload of peat?

7   is from the world's oldest whiskey distillery?

8   is not the Pontiff's phone number?

9   is just as it was in the beginning?

10   is perfected by 16 men?

• 16 • *Who or what:*

1   is neither perch nor pike?

2   is one of the most poisonous of all shrubs?

3   do the streamlets do down yonder green meadow?

4   port saw a cargo of over 50 tons of dynamite kill over 500?

5   was the first cadet from the subcontinent to graduate from the RMA?

6   grape was exploited by a Speyer merchant in the early part of the eighteenth century?

7   is an incredible story of survival during the war in the Far East?

8   tetrapod was supposed to act as a fire extinguisher?

9   class of 26 included Scylla and Charybdis?

10   turned out to be Bodin's daughter?

• 17 • *Which schoolboy:*

1   reminded Walter of his little brother?

2   gained the Bootlesworth Exhibition in 1898?

3   played 'Pop Goes the Weasel' on the vox humana?

4   burst into tears on attempting to construe:

> αλλα συ τόν γ' επέεσσι παραιφάμενος κατέρυκες
>
> Ση τ' αγανοφροσύνη και σοις αγανοις επέεσσίν?

5   was able, in speech and manner, to imitate Marcellus Stengel who taught drawing and singing?

6   was required to give a sketch of the rise and history of the Dominicans from the time of Herod the Conqueror to the death of Titmus?

7   decorated the study with a dado, a stencil, and cretonne hangings?

8   was confined in an upper room at the Fighting Cock?

9   was reported upon in glowing terms by Craw?

10   first began to crib in the Lower Fifth?

• 18 • *During the reign of our eponymous monarch:*

1   what began at 35 King Street?

2   who was hit by a rocket at Parkside?

3   how did a button, a basket and another return to their homeland?

4   which new replacement structure would eventually be moved to Arizona?

5   how did Parliament act in response to the receipt of material by Robert Knox?

6   whose lack of 'the true faith of a Christian' led to the Sheriff's Declaration Act?

7   for what were the premises in Charles II Street quickly found to be too small?

8   what was the result of inappropriate disposal of split notched sticks?

9   who found himself far from home in the Strait of Bonifacio?

10   who bought out West & Wyatt?

Win £1000-worth of books!

The bespoke set of questions (see p. 309) has been compiled especially for this book by Pat Cullen, and just to tantalise quiz aficionados, the answers are not given here…

Answers will be published online at www.liverpooluniversitypress.co.uk and on Twitter (https://twitter.com/LivUniPress) on 30 June 2012 and will also be available on request from the publisher from that date onwards.

To enter a competition for a prize of *£1000-worth* of Liverpool University Press books, send in the answers by **15 June 2012** to:
LUP World's Most Difficult Quiz
Liverpool University Press
4 Cambridge St
Liverpool
L69 7ZU

or email entries to lup@liv.ac.uk with the subject line 'World's Most Difficult Quiz'.
Entries should include full contact details
(name, address, phone number and email address).

All the correct sets of answers will be placed into a prize draw and a winner picked out on 30 June 2012. The lucky (and erudite) victor will be given £1000-worth of Liverpool University Press books of his or her choice.

For any enquiries about the competition, or to request a set of answers, please contact the publisher at:
Liverpool University Press
4 Cambridge Street
Liverpool
L69 7ZU, UK
Tel: +44 (0)151 795 2149
Email: lup@liv.ac.uk
Twitter: https://twitter.com/LivUniPress
Web: www.liverpooluniversitypress.co.uk

Good luck!